THE
SPIRITUAL
LIFE
OF
WATER

THE
SPIRITUAL
LIFE
OF
WATER

Its Power and Purpose

ALICK BARTHOLOMEW

Park Street Press
Rochester, Vermont • Toronto, Canada

Park Street Press
One Park Street
Rochester, Vermont 05767
www.ParkStPress.com

Text stock is SFI certified

Park Street Press is a division of Inner Traditions International

Originally published in the United Kingdom by Floris Books under the title *The Story of Water*

Library of Congress Cataloging-in-Publication Data
Bartholomew, Alick.
  [Story of water]
  The spiritual life of water : its power and purpose / Alick Bartholomew.
    p. cm.
  "Originally published in the United Kingdom by Floris Books under the title The Story of Water."
  Includes bibliographical references and index.
  ISBN 978-1-59477-360-0 (pbk.)
  1. Water. 2. Water—Social aspects. 3. Hydrology—Popular works. I. Title.
  GB665.G365 2010
  202'.12—dc22

                                                          2010032071

Printed and bound in the United States by Lake Book Manufacturing
The text paper is SFI certified. The Sustainable Forestry Initiative® program promotes sustainable forest management.

10 9 8 7 6 5 4 3 2 1

Text design and layout by Priscilla Baker
This book was typeset in Garamond Premier Pro with Augustea and Gill Sans used as display typefaces

To send correspondence to the author of this book, mail a first-class letter to the author c/o Inner Traditions • Bear & Company, One Park Street, Rochester, VT 05767, and we will forward the communication.

For Mari et amicis

To Mae-Wan Ho for her inspiration and for generously allowing me to quote from her books and articles. To Martin Chaplin for permission to quote from his useful website, to Callum Coats for his diagrams, to Chris Weedon of the Water Association for his encouragement and helpful suggestions, and to Christopher Moore of Floris Books and Laura Schlivek of Inner Traditions for their helpful editing.

And special thanks to Caroline Way for allowing me to quote her poem "Still Water Meditation," which aptly sets the theme for this book.

CONTENTS

FOREWORD

I have a great fondness for water bears. Less than a millimeter long, water bears—or tardigrades—clamber about on eight stubby legs, tipped with the tiniest of claws, like minute animated jelly-teddies in a watery micro-world. Endearing! But water bears are much more special than that. When dry conditions arrive, instead of succumbing to death, water bears survive by just drying up . . . completely! Well, almost. Drying to a body content of 1 percent water, from close to 100 percent, the creature transforms into a microscopic speck of organic dust, utterly resistant to drought, extreme cold, vacuum, and even radioactivity. In this dormant, desiccated state, a water bear can survive for thousands of years. It's a good trick if you can do it!

Yet, however remarkable the resilience born of desiccation seems, surely the greater miracle is the life that water brings! For, with even a single drop of water, the sleeping water bear bounces back into action, striding again through mossy jungles. How is it that one extra ingredient has the power to awaken a mote of dust? What has happened? What is water doing? What *is* water that its presence facilitates and empowers life?

The Spiritual Life of Water sets out in answer to these questions, probing much further than merely repeating that favored adage that "Water is Life." Here is a tale of wholeness and connectivity told through water; of the interplay between material and nonmaterial, enacted on Earth, yet influenced from far beyond the bounds of our planet.

The extraordinary subtlety and complexity of water's roles are vividly illustrated. And having done so, the book then asks: What are the qualities of water that best support life? The quest for a comprehensive answer to this question has been the research focus of the "heroes" of Alick Bartholomew's story. By drawing together the findings and insights of these researchers into so many aspects of water's reality, a picture emerges of a seemingly infinite array of interrelating properties and qualities, which we are only just starting to comprehend. And by analyzing and then synthesizing these insights within a single volume, Alick has taken us a step closer to answering that related and most fundamental of questions, "What is Life?"

CHRIS WEEDON,
COFOUNDER OF THE WATER ASSOCIATION,
SOMERSET, UK

Still Water Meditation

Place a drop of water in the palm of your hand.

The drop that you hold in your hand
Is part of the water which was the cradle of all life
On this planet Aeons ago
The first rain that splashed down on the hot earth
To form the first sea.
Each drop, in sunlight
Has risen from the sea in countless ages
And fallen to the earth again
As rain

The drop that you hold in your hand
Has been a prism forming myriad rainbows
Has travelled underground streams
Bubbling through dark caverns
The Architect of cathedral caves
Formed valleys
And split granite

The drop that you hold in your hand
Has flowed down broad rivers
Has risen in the sap of trees
Has been the sweat of slaves
And the tears of children
It has become the foam topped waves
And deep unfathomable depths
Of vast dark lakes
And seas

The drop that you hold in your hand
Has been part of the great flood
It has been a dewdrop on a blade of grass
A drop that has been pounded
Through the hearts of whales in blood
And lain in an eagle's egg
It has travelled in the fluid of a poet's brain
And dripped from the wounds of the dying

The drop that you hold in your hand
Has been trapped in the snows of the arctic
Reflected the sun in a desert oasis
And refreshed the weary

This drop
Unimaginably old
Yet fresh and new
Is evaporating slowly from your hand
To mingle with the air you breathe, perhaps
Or drift in a sun-topped cloud
A thousand feet above the earth
Imagine its journey from your hand
Where will it go?
You can direct its journey
As it evaporates
Send your consciousness with it
It is the water of Life
It is still water.

CAROLINE WAY

INTRODUCTION

Water is good; it benefits all things and does not compete
with them.
It dwells in lowly places that all disdain.
This is why it is so near to Tao.

LAO-TZU

Why is water such an evocative subject? It influences the emotions, the imagination, and creativity—artists and poets find inspiration in it. So many words in our language are stimulated by water: outpouring, flowing, bubbling; well up, swell, drain. Yet we take it for granted, treating it as a convenience—something to quench our thirst, bathe in, and use for washing our homes and cars. Water is the most familiar—yet, at the same time, least understood—of all substances on our planet.

Widely published reports that climate change will alter the reliability of freshwater supplies have caused people to begin to think more seriously about the problem. We are already fighting wars over access to oil, which we worship for its huge energy potential and ability to create enormous wealth. In conflicts over water, which have also begun in the American Southwest and elsewhere, there is even more at stake—our survival.

Water is essential to human survival, yet we waste it profligately, taking for granted that it will issue forth at the turn of a tap, and abuse it in ways that belie its noble character and function. In a real sense, water *is* life, yet we treat it with neglect and contempt.

This precious substance is an essential component of our physical and spiritual being. We *are* water, and it is in our genuine interest to understand the true nature of this substance that plays such extraordinary roles in the creation, maintenance, and evolution of life. Some see it as an organism with its own life cycle.

Water carries all life but is beyond time, for it bears in its flow the seeds of future life, as well as the memory of past life. We have lost touch with the magic of water—the freshness of a natural spring, reflections in a mountain lake, the mystery of a sacred well. Water mediates between life and death, between being and not being, and between health and sickness, yet we have allowed water to spread illness and disease.

Much is spoken these days of the destructive nature of water. Such water is Nature on the rampage, perhaps flaunting her power in response to the reckless damage humanity has wrought on Earth's ecosystems.

Humans resonate with water. So closely is water linked to human emotions that just sitting at the edge of the ocean on a sunny day imbues many of us with a sense of inspiration and joy. Our ancestors were fascinated by its magic and generated a vast water mythology. Mainstream science does not tell us about this, but we will be examining holistic scientific research that may give us some clues.

Earth, with more than 70 percent of its surface covered by ocean, is known as the planet of water. Even our human bodies are more water (60 percent) than anything else. But water is also believed to exist or have existed on other planets. Where did it come from?

It is impossible to destroy water. Nature is very good at recycling, and recycles water best of all. As far as we know, planet Earth has about as much water in one form or another as it has had for billions of years. It seems as if water was intended for life; certainly life could not have come without it. It has three basic states: solid (as ice), liquid, and gas; mist could be called a fourth state. There is no other substance that can exist in Nature in these states, within a temperature range of about 100°C (180°F).

There are at least sixteen different forms of ice. There are likely to be as many different forms of liquid water; we don't know as yet. There are dozens of different roles played by liquids that are basically water, including blood, sap, and about thirty different human bodily fluids, each with its specific purpose.

Caroline Way's poem that opens this book, "Still Water Meditation," echoes precisely this thought of the indestructibility of water and its many roles in life. But it also illustrates wonderfully that it is through the medium of water that we all share a common heritage. We are all one—water is the epitome of holism. The mystical naturalist who inspired my pilgrimage with water, Viktor Schauberger, talked of the whole universe being held in a drop of water.

This study is also a celebration, because it is to water that we owe our very existence. Our biology and physics textbooks tell us that water is merely an inorganic compound through which various chemical processes take place, but our aim is to raise the awareness of water as a source of inspiration. The story of water as the stage manager of life, communicating to our bodies' cells how to be part of a vast orchestra, distributing energy in the landscape to make it balanced and productive, has not yet been simply told. Indeed, the very laws that govern the harmonious movement of the planets also determine the form and behavior of our organic life, through water. This extraordinary picture of water's part in the evolution of life derives from the discovery of quantum physics that we are embedded in a vast web of energy that interconnects all of creation. What this book proposes is the novel idea that water and the quantum field are two complementary aspects in the balanced mediation and sustenance of life.

One of the reasons we know so little about water may be our obsession with the physical nature of life. Older cultures did not suffer from this limited worldview and consequently had a greater appreciation of water's special qualities than we do today.

The poet, philosopher, and scientist Johann Wolfgang von Goethe (1749–1832) was, more than anyone, a bridge between pre- and post-Enlightenment thinking. He sensed the profound difference in outlook between the new rational, mechanistic, and more exclusive worldview, and the more traditional inclusive, Nature-centered view. He called the latter "holistic" science, in contrast to "reductionist" science. Goethe understood that all of life is one, closely interconnected and interrelated, and that water—sustainer of life—is the very symbol of holism.

The international forum known as the Scientific and Medical Network, of which I'm a member, challenges the adequacy of scientific materialism as an exclusive basis for knowledge and values.* We discuss ideas in a critical but open-minded way that goes beyond the science of splitting and specializing. We integrate intuitive insight with rational analysis and encourage a respect for the earth and community with a holistic and spiritual approach.

We are here in the boundary zone between the known and the unknown. We shall try to maintain some rigor as to the deductions made from the phenomena we describe. However, the scientific quest must embrace intuitive insight as well as proof; otherwise, there is no progress.

Much of what is proposed may seem to some mainstream scientists as mere supposition, but in the interest of advancing understanding, I ask you to continually consider the whole picture—for that is surely what life is about.

The book is divided into three parts. The first part deals mostly with facts about water that are acknowledged by mainstream science: its anomalous nature and the purpose of the great water cycles—in the oceans and atmosphere; on and beneath the land; in forests, trees, and other organisms; and in humans. We also introduce the insights

---

*The Scientific and Medical Network (SMN) is a leading international forum for people engaged in creating a new worldview for the twenty-first century, bringing together scientists, doctors, psychologists, engineers, philosophers, complementary practitioners, and other professionals. Formed in 1973, it has members in more than thirty countries.

of Viktor Schauberger, the Austrian naturalist, into water as a bridge between conventional and newer, more radical ideas about water. The second part provides insights from holistic science, and flowing through the entire book is the theme that water is inseparable from a holistic view of life. The third section considers aspects of the current water crisis in the world, and how we can learn to adapt and reduce its effects.

We will examine how water is created, its physical and chemical characteristics, and its role in shaping our planet. However, we cannot get far in understanding water by dwelling on its physical characteristics. Water has no identity, separateness, or form (temporary ice crystals being the notable exception). The real significance of water is its role as a medium—for metamorphosis, change, building and recycling, nourishment, information transfer, energy exchange, and balancing.

Water has unique qualities that make it quite different from any other substance or compound. The fact that these anomalies all seem to be weighted toward creating the most favorable environment for life begs the question: Could water be the exception to evolution by natural selection? Could it have been specially "designed" for our evolutionary potential? This study investigates whether water's extraordinary story might illuminate a quest for meaning.

I believe that the subtle properties of water and its role in the ecosystem are groundbreaking discoveries that place it at the heart of all life processes. Water could be the handmaiden of that mysterious field of creative quantum energy that surrounds us. Perhaps it could even be called a medium of consciousness. Our forebears regarded water as sacred. Was this just superstition, or did they know something we don't? When Man lived close to Nature, and considered himself to be part of it, there was not yet the feeling of self and other, of separation. The implications of rediscovering this truth through the quantum view of holistic science are profound for the future of human society. This will gradually become clearer as we progress in the latter part of this study.

The book has a radical message: that water as "the ground of all being," the "primal substance," is an organism that is self-creating and self-organizing. It governs both life and death. Living, highly structured water is healing and life enhancing. Conversely, debased and polluted water can carry deadly disease and the message of death. Between those two opposites are qualities of water we tolerate when we should not. We need to be much more discriminating and learn how to support life.

Every living thing, from Earth itself to the tiniest single-cell organism, needs to both contain and be surrounded by vibrant water. Water is what brings interconnectedness to all of life. The story of water is a parable for "all is one," a lesson we urgently need to learn. Amid our cultural emphasis on individual wants and the prevailing scientific, medical, and educational models of splitting things into parts, water can teach us many things.

WAYS OF KNOWING

Science is about knowledge of our world—of life. Its Latin root, *scire,* means "to know." Yet, there are different ways of knowing. When Carl Gustav Jung, originator of analytical psychology, was asked if he believed in God, he replied: "I don't believe; I *know.*"

The natural world is essentially an indivisible unity, but our present culture is condemned to apprehend it from two different directions: through our senses (perception) or through our minds (concepts). A child simply observes and marvels, but as our rational minds develop, we are taught to interpret what we see, usually through other peoples' ideas, in order to "make sense" of our sensory experience. Both are forms of reality, but unless we are able to bring the two aspects together in a meaningful way, the world will present nothing but incomprehensible riddles to us.

The Enlightenment was a triumph of reason over authority and superstition. It brought about an immense advance in knowledge and developed the modern subjects of physics, chemistry, geology, and astronomy. It also helped sever our ties to the natural world and put an end to any pretence of being subservient to Nature. This resulted in a philosophy that perceived Earth as basically dead, her resources to be plundered without question. A bias developed toward a more mechanistic worldview and a distrust of nonrational ways of knowing.

Our current societal identification with the conceptual is the weakness of the prevailing scientific orthodoxy. Some of the pioneers of science were able to immerse themselves deeply in pure observation and allow concepts to speak for themselves.* The trained scientist today, however, burdened with preconceived ideas or principles, is likely to come up with either isolated phenomena or a very fragmented picture.

IS THE UNIVERSE A MACHINE?

Isaac Newton's *Principia* described the universe as a machine, and our worldview to this day is based on that premise. Our new technologies are trying to fix the world as though it were an automobile, disregarding the exquisite harmony that holds everything in balance. A machine is predictable because it stands alone and cannot change. A living system is unpredictable, connected to its environment, self-organizing, and creative. If I am encouraged to see myself as a separate part of a world machine, I will feel divorced from my environment with an inevitable sense of alienation, in denial, and with a temptation to escape into addictions.[1] In making our way in the world our hearts are pulled in one direction (yes, I can) while the machine image pulls us in another (no, it's impossible).

In biology, the quick fix is to develop manipulative technologies, such as genetically modified (GM) crops or horizontal gene transfers, regardless of the inherent dangers of pollution and monocultural devastation, or harm to the wider community. One suspects that the priority of GM companies is to maximize profits rather than quality of food or

---

*Viktor Schauberger possessed this rare gift. He noted: "The majority believe that everything hard to comprehend must be very profound. This is incorrect. What is hard to understand is what is immature, unclear, and often false. The highest wisdom is simple and passes through the brain directly into the heart."

the environment. Unfortunately, politicians seem to get caught easily in this web of self-serving corruption. In environmental policy, the quick fix is to jump into unsustainable technologies in order to maintain the profligate lifestyle to which we are accustomed, rather than trim our way of life to live in harmony with Earth's bounty.

THE POLARIZATION OF SCIENCE

The enormous energy released in the past two centuries by the exploitation of fossil fuels has accelerated the development of prodigious technological achievements. More crucially, it has given pioneers of new technologies a sense of dominance over Nature, as well as money, power, and global influence. Inevitably this worldview has influenced the politically inclined and educated among us. It has led to a growth in materialism and the commercialization of values.

On the other hand, discoveries in quantum physics, fractal geometry, and the physics of the organism are leading to a new science that is at odds with the orthodox Newtonian theories now understood to have relevance primarily in the physical domain. This new holistic science can contain the old orthodoxy, but the Newtonian understanding cannot easily cope with the quantum; hence, their antagonism. It is as though we are now seeing two incompatible kinds of science.

Before the 1970s, scientific research was funded largely by government. To a great extent this guaranteed its independence. Today nearly all scientific research is funded by business, which naturally has its own agenda that limits the objectivity of the research. This is particularly true in biology, where there is so much profit to be made, but also to some extent in physics and chemistry. The independent Institute of Science in Society is one of the few research centers that subscribe to a holistic view of society.

The media's bread and butter is that which is new or unusual, but it also thrives on controversy, which can confuse the public. They don't know what to believe when climate change skeptics are presented as credible, or "bad science" reporters are encouraged to start a witch hunt against forms of subtle energy medicine, such as homeopathy or acupuncture. The cultural climate today is hardly sympathetic to a holistic worldview, yet this is beginning to change as more people realize that the established symbols of authority do not have the answers.

WATER AND ENERGY

In part 2 of this book, we will look more closely at the lesser-known energetic and quantum qualities of water that enable it to perform its incredible functions of initiating and sustaining life. We'll also study other pioneers of a new understanding of water: Mae-Wan Ho, Theodor Schwenk, Patrick Flanagan, Jacques Benveniste, Masaru Emoto, and Cleve Backster.

In discussing holistic research on water's extraordinary qualities, we will be talking about energy in rather different terms from mainstream understanding. What is the essential nature of energy? There is much confusion around the term, and if we are honest, we don't really know, except that it always seems to be connected with motion.

Conventionally, energy means the power to do work and refers to the gross physical energies, such as those produced by a hydroelectric power generator or an internal combustion engine—any force that produces change. These physical energies are usually termed "kinetic" energy; or if they are stored and as yet not manifest, they are called "potential" energy.

We cannot see energy, only its outward manifestations; its origins lie beyond our senses. There are many forms of extremely high energy that have been measured by science (for instance, nuclear energy), but there are other forms of energy that defy measurement. They are too subtle and cannot be detected by even the most sophisticated instruments. Although science can detect brain activity related to human emotions, it cannot measure their intrinsic power, frequency, or vibrational rate (velocity of atomic rotation), nor their true point of origin.

We refer to these as "dynamic" or "subtle" energies (for instance, quantum energy). They are part of energizing life processes and appear to operate under different laws from the Newtonian. Viktor Schauberger claimed that they respond to the law of anticonservation of energy,* and are therefore conveniently ignored by materialists (see box).

Energy Is Immaterial

H. H. Price, Wykeham professor of logic at Oxford University, writes: "We must conclude, I think, that there is no room for telepathy in a materialistic universe. Telepathy is something which ought not to happen at all, if the materialistic theory were true. But it does happen. So there must be something seriously wrong with the materialistic theory, however numerous and imposing the normal facts which support it may be" *Hibbert Journal* (1949). Goethe, too, said of conventional scientists: "Whatever you cannot calculate, you do not think is real."

Immaterial, or life energies have been recognized and worked for thousands of years not only by indigenous people living close to Nature, but also by sophisticated cultures, such as the Chinese. One example from that culture is *feng shui,* the knowledge of placement in the environment.

The Chinese also developed the sophisticated medical treatment of acupuncture, using fine needles to correct imbalances of *chi,* the life energy that moves along energetic meridians of the body. Although this practice is widely used throughout the world by accredited practitioners

---

*The law of conservation of energy states that the amount of energy throughout the universe is finite; energy merely transfers from one form to another—potential to kinetic, and vice versa (the physical sphere). The law of anticonservation of energy postulated by Viktor Schauberger holds that the amount of available energy—potential, kinetic, or dynamic—can be increased at will to virtually any order of magnitude (the quantum sphere). Schauberger saw the two as dialectic counterparts.

and some progressive doctors, it is still not recognized by all orthodox doctors of Western medicine. Holistic science, however, is now beginning to identify the nature of chi energy.[2]

YIN/YANG BALANCE

The sun is our main source of energy. In Chinese tradition, it emits a *yang* (masculine/positive) energy. Earth balances this with a *yin* (feminine/negative) energy. The world is governed by the yin and the yang. They are the essential components for all biological and physical processes, and water's working depends on them. Polarities are the mechanism of creation and water is their vehicle.

Yin and yang are dynamic in the sense that their energy fluctuates—when one expands, the other diminishes. The concentration of energy is a yin process, while the tendency to move and disperse it is yang.

Western thought holds yin and yang as fixed states, but in the Chinese tradition they are constantly shifting. Thus, in every man there is feminine energy and in every woman there is masculine energy, these tendencies varying in different situations. It is the same in Nature. Mornings tend to have yang energy, and evenings, yin.

In Chinese terminology, yin corresponds to all that is contractive, responsive, and conservative; yang corresponds to the expansive, aggressive, and demanding. It is thought that all men and women go through yin and yang phases. In Western thought all men are supposed to be masculine, creative, and active, while women are considered feminine, receptive, and passive—a rationale for keeping women in a subordinate role, and for men taking the leading roles and most of society's privileges.

Rather than the Western concept of passive/active polarity, the Chinese view yin as responsive, consolidating, cooperative activity; and yang as aggressive, competitive, expanding activity; yin is conscious of the environment, and yang is more about self. One can see that our society has favored yang over yin—rational knowledge over intuitive wisdom, science over religion, competition over cooperation, and exploitation over conservation.

In the West we give yin and yang a moral connotation, seeing them as "either/or." The classical Chinese tradition, however, views them as extremes of a single whole—a constantly changing dynamic balance; only what is out of balance is harmful.

Physicist and author Fritjof Capra believes the roots of our problems lie in a profound imbalance in all aspects of our culture—our thoughts and feelings, values, and social/political structures. Capra writes: "Excessive self-assertion, which is characteristic of the yang mode of behavior, manifests itself as power, control, and domination of others by force; and those are, indeed, the patterns prevalent in our society."[3]

All processes depend on an unstable reciprocity between extremes. As soon as a process becomes stable, it stagnates. It's the same with water. Moving, circulating water is energized; still water is effectively dead. Water is the ideal medium for processes because it is an unstable and dynamic medium, and without water, nothing in the environment of Earth can change.

With the rising concern over ecology and sustainability there is a profound shift in values taking place—admiration of large-scale enterprises is giving way to "small is beautiful," material consumption is shifting to more voluntary simplicity. This shift is being promoted by the human potential movement, feminism, holistic approaches to health, and a growing cultural emphasis on the quest for meaning and spiritual connection.

We will employ the Chinese use of yin and yang as tendencies toward extremes of the whole in this part of the book, particularly in connection with Viktor Schauberger's work.

WATER RETAINS AND COMMUNICATES ENERGY

Evolution could not progress without the extraordinary ability of water to retain energy. There would be no raising of quality, no healing. The process seems to be tailored to the uplifting of human consciousness, as it is linked to the quality of free will or the ability of choice given to our species.

The health of the body is affected by the quality of thoughts. Having a positive state of mind can promote healthy, balanced cellular health, while anger, negativity, and limiting thoughts can result in health imbalances and illness. Our thoughts are extremely powerful.

Our biological water is the medium for all communication, internal and external. Recent biological research shows that as the "intelligence" of our whole organism, water chains allow electrical impulses and information to reach all parts of the body much more quickly than is possible through the nervous system (see p. 169).

Emotional blocks, which are a common hindrance to our ability to live up to our individual potential, can be released through working on the water meridians, as well as through acupuncture, shiatsu, or such processes as Emotional Freedom Technique (EFT) (see p. 137).

One of the misconceptions of mainstream biology is that our constitution and our potential are fixed by our DNA. In fact, our experiences and how we respond to life significantly affect our personal evolution (see chapter 2).

Perhaps humanity's purpose at this time may be to initiate healing and a raising of consciousness in the soul of our planet. Earth has its own sense of purpose, which may have contributed to, or even determined, the environmental upheavals that have led to evolutionary changes. Earth, however, required water to transmit the new information necessary for creating new species and optimizing conditions for a flowering of biological life-forms.

THE QUANTUM FIELD

Nearly a century ago, early pioneers of quantum physics discovered through their microscopes that tiny subatomic particles sometimes behave like vibrant, continually changing subtle energy rather than matter, defying the Newtonian laws of space and time. They named them "quanta."

This promising research was distracted in 1939 by the demands of our society's burgeoning atomic industry and war machines. However, a new generation of physicists has found that quanta do indeed fill the macro environment as well, making an enormous web of interconnected dynamic energy that seems to continue infinitely through space in a kind of communication system.

It resonates with the Hindu concept of *akasha,* an etheric substratum from which all matter was created, as well as the traditions of many other early civilizations. This theory attracted considerable scientific credence over the years but lost its credibility to the materialist worldview in the latter part of the nineteenth century and is no longer discussed in science textbooks.

Is the quantum field the same thing as the etheric field? Not if you go by current attempts to mathematically interrelate nuclear, electromagnetic, and gravitational forces among particles. The quantum field may well be identified with the etheric, but this will require an acceptance that the physical domain is not the only reality. The etheric field in Eastern science is understood to be pure dynamic energy—a difficult concept for Western science. It is just there; it doesn't do anything obvious.

Quantum physics is a new science in process. There is still disagreement as to whether the quantum domain applies to the macro environment, which might open a Pandora's box. The metaphysical implications that can be drawn from the idea of an interconnected field of energy are legion, and one should be wary about jumping to too many philosophical conclusions. Many quantum physicists are skeptical of esoteric and mystical theories. The principles upon which there is general agreement are the uncertainty principle, which put an end to the Laplacian view of a deterministic universe,* and that

---

*Pierre-Simon, marquis de Laplace (1749–1827), was a brilliant mathematician and astronomer often referred to as the "French Newton." He proposed a "demon" who understood all the forces that set nature in motion and would therefore be able to foretell all future events, based on the theory of causal determinism. This popular theory went against the idea of free will and particularly the theories of quantum mechanics, which state that unpredictability plays an important part in evolution.

All Is One

"Quantum theory reveals a basic oneness of the universe . . . As we penetrate into matter, Nature does not show us any isolated 'basic building blocks,' but rather appears as a complicated web of relations among the various parts of the whole . . . The human observer constitutes the final link in the chain of observational processes, and the properties of any atomic object can be understood only in terms of the object's interaction with the observer." Fritjof Capra, *The Tao of Physics*, rev. ed., (1991).

Eastern mysticism shares similar concepts: "The material object becomes . . . something different from what we now see, not a separate object in the background or in the environment of the rest of Nature, but an indivisible part, and even in a subtle way an expression of the unity of all that we see." Sri Aurobindo, *The Synthesis of Yoga*, Lotus Press (1990).

of entanglement, which challenged the idea of completely isolatable systems (see p. 209).

Ancient mystical systems, especially Hindu, Taoist, and Buddhist, held water in particular reverence and understood some of its quantum qualities, even if they did not describe it in those words. Niels Bohr and Robert Oppenheimer, pioneers of quantum physics, found remarkable similarities between their new worldview and the concept of the oneness of all creation held by these mystical systems.

The idea that everything is connected energetically is the foundation of the principle of holism. A discussion of holism can end up as teleology—an argument for a higher, designing power in the universe (see p. 16)—which is anathema to many mainstream scientists. However, I have elected to go with the holistic version of the quantum field because this is the only theory that seems to support, or possibly explain, the weird qualities of water. When I speak of quantum water in part 2 of this book, I am particularly thinking of those qualities or characteristics related to its role in communication and storage of information that seem to contravene the normal theories of locality and time.

A QUESTION OF MEANING

As far as we can discern, humans are the only order of life that has the ability of self-reflection. We have a need for meaning.

This literary journey we're taking is a mirror of my own personal search for meaning. When I discovered that water was the key to my experience of life, everything else started to connect, like pieces of a jigsaw puzzle. My fascination with water's role in the environment was enkindled by Viktor Schauberger and expanded into a sense of personal connection with the wonders of coherence described by Mae-Wan Ho and other quantum biologists. These interconnections opened up the vast landscape of holism—the view as though from a mountaintop. Because of water's multidimensional nature, water is the key to a holistic worldview.

It is difficult to understand the importance of water through a rational process. When we use our imagination and our intuition, the meaning starts to unfold. It is an exciting path that may illuminate your own vision about the meaning of life. We will start with the nature of the organism, and then expand into the world of subtle energies. I hope you will find the journey stimulating.

> *There is no such thing as a logical method of having new ideas, or a logical reconstruction of this process . . . Every discovery contains an irrational element or a creative intuition.*
>
> KARL POPPER

PART ONE

OUR USUAL VIEW
OF WATER

ONE

THE IMPORTANCE OF WATER

All is born of water and upheld by water, too!

JOHANN WOLFGANG VON GOETHE

The eighteenth-century poet and scientist Johann Wolfgang von Goethe (1749–1832) referred to water as "the ground of all being."* Thales of Miletus (640–546 BCE) also believed water to be infused with being, believing it was the original substance of the cosmos. The Austrian "water wizard" Viktor Schauberger (1885–1958) had a similar view, saying that water is the product of the subtle energies that brought planet Earth into being and is itself a living substance. "The upholder of the cycles that support the whole of life is water," he wrote. "In every drop of water dwells a deity, whom we all serve; there also dwells life, the soul of the 'first' substance—water—whose boundaries and banks are the capillaries that guide it and in which it circulates."[1]

To taste cold, fresh water from a mountain stream is to experience the elixir of life. But what of its sounds? Do you know anyone who is not affected by the evocative sound of water? The thunder of waves

---

*This describes water perfectly: the ground is our base, where we come from, our common denominator; our being is our very nature, our true integrity, our wholeness. Goethe was a scientist and polymath, as well as philosopher and poet.

crashing on a rocky headland is awe inspiring, and a raging tsunami is terrifying. But usually the sounds of water are relaxing and healing: the quiet slap of the tide against the shore on a still day, the burbling of a brook, or the plip plop of water dripping in a cave.

In all symbolic traditions, water is linked with the emotions that make us sensitive, receptive, and compassionate. Artists love water for its inspiration; it has the ability to stimulate awareness and imagination. Why does water affect us so profoundly? Might it be because we are composed mostly of water? It is what unites us with all of life.

The moon is water's cosmic partner, for it controls the tides. Almost every rhythm—from moon rhythms reflected in the hydrosphere and planetary rhythms known to biology, right down to the many physiological rhythms found in every living organism—is based on the pulsation of water.

THE INSPIRATION OF WATER

As if it were not enough that life is totally dependent on water in all its forms for creation and sustenance, we are given extraordinary bonuses in the form of the magical beauty that it displays for our wonder and enjoyment. What would life be without rainbows and sunsets, thunderstorms and cloudscapes, waterfalls, and waves breaking on a rocky shore?

How many great painters and musicians have been inspired by streams, by mighty rivers and the ocean? It is hardly surprising that water plays a central role in many of the world's religions.

We all need to get away from the daily grind, and many of the ways people relax involve water. My cat likes me to take her for a daily walk, and we have a ritual of sitting together on a log by a sharp bend in the river where the trees on the bank form a tunnel (see plate 1). I watch the clear water's surface while she observes the squirrels and little birds. Now and again a sunbeam pierces the canopy and reflects off the rippling water's surface, making light waves on tree trunks and the undersides of leaves. As the sunlight becomes softer and more golden in autumn, these reflections are as inspiring as a Mozart symphony.

What a contrast it is to go to the same bend on a stormy winter's day when the swollen river is boiling with murky turbulence. The ford below my home becomes impassable, and fallen branches get trapped on the depth indicator that rises to the two-foot mark. Cars trying to navigate this amount of river have, in the past, been swept downstream.

We forget how inspiring different forms of water can be. For many, winter is a depressing season, but how beautifully the land is transformed after a fresh snowfall (see plate 2)! If you ski, you know how wonderfully refreshing it is to get out on the slopes, whether you prefer fast downhill runs or the more peaceful gliding through trees. One poignant memory of mine is of the winter stillness of a New England pond, the swishing of my ice skates harmonizing with the wind in the trees lining the banks.

When I lived in Boston, I used to escape to the Charles River basin after work and sail a little Mercury sloop. Now that was relaxing, even though I was still in the big city. Sailing is a great way to let go of life's worries and be at one with the wind and water.

I first crossed the Atlantic by sea in a troop carrier in 1948. It was fun later to go on the big Cunard ships, in the days before commercial airlines; the ocean helped me to lose the sense of time. But what I enjoyed most was to go on a small cargo boat where I could spend all day in the bow watching dolphins or long-distance seabirds. The ocean is mesmerizing, calms the busy mind, and stimulates the inner philosopher.

Surfing provides the most intimate contact possible with water. It offers the rare opportunity to be at one with the water and its energies. The vast, curling tunnel of the mega wave creates a powerful energy vortex down its center.* Aficionados say that "going down the tube,"

---

*A BBC film crew shot a remarkable film of a surfer inside a four-meter (about thirteen feet) barrel wave for a Natural History Unit series on the South Pacific, which aired in 2009. Filmed in super-slow motion using a high-definition camera, it shows the wave forming recognizable multiple fractal-like vortices shooting back from the face of the wave.

being totally enclosed by a fast-moving tubular wall of liquid energy, is the ultimate experience (see plate 3). "Hanging ten" on the crest of a big breaking wave conveys the sense of going over a precipice; a surfer's mind is lifted by the vortex onto a higher energy level for a timeless moment that can give a sense of oneness with the whole ocean and all of Nature. To experience this even once can be a life-transforming experience, which may be why many experienced surfers become mystics (see box).

A Door between Dimensions

The vortex is like a door between dimensions. Black holes are vortices, connecting universes. One is reminded of what people describe who have had a near-death experience—going through a tunnel to meet their loved ones on the higher plane.

The common thread in all these experiences is that they give a sense of timelessness, as well as a specific connection with the natural environment. It also gives us a sense of "the spaces in between" and makes us yearn for solitude and silence. Water is an integral part of the human on a physical level, but perhaps even more so on psychic and spiritual levels. As we will examine later, water gives us a connection with the cosmos.

WHAT IS WATER?

Because we are composed mostly of water, it ought to be the most familiar substance imaginable, yet we actually know very little of its mysteries. Even the new sciences throw little light on it. One difficulty in grasping the whole nature of water may be that our intimate physical relationship with it—it is a large part of our being—may make it more difficult to form a detached view about it.

Second only to hydrogen, water is the most common molecule in the universe and is fundamental in the formation of stars. It is found in the form of dispersed gaseous molecules and as amorphous ice in tiny grains, as well as in much larger asteroids, comets, and planets, but water needs particularly precise conditions in order to exist as a liquid, as it does on our planet. It is thought that this water was transported to Earth by comets and asteroids, and also arose out of the interior some time after the planet acquired a crust.

STATES OF WATER

There is no compound other than water that can exist in its three basic states within such a narrow band of temperature and pressure. Each state has its vital and special purpose: ice, for weathering of rock, is the most stable state; liquid water, for energy transmission in the earth and in organisms, is chameleon-like and sensitive; vapor, for driving the atmospheric and greenhouse systems, is the most unstable.

We tend to think of each state of water as specific and lasting, but there is an incessant interchange between them. One of the principal features of life is constant change and transmutation, and that is because of these qualities of water.

Water's quality of absorption is absolutely crucial to all environmental processes. In a sense, the separation of ocean from atmosphere is arbitrary. Water is constantly evaporating from any body of water, leaving impurities behind as it forms the important atmospheric gas, water vapor. Mist is tiny droplets seeking bits of dust in order to make larger drops of water. When you go out walking in a thick fog, your coat allows the mist to condense as wet water (see plate 4).

Water also absorbs gases, a very important aspect of the greenhouse effect. Its ability to contain gas depends on temperature—the cooler it is, the more it can hold. (This is opposite to the atmosphere, which can hold more water vapor if it is warmed.) The principal greenhouse gas is carbon dioxide (CO_2), which is absorbed by oceans and forests that serve as "carbon sinks" (absorbers of excess CO_2 in the environment). We do not yet understand the mechanism by which oceans normally increase their rate of absorption of CO_2 when the level of this gas starts to raise the greenhouse effect above a balanced level. Unfortunately, we are now in abnormal times, and global warming is reducing the efficiency of forests and oceans to perform this vital function.

As a greenhouse gas, methane is twenty times more powerful than CO_2 in trapping heat close to Earth's surface. When the Arctic tundra melts, masses of methane and CO_2 are released. There are enormous amounts of methane hydrides locked up in the ocean shelves that might be released into the atmosphere if the temperature of the sea rises to a critical level. All these changes influence each other as positive feedback effects, creating magnified outcomes we are only just beginning to appreciate.

Because ice also absorbs gases, information on the oxygen content of the atmosphere in prehistoric times can be gained from analyzing oxygen bubbles in ancient ice fields. Recent research shows that oxygen levels are being depleted faster than those of CO_2 are increasing.*

WATER IS A NEUTRAL MEDIUM

Water is an unselective host body for nutrients and pollutants alike. Holistic biology reports that water also stores and communicates subtle energies, both those that enhance life and those that destroy it. The quality of the water determines which role it is able to play, and this is governed by general environmental factors, the shapes and forms of organisms, and the particular response of water to temperature and certain types of movement.

Pure water exists in Nature only in evaporated form. This is not

---

*New research shows oxygen depletion in the atmosphere accelerating since 2003, which is bad news for mammals. Mae-Wan Ho, "O_2 dropping faster than CO_2 rising," *SiS,* August 19, 2009.

healthy water; in order to become healthy it must acquire its complement of minerals, salts, and trace elements. Radical scientific thought believes it is then "mature" and ready to perform its role as the nourisher and sustainer of all life.* But water is easily degraded, and we need to understand how to help water retain its life force and support health.

Because it is so familiar, we regard water as an ordinary liquid, yet it is anything but ordinary. Its "anomalies" (see pp. 52–53) are very different from those of other liquids and suggest that water was intended specifically to bring forth life. Life cannot evolve or be sustained without liquid water, which is why we are eager to find water on other planets and moons. Enzymes, which are actually proteins that increase the efficiency of biological cells, cannot function without water molecules.

The most important of water's anomalies are those that orchestrate the temperature range of liquid water (0°–100°C, or 32°–212°F). This range is wider than the liquid states of other similar compounds. It neatly encompasses the range required to sustain organic life.

The properties of water are so unique and clearly adapted to the requirements for life that the living world should be seen as a partnership between biological molecules and water. It performs so many functions that you might even think it *is* life. It energizes, nourishes, transports, lubricates, reacts, stabilizes, signals, partitions, structures, and communicates.

The prophet Nostradamus believed water even held information about the future. He used a bowl of water as a skrying tool for helping him to make predictions.

WATER AS FACILITATOR AND STAGE MANAGER

Earth's most important substance is, without doubt, water. It drives everything, from the most delicate metabolic processes in our bodies,

---

*The research of Viktor Schauberger supports this view and will be more fully explored in later chapters.

to creating environments favorable to life, to weather patterns, and to climate change.

Dynamic water, when it is alive and energized, initiates and operates all the processes of life. The most important function of biological water is to facilitate rapid intercommunication between cells and connective tissues so that the organism can function as a coordinated whole.

Though not recognized by mainstream science, living water performs this intercommunication function among organisms, groups of organisms, populations, natural kingdoms, and worlds, creating a network of sensitivity throughout all of life so that nothing can happen without affecting other processes; all are linked together by water. In this way, it drives evolution.

However, its workings are ambiguous. On the one hand it seems to initiate processes, and yet its role is the more passive one of facilitation. This should become clearer as we progress through this study. It is similar to a doctor or healer who initiates the healing process and facilitates the subject's own potential for healing, rather than actually healing the patient.

Our incomplete knowledge of water's role and function makes it difficult to predict processes of instability and change such as those we are experiencing today. Water magnifies and accelerates a process like that of global warming (or cooling) and can be either beneficial or destructive. It is vital that we understand water's role in the critical tipping points of the warming cycle, especially positive feedback loops.

WATER'S SHAPE

The ideal form for water is the sphere (see plate 5). This shape gives water integrity and allows it to circulate and retain its energy. (The egg shape, which we shall study later, has a more specialized purpose.) Water is alive only when it moves and is able to develop layers and filaments. These structures are invisible unless something like potassium permanganate, an oxidizing agent that turns water dark purple, is added.

When the drop hits the ground its shape is lost, but it will seek a slope down which it can develop these structures in its flow. A good place to observe water movement is on a smooth, inclined road surface where it's easy to see its constantly changing direction, back and forth, like a dance. In the same way, a stream will erode the bank on the outside bend and deposit sand on the inside bend.

The strangest thing about water is that it moves rhythmically. On the slightest slope the water's surface starts to move and its structure becomes laminar, that is, filled with surface-like plates of vortical structures. Indeed, water is the element of movement; it is a carrier. This movement is its function and its magic.*

As soon as it is moving it can perform its real function, which is to open up to the environment; in movement it fulfills its potential, which is to bring life. Water sacrifices itself entirely to its surroundings, and everything in Nature depends on it. Movement is influenced constantly by its very presence.

CARING FOR THE STREAM

Do your own simple experiment. Wade into a small stream on a warm day with a butterfly net, disturb the gravel and mud on the stream bottom with your feet, let the net sieve some of this water, and drop the contents of the net into a tray of water. You will be astounded by the variety of invertebrate life, from tiny shrimps to insect larvae, to worms of many kinds. The presence of dragonfly and damselfly larvae indicates a healthy stream. They spend six to seven years as larvae in the mud of the stream's bottom and on pupating have only several weeks in the sun.

With control of pollutants, the water quality of our rivers has improved enormously in recent years, and conservation authorities are

---

*In 1913 the chemist and natural theologian Lawrence J. Henderson pointed out that the strangeness of water consists in its possession of the precise properties that make it "fit" for life on Earth. See *The Fitness of the Environment*.

trying to encourage a wide biodiversity of fauna in rivers. Typically there may be thirty family groups of invertebrates, some of which may contain two hundred to three hundred species. This is a sign of good water health, which increases the number and variety of fish and brings back animals like otters and water voles.

Schauberger, the Austrian naturalist, posited that streams attract trees to their banks to keep the water cool.[2] Through careful study of the ecological balance, sensitive management schemes can be put in place to protect their ecosystems and maximize their biodiversity.

THE SEASHORE

The intertidal seashore is hybrid territory with unique fauna and flora. Rocky pools are home to a fascinating population of tiny crabs, mussels, and worms. The tangle of bladderwort and other kelp—with their attendant insect life, abundant when the sun comes out—creates a pungent aroma. It makes a rich compost, traditionally used in the Scottish Hebrides and the British Channel Islands as a fertilizer. During the Second World War there was a seaweed research laboratory in my village; it created such products as a powder surgeons used inside their rubber gloves.

A sandy beach looks quiet and peaceful, but under the surface are insect larvae and worms, which throw up their casts in little spiral pyramids. When the tide retreats, flocks of wading birds are attracted to the rich takings.

I never did enjoy building sand castles, preferring to divert the little streams coming down the beach into pools and harbors. My favorite pastime, however, was searching for the elusive little pink cowry shells, which still fill jam jars in my home.

Perhaps this special environment reminds us that part of us still belongs to the sea. Certainly it draws us, and many would regard the seaside as the only appropriate place for a relaxing vacation.

LISTENING TO THE STREAM

Indigenous peoples, who lived closer to Nature, understood the importance of water and took great care to protect it.

One of the principal cultural ceremonies of the Pacific Northwest indigenous tribes in British Columbia was the "potlatch," believed to have been practiced for thousands of years. Usually a part of this complex ceremony was given to the recitation of the spiritual traditions of the tribe. The "speaker," a position often handed down in one of the chief families, performed this important role.

The training of future speakers was a long-observed ritual in which young people were taught to listen to the wind from mountaintops, ocean waves on the rocky shore, and the music of the rushing stream. In this way they learned to incorporate Nature's sounds and cadences in telling stories of the tribe's wisdom. To these people water was a sacred medium of communication, and they felt its sounds should be the vehicle for teaching their traditions.

How water informs language is hinted at by many of the ancient scripts, which employ flowing lines like water in their characters (for instance, Hebrew).* Greek became more disciplined, but it was Latin with its upright, straight characters that forgot the memory of water.

Viktor Schauberger had a remarkable experience while sitting by a rushing stream in his pristine Alpine refuge. Listening to its vivacious music, he intuited how water needs to move and behave in order to stay healthy, which was to inform the groundbreaking research that earned him his reputation as a water wizard.

---

*The Phoenicians called water *mem,* the root for "memory," a reminder of the ancient belief in water's ability to record and transfer information. Mem is also the thirteenth letter in the Hebrew alphabet. The Hebrew word for "water" is *mayim.*

HOW WE REGARD WATER

Until quite modern times, water was always regarded as sacred. This precious substance used to require a great deal of effort to collect for domestic use (and still does in some parts of the world). It was treated with reverence and believed to be protected by divine beings.

Our attitude toward water has changed enormously in recent centuries. With the advent of rationalism and the denial of spiritual influences on humanity came the great explosion of technology that loudly proclaimed human supremacy over Nature. Since we decided we were not part of Nature and devised our own self-centered laws, we have lost touch with the magic of water. We have forgotten its true nature and the meaning of its pulsating movement.

The key to understanding water and living more in tune with our environment and with Nature is to learn to see and feel holistically as part of a community of beings—human, animal, microbial, and botanical—united by the common bond of water.

> *Water is the source of all life.*
> ATTRIBUTED TO THALES OF MILETUS
> (634–546 BCE)

TWO

THE COSMOS AND THE SOLAR SYSTEM

*God is a mathematician, and the universe is beginning to
look like a big thought rather than a big machine.*
ASTRONOMER SIR JAMES JEANS

WATER IN THE UNIVERSE

Hydrogen (H_2, twinned atoms), the main product of what is commonly
referred to as the big bang, is still the most plentiful element in the universe. The prevailing theory of water's origin is that the process of star
creation broke down and re-formed the primitive elements into oxygen
and all the other elements that make up our world, including hydrogen
(which comes from the Greek words for "water" and "creator"). As the
gas collapsed to form a new star, the hydrogen combined with oxygen to
form water (H_2O).

Forty years ago scientists had only one solar system to study—our
own. A recent revolution in astrotechnology means astronomers can
now spot Earthlike planets orbiting faraway stars, raising the hopes
of finding extraterrestrial life. In the past twelve years more than two
hundred planets have been detected outside our solar system by mea-

surements of tiny gravitational wobbles of distant stars. Many of these reveal the presence of water.

In some parts of the galaxy, free gas and dust among the stars form opaque clouds that block out the light (like Orion's Horsehead nebula). It was in one of these, in 1969, that physicist Charles Townes discovered a bright peak in a microwave spectrum of the cold interstellar gas that indicated an abundance of water. It seems that there is plenty of water in these star nurseries as ice or steam, but seldom as liquid water.

James Lovelock, proponent of the Gaia hypothesis, described a habitable zone, or "Goldilocks zone"—from the fairy tale about the little girl who preferred porridge that was "not too hot, and not too cold"— to describe the necessary planetary conditions to be "just right" in order to sustain life. According to this theory, water in liquid form can exist only in a Goldilocks zone (see box on p. 32). So far, telescopes have been unable to identify extraterrestrial bodies that meet the Goldilocks criteria in terms of size and temperature.*

Earth's temperature range, which is suitable for life and for liquid water, is less than 2 percent of the average temperature range found among the planets in our solar system. Earth has been able to compensate for the cooling of the sun since it was formed by virtue of the heat distributed by water.

WATER IN THE SOLAR SYSTEM

Our solar system is thought to have formed from a nebula more than five billion years ago, some of the pristine remnants of which are found in its outer reaches. The Oort cloud—a hypothesized cloud of comets believed to extend from 50AU to 50,000AU (astronomical units), or up to a light-year from the sun—consists of debris left behind from

---

*The most recent mission to search for planets like our Earth is the Kepler probe, which NASA launched March 7, 2009, from Cape Canaveral. This three-and-a-half-year mission is searching our galaxy for Earth-size planets in habitable zones around stars. It would take more sophisticated future missions to analyze their atmospheres to detect whether they could support life.

Life on the Margins of Possibility

The postulation of a Goldilocks zone has its limitations. For one thing, even on our own planet certain microorganisms such as bacteria or microbes can live, or even thrive, in conditions that are prohibitive to most of life on Earth. These are called extremophiles and include, for instance, an organism that can thrive at temperatures between 176°–250°F, such as those found near volcanic vents on deep ocean floors; and organisms adapted to the very high oxygen levels of the subglacial Lake Vostok in Antarctica.

It is possible, even likely, that forms of protolife are much more common than we think—bacterial life that existed on Earth two billion years ago (and still does today) may well exist under the surfaces of some of the solar planets' moons.

the condensation of the solar nebula and probably trillions of comet nuclei.* These objects are composed mainly of ice (predominantly water, but some methane and ammonia) and represent a gigantic reservoir of water.

So how did our oceans become filled? The solar system, when it started to coalesce, would have contained a great amount of water to be distributed among the bodies that condensed out of it. Earth would have released much of this interior water as a vapor held near the surface by its gravitational field. In the mythology of Earth creation there were rains lasting for centuries.

For a billion years after the formation of our solar system, comets were extremely numerous. Earth was most likely bombarded by these wanderers that typically are several hundred feet to several miles in width and composed principally of ice. It would take half a million of

---

*An astronomical unit (AU) is the distance from Earth to the sun—approximately 93 million miles.

these icy entities to provide half of the water in our oceans. In addition, comets contain a high content of heavy, deuterium-rich hydrogen, the heavy form of hydrogen that originated with the big bang and that is still commonly found in the universe. Primary water, from Earth's interior, lacks this deuterium content. Oceanic water, which has a lower level of deuterium, is therefore believed to be a mixture of the two sources of water.

When Earth was formed, the early magmas contained a lot of water. Rachel Carson suggested in *The Sea Around Us* that about half the ocean water would have come from deep inside the planet. More recent theories suggest that new primary water is constantly being produced in Earth's mantle. John McCreary postulated in *The American Dowser* that "primary water is generated in the rock strata when the right temperature and pressure are present. It is then forced into fractures and fissures in the rock where it can traverse large distances, hundreds of kilometers. Some of this water is expressed as springs that can be either hot or cool. This water is always moving and therefore can be detected by dowsing."[1]

A major repository of comets is the Kuiper Belt, which extends outward from Neptune to about the orbit of Pluto. There are also thought to be ice-encrusted objects in the asteroid belt between Mars and Jupiter. There is no shortage of frozen water in our solar system, and it seems to have been present since the beginning of time, but liquid water has been more elusive.

Comparison of photographs of the surface of Mars taken in 1999 and 2006 by orbiting satellites shows recent deposits in two gullies that could have been made only by flowing water. It is now thought that the planet may have large underground reservoirs of water that occasionally gush up as aquifers.

Astronomers have found evidence of liquid water on Saturn's moon Enceladus, a discovery that raises the possibility that it could support life.[2] Images from the Cassini spacecraft showed that the south pole region was geologically active with erupting plumes of water.

Why is Earth the only planet to have oceans? There is a narrow temperature range that allows liquid water to accumulate, and because Mars is the only other planet in our solar system within that range, it is probable that it once carried oceans on its surface. Its smaller mass and lower gravity would have made it difficult for Mars to retain its atmospheric water. However, it is now thought that Jupiter's planet Europa may have abundant water *below* its icy surface, because the interior is warm enough to liquefy water.

A study of the links between Earth's physical processes and life can help an understanding of evolution. Earth is generally thought to be about four-and-a-half billion years old. The first two billion years are clouded in mystery. But let's say that it would have taken about half a billion years for the planet to develop a crust and start to form oceans. Probably about two billion years ago the oceans became the womb for primitive forms of organic life, initially bacteria, worms, and algae. It was impossible, then, for life to gain a foothold on land that, up to four hundred million years ago, had a most inhospitable environment.

There was no climate as such. How and when the atmosphere formed is also a mystery. The early atmosphere must have been composed mostly of CO_2, creating a very hot surface temperature (similar to the planet Venus). It is thought that a cosmic impact (for example, when the Earth/moon system was created) may have removed this heavy atmosphere, to allow a thinner, life friendly one to develop. Once photosynthetic plants became established on land and microorganisms in the oceans, the formation of an oxygen-rich atmosphere would be able to proceed.

THE EARTH/MOON SYSTEM

We cannot understand water without accepting its intimately intertwined relationship with the moon. All ancient cultures celebrate this, and in many traditions the moon has had a strong influence on the understanding of life cycles and on planting times for crops (see p. 192).

There are many theories of how the moon was created, but most agree that its age is similar to that of Earth. There are two principal theories of the moon's origin. One is that it was formed as the result of a collision of a Mars-size object with a very young Earth; the other is that it was formed by an accumulation of leftover debris from the formation of Earth.

We know of no other planet-moon combination in which a moon is as large or as close as our moon in relation to its planet (one-quarter the size of Earth, it has been called a "binary planet" system). The generation of our planet's strong magnetic field, which lessens damage to life systems from cosmic rays, was probably due to prolonged heating following the likely impact that created the Earth/moon system.

The evolution of terrestrial life as it has unfolded would have been impossible without the planet's extraordinary partnership with the moon. It has stabilized Earth's obliquity (inclination of its axis to its plane of rotation) at 23°27', which allows predictability of seasons, climate, weather patterns, and plant and animal environments. (Ours is the only planet in the solar system that has a stable obliquity. Mars's, for example, swings between 0° and 60°.) It is possible that the stability of the Earth/moon system has also limited disruption from cosmic impacts, always a threat to the development and maintenance of life. Clearly, Jupiter and Saturn, because of their enormous masses, have been our first line of defense (for instance, when the Shoemaker-Levy comet struck Jupiter in 1994), but our moon is an inner defense system.

The moon's ability to generate large tides created a littoral environment with tidal pools to encourage polymerization of organic molecules and would have facilitated the emergence of life from the ocean onto dry land. The moon's gravitational effect on water in organisms is clearly extraordinarily important in promoting growth patterns. (See chapter 13.)

The inevitable conclusion is that it is difficult to see how other planets fulfilling the Goldilocks criteria could produce organic life as we know it unless they had a moon like ours.

GATEWAYS IN TIME

Geological periods are quite distinct (see time chart in figure 2.1). They are typified by specific geophysical conditions, climates, and life-forms. Very often the opening of a new period is heralded by one of four agents of change: the shifting of continents (with mountain formation), cosmic collisions (for instance, the demise of the dinosaurs), climate change driven by changes in CO_2 (for instance, the end of the Permian period), or worldwide glaciation. These gateways often cause species extinction, but they bring in new species or life-forms with an escalation in complexity, which is an essential part of evolution toward higher quality, or "consciousness."* They can be seen as either setbacks or times of great opportunity for life. It seems that our planet's evolutionary path is closely connected to the evolution of life.

A dozen or so causes of mass extinctions have been proposed, including supervolcano eruptions, changes in sea level, meteor collisions, and sudden or lasting cooling or warming. There is as yet little appreciation of the mass extinction that is now in process. Julian Caldecott presents some sobering statistics on this species extinction in his book *Water*.

> There are millions of species on Earth, but 70 percent of the terrestrial ones are concentrated in only thirty-four biodiversity hotspots. These biodiversity areas formerly amounted to 15.7 percent of the planet's land area. The terrible judgment on our species is that 86 percent of this habitat has been destroyed, mostly since 1950.
>
> These small and declining patches shelter many species that occur nowhere else: at least 150,000 endemic plant species, almost 12,000 endemic invertebrates, and many millions of other invertebrates, mostly unknown to science.
>
> It is not possible to slash and burn 86 percent of the habitats of tens of millions of species without at least half becoming extinct. Not necessarily at once, but committed to extinction they will be, due

---

*The idea of Earth having a "consciousness" as part of its evolution is a variation of James Lovelock's Gaia hypothesis.

Eras	Periods	Million Years	Earth Movements & Glaciation	Life-Forms
QUATERNARY	Holocene Pleistocene	— 2 —	(glaciation)	man
TERTIARY	Pliocene Miocene Oligocene Eocene	65	(ice caps) **ALPINE** (vulcanism)	higher mammals **modern forests** bony fish
MESOZOIC	Cretaceous	144		***5th mass extinction*** (dinosaurs) reptiles flowering plants ammonites
	Jurassic (New Red Sandstone)	205		**more diverse forests** first mammals & birds dinosaurs
	Triassic	248		***4th mass extinction*** **coniferous forests**
PALAEOZOIC / UPPER	Permian	290	**HERCYNIAN** (glaciation)	***3rd mass extinction*** (oceanic)
	Carboniferous	354		**coal forests** first land vertebrates sharks
	Devonian (Old Red Sandstone)	417	Late **CALEDONIAN**	***2nd mass extinction*** **primitive trees** first plants & animals **soils form** climatic zones
PALAEOZOIC / LOWER	Silurian	443	Early	
	Ordovician	495		***1st mass extinction*** first fishes
	Cambrian	545		Cambrian "explosion" abundant marine life esp. trilobites
PRE-CAMBRIAN / PROTEROZOIC	Vendian	650	**CADOMIAN** (Snowball Earth) glaciation	precursor to explosion of oceanic life-forms
	Cyrogenian	1 bn		ocean salinity present level primitive oceanic life
		2.5 bn		*Eukaryotes* bacteria
PRE-CAMBRIAN / ARCHEAN		3.5 bn 4.6 bn		oxygen reltd blue-green algae *Extremophile prokaryotes?* Moon lavas (maria) oceans forming oldest rocks crust forming Moon's cosmic bombardment Earth's & Moon's births

Figure 2.1. Geological time chart. Note the periods of "Earth restlessness" in which traumas caused by orogeny (mountain formation), glaciation, rapid global warming, or cosmic collision bring mass extinctions followed by evolutionary explosion. (A. Bartholomew)

to the reduction and fragmentation of their habitats and the death of partner species, such as their pollinators and seed dispersers. If the whole dynamic were stopped today, we would still be looking at millions of species continuing to die out, probably at an accelerating pace as the struggle ends for thousands of ecosystems. This process seems set to peak in the period 2000–2025, when half the world's species are likely to be lost, at a rate of about a million a year.[3]

Mountains eroded by ice and water provide the nutrients for evolutionary advance. There is little evidence of cosmic collisions far back in the record, but undoubtedly there were a number, some of which might have been responsible for gateways in time. We know only of more recent ones where the evidence still exists on the earth's surface, such as the extinction of the dinosaurs about 65 million years ago at the end of the Cretaceous period. There is also evidence of one much more recent, about ten thousand years ago near the end of the last ice age, which may be connected with the myth of the great flood described in Genesis.[4]

GLACIATION

The most recent theory about the global thermostat is that it is controlled through the action of CO_2. The global thermostat takes care of most variations of the heat received from the sun. Earth has been ice free for 90 percent of its existence. However, for at least the last thousand-million years, our planet has switched between a balmy greenhouse climate and one in which significant amounts of ice covered its surface.

There are two factors that may have contributed to the onset of glaciations. First, our planet is in an elliptical orbit around the sun; when farthest from the sun, it might have cooled sufficiently for ice sheets to form. Second, the continents move on the surface of the globe, and if they were to group near one of the poles when farthest from the sun, this could have caused worldwide glaciation.

Polar ice caps have formed at least four times, creating a condition that, as we have noted, results in a world climate balance that seems to favor biodiversity.

EARTH RESTLESSNESS

Earth went through an evolutionary advance at the dawn of the Paleozoic era, some 545 million years ago. At that time there was an explosion in the biodiversity of ocean life-forms; quite complex organisms started to appear—vertebrates and hard-shelled creatures, such as the easily recognized trilobites, a type of arthropod. An abundance of oceanic fossil remains is found in the geological strata from this time onward.

Then, about two hundred million years later, halfway through the Paleozoic era (still 400 million years ago), there was another great planetary restlessness—the Caledonian earth movements. These raised great mountain chains in Ireland, extending through Scotland and into northern Scandinavia, as well as in other parts of the world, repositioning landmasses.

Earth's four billion years prior to this time could be described as a long period of gestation involving gradual surface cooling, establishment of solid crust with continental roots, formation of oceans, balancing of water chemistry, creation of a primitive atmosphere, and, eventually, basic life-forms in the womb of the ocean.

LIFE EMERGES FROM THE OCEAN

The first terrestrial life-forms were types of seaweed that absorbed CO_2 and produced oxygen: mangrovelike semiaquatic plants and primitive ferns. Then the first nonaquatic plant life appeared, enabled by the creation of soils that could later support the first forests in the Carboniferous period, which subsequently allowed the first land vertebrates to emerge—amphibians and early vertebrates. The chemical composition of seawater creates an environment that limits the evolutionary potential of sea creatures, but, much later, ocean mammals got around this obstacle by developing a heart and blood circulation that depends on oxygen.

Life has had a more tenuous hold on the dry land of this planet than would appear from its success in the current age. However, during the Ordovician, Devonian, Permian, and Cretaceous periods (see time chart in figure 2.1 on p. 37), there was mass extinction of oceanic species due to the overacidity of the surface oceans.[5]

EARTH AS AN ORGANISM

When James Lovelock first proposed his Gaia hypothesis around 1971, mainstream science castigated him as a romantic. However, the concept of our planet as an organism is really quite ancient. It had been given scientific credence by Viktor Schauberger in the 1930s, but his ideas remained in the German esoteric field until the 1990s.

Earth's identity as a living, breathing organism that is constantly evolving and maturing, able to sustain life-forms of ever-increasing complexity, is something that mainstream science still finds very difficult to accept. Earth's ability to regulate the biosphere's environment, control its temperature, and renew its skin is a remarkable story. Even when faced with cataclysmic events, Gaia demonstrates the ability of self-healing.

The Darwinian view is that life evolves by selection in the face of environmental influences, whereas the Gaia hypothesis claims that life influences its environment in such a way as to optimize its own future. Earth, it seems, may actually create these events in order to stimulate evolution. Just as forest fires support biodiversity, in the longer scheme of things, orogeny and continental lift and submersion help to rejuvenate fertility.

There is much talk today of the need to "save the planet." Earth has brilliant resilience to adapt to change, and the present threat will be no exception. It is humanity that is facing destruction, by its own hand.

LIFE IN THE OCEANS

Life originated in the oceans, some 3,600 million years ago. Beneath the surface of our planet, as far down as eleven kilometers (nearly seven miles), millions of species and countless ecosystems flourish. It is easy to think of life on planet Earth primarily as a terrestrial phenomenon, with fish and whales in the oceans as a bonus. Actually the reverse is the case, but it's only with modern research techniques that the extraordinarily rich life of the oceans is beginning to be known. Some 13,000 new species were discovered in 2003 alone, out of a known total range of 38,000 species, from plankton to whales. More than 90 percent of our planetary biomass (in weight of living matter) is found in the oceans, 90 percent of which are single-celled and microbial species. Fully 80 percent of ocean species depend on endangered coral reef environments.*

We think of the forests as the producers of oxygen, but marine plants, phytoplankton, and algae convert much greater amounts of CO_2 into oxygen. Water vapor rises from the ocean surface to form clouds that release fresh water over the land. Ozone rising from the ocean's surface protects life from ultraviolet radiation. These sources of oxygen are under the same threat as our forests.

The average depth of the oceans is almost 4,000 meters (2.4 miles) and includes approximately 97 percent of the water on our planet. It is thought that life started with extremophile species around the hydrothermal vents in the deep sea floor, which can heat the water to 450°C (842°F).† Similar rare creatures are still found today. They do not need photosynthesis for food, as does 97.7 percent of the biosphere. They obtain their energy solely from chemical reactions and were the first step in the evolutionary process.

Sun, oceans, atmosphere, and the equatorial rain forests are the principal drivers of climate. The oceans moderate it by removing excess heat from the tropics through the thermohaline oceanic circulation system. Although phytoplankton comprise only 0.2 percent of

---

*See the box in chapter 17 titled "The Growing Acid Problem in the Arctic Ocean," which discusses how acidity in the oceans threatens life at the bottom levels of the ocean food chain. Chris Bowler, a marine biologist on the EU Tara Ocean project in Barcelona is setting out on a three-year survey of the world's oceans to study marine life-forms. His research should provide valuable data on the state of the ocean ecosystem.
†An extremophile organism is one that lives under extreme environmental conditions.

the world's biomass, their prodigious reproduction rate helps account for nearly 50 percent of our primary food source and supports the incredibly rich marine community, from zooplankton to whales; but phytoplankton thrive only in cold water. Global warming is threatening the base of the food chain found in the rich biodiversity of the oceans, and the higher part of the food chain is under siege from industrialized overfishing and pollution.[6]

THE IMPORTANCE OF WATER FOR EVOLUTION

Ecologist Viktor Schauberger saw water (including sap and blood) as an organism, the vital life-giving and energy-empowering vehicle that intelligent Nature uses for all forms of transmission and communication, energetic as well as physical. He understood water to be a medium linking earth and cosmos, with a vital role in promoting higher evolutionary life-forms.

Schauberger emphasized the importance of the water cycle, with the nourishment it provides for evolutionary biodiversity. Water, as the vehicle for life, may indeed have its own evolutionary journey. Fresh water in Caledonian times may have been much less complex than today's, not in its chemical composition, but in its structure.

As we shall describe in later chapters, water is able to carry more intricate information when its structure is more complex. In Caledonian times, four hundred million years ago, a simple laminar structure was perhaps all that was required of water. To support the evolutionary demands of new life-forms for more complex DNA and chromosome forms, water would need to develop more complex geometric structures, such as three-dimensional geometry, complex octahedrons, molecular clusters, and Platonic solids and their derivatives. These structures appear now only in the highest quality water, indications being found in techniques like the drop water method of analysis (see chapter 13).

The evolution of mammals was a further giant step forward in evolutionary sophistication and could not have arisen without the development of water structures more similar to the complexity we find today (see chapter 3).

The civilizations of Man could not have evolved without mountains providing the minerals, water, and fertile land. Ice and water erosion were the drivers of this vital process. Great alluvial flood plains became the cradles of civilization—Mesopotamia, the Indus Valley, the Yellow River, the Nile Delta. Because mountains provide the minerals that are the source of the great rivers, it is not surprising that many people find mountains spiritually nourishing.

THE SKIN OF THE EARTH

The skin of any organism performs a number of important functions. As the outside layer, it defines the integrity and coherence of the organism and protects it from physical assault and infection. It is the vital heat-balancing organ for most organisms. It is also the antenna for receiving deeper cosmic or earth energies (see chapter 13).

Earth's "skin" operates by similar principles. It is composed of atmosphere, oceans, mountains, ice, and land. They work as a single system, for if one part of the system becomes unbalanced, the integrity of the whole is affected. In the current epoch, 90 percent of the ice-free landmass was historically covered by vegetation. Of this, 75 percent had forest cover; this has been reduced to only 25 percent, causing modification of the world's climates, loss of fertility, and soil erosion. On "the planet of water," it's no surprise that the land skin is water-dependent. Its absence causes desertification.

THE MOON AND ITS TIDES

When you consider that the oceans are a thin, fluid skin on the planet, it is easy to see why the moon's mass exerts a gravitational pull on them. The sun does as well, but being 390 times farther away, its gravitational influence is much smaller. As it circles Earth, the moon pulls all the water bodies, affecting not only ocean tides but also lakes, rivers, air masses, and rainfall.

Earth has tides as well. A national study by Columbia University in 1970 found that the land surface rises and falls an average of twelve inches each day. There are also detectable lunar winds, flowing east in the morning and west in the evening, affecting plants. Water-based organisms demonstrate either pulsations or rhythms that are connected to lunar gravitation (see chapter 13).

The moon's orbit is elliptical; when it is closest to Earth (its perigee), the tidal effect is stronger. Its orbit is also tilted; when it crosses Earth's orbital path (the nodes), it can eclipse the sun's light. Spring tides are caused by sun and moon being in the same line, which happens every fourteen days. The highest tides occur every seven and a half lunations, when the perigee coincides with a new or full moon. If a storm happens to be moving onshore at this time, flooding and property damage can be severe.

Long estuaries or narrowing bays, like the Severn Estuary on the west coast of England or the Bay of Fundy in Nova Scotia (Canada), can have forty-foot variations between high and low tides. There are also nodal points where ocean currents meet, which can cause larger variations.

Intertidal environments are very productive ecosystems, often having the widest biodiversity in rock pools, coastal marshland, and mangrove swamps. Inevitably their rich nutrients attract a wide range of small marine animals, insects, and birds. They were the stepping-stone for life to emerge from the sea and tentatively colonize land.

The moon has a strong effect on many biological processes in organisms, such as reproductive and plant growth cycles. Ancient peoples, understanding this, regarded the moon's influence as more personal than the sun's and used the thirteen-month moon calendar for the year. Because the moon affects all growing things, a system of lunar-based horticulture has evolved, which we will consider in chapter 13.

First, we'll look more closely at the nature of water, this most familiar, yet strange, substance.

THREE

CHARACTERISTICS OF WATER

It is clear that life on Earth depends on the unusual structure and anomalous nature of liquid water. Organisms consist mostly of liquid water. This water performs many functions and it can never be considered simply as an inert diluent. It transports, lubricates, reacts, stabilizes, signals, structures, and partitions. The living world should be thought of as an equal partnership between the biological molecules and water.

MARTIN CHAPLIN*

After hydrogen, water is the most common molecule in the universe. It is the most common substance on our planet and its molecular structure is woven into all biological molecules. Water vapor is the principal greenhouse gas and is also responsible for absorbing 70 percent of cosmic radiation.

*Martin Chaplin is a professor and biochemist at London South Bank University, to whom I am grateful for permission to reprint models of the geometry of water structures from www.isbu.ac.uk/water. He identifies sixty-seven anomalies of water: twelve of phase (states controlled by temperature or pressure), twenty of density, twelve material, eleven thermodynamic (for instance, specific heat), and twelve physical (such as viscosity). A summary of the less complex is given in appendix 2.

BASIC WATER

Many of the characteristics of water are well known. It might be useful, however, to consider its main chemical and physical properties.

- Under normal conditions, water has neither smell nor taste. The intrinsic color of water and ice is a very pale blue.
- Water vapor is invisible; mist and cloud are a mixture of vapor and small liquid particles.
- It is transparent, allowing light to penetrate for photosynthesis in aquatic plants.
- Water as H_2O is an electrically polar molecule: the electronegative oxygen atom ensures that the two hydrogen atoms are relatively positively charged. This charge difference, called a "dipole," makes the molecule polar and stable.
- The unusual geometry of water molecules allows tight three-dimensional bonding that produces a particularly strong and stable structure. This means that although more kinetic energy is required to change water's state—for instance, a higher temperature to boil it—the bonds can also easily come apart.
- These hydrogen bonds are the clue to water's behavior; they assemble and pull apart millions of times a second, giving water its extraordinary adaptability. For example, water can climb up a tube by capillary action, which is a primary process of biological life.
- The boiling point of water is related to barometric pressure; at sea level water boils at 100°C (212°F), but at the top of Mount Everest it boils at 68°C (154°F). In the intense pressure of deep ocean trenches, water is still liquid at very high temperatures.
- If water behaved normally (that is, in the same way as its chemically related compounds), it would be a gas at ordinary temperatures and there would be no rain, rivers, vegetation, or body fluids. It is the only compound that is found in Nature in all three basic states—solid, liquid, and gas.

- Earth's climate is largely regulated by the ability of water to absorb and retain heat (called latent heat). This enables water vapor in the atmosphere to condense, form clouds, and produce rain. The amount of water vapor that the atmosphere can hold increases with rising temperature.

- Water has the highest specific heat of vaporization (the amount of heat energy required to raise the temperature of a given amount to form vapor from the liquid state) of any compound other than ammonia. This consequence of the strong hydrogen bonding helps to control large fluctuations in temperature, thus moderating climate. It is also related to water's capacity to retain heat.

- Water has a high surface tension because of the strong bond between the atoms—it sticks to itself and to other surfaces, assisting its capillary action in plants. Surface tension also causes water to form naturally into drops.

- Spring water often has the highest surface tension. The strong skin of this water surface is called the "meniscus." Damaging water's skin can affect its ability to form membranes within its body.

- Water's most important quality is as a powerful solvent. Substances that dissolve easily in water (hydrophilic, or "water loving") are salts, sugars, acids, alkalis, and some gases, especially oxygen and carbon dioxide (carbonation). Those substances that do not mix well with water (hydrophobic, or "water fearing") are mainly oils and fats, which are nonpolar molecules.

- The components for cell functioning (proteins, polysaccharides, and DNA) are also dissolved in water.

- Pure water has low electrical conductivity (permitivity), but as soon as salts are absorbed, it becomes a good medium for bioelectrical storage and transmission, which explains why biological water and sea water are saline.*

---

*Electromagnetic fields are produced by living organisms; for example, the electric currents that flow in nerves and muscles.

- Water achieves its maximum density at 3.98°C (39.16°F), expanding 9 percent on freezing. This causes ice to float, allowing life to flourish below the frozen surface.
- Water is responsible for aromas. Hydrophobic oils and volatiles were converted from water by alchemical processes.

WATER'S STRUCTURE

We think of a substance's chemistry as a description of the particular chemical elements it contains (like H_2O), but the way that the atoms, electrons, and nuclei are arranged (their shape and structure) is vital to the behavior of the substance.

In water's case the geometry contained in the molecule determines what is unusual about it. Many chemists say that it is precisely the asymmetry of its molecule that allows water to perform its life-creation role.

The water molecule is a simple union of two small hydrogen atoms that have a positive electrical charge and one relatively large, negatively charged oxygen atom, arranged at an angle of 104° (see plate 6). The oxygen atom has two very negative electrons, which drive the hydrogen atoms closer together, making the valence angle tighter. The inherent instability in this geometry may explain water's extraordinary adaptability in a world comprised of imperfect structures but nevertheless programmed toward a state of equilibrium, harmony, and beauty. As author Paolo Consigli states so beautifully, "The imperfect symmetry of the water molecule, with its bifurcated disposition, holds the secret of matter's very existence: instability and imperfect symmetry belong not only to the aquatic sphere, they are the guiding law of the universe since its inception."[1]

Oxygen's negative charge holds the much smaller hydrogen atoms in close embrace, which makes for a very strong covalent bond that is easily made but difficult to break.*

---

*A covalent bond is a sharing of pairs of electrons between atoms.

We normally associate the term "structure" with solid matter in which the stable matrices of atomic bonds keep their shape and form. Water is a medium that is constantly changing; how can it have a structure? Certainly, it seems that ordinary water cannot have a long-term order, but the key to its structure lies in the fairly stable noncrystalline clusters.

One of the most exciting areas of biological research is how water's structures influence the role of biological water (in the body). Most chemists identify a tetrahedral (four-sided) structure to the water molecule. Martin Chaplin of London's South Bank University, who specializes in water's role in health, has proposed for the structure of water an ingenious model of a 280-molecule icosahedron water cluster, which is a highly symmetrical and aesthetically pleasing structure (see plate 7). It is possible with this model to map all the anomalous properties of water.

The icosahedron is a twenty-faced polygon and the most complex of the five Platonic solids, which, in classical times, were thought to represent the building blocks of all of life and of the universe (see plate 8). The icosahedron was identified with the water domain, with the qualities of personal transformation and sexuality, and with the emotions.

TWO STATES OF WATER

The great mystery is: How is it possible for water to behave quite differently from ordinary liquids? The icosahedral model facilitates the mapping of the controversial idea, first proposed in 1901 by Wilhelm Röntgen (who discovered X-rays) that water exists in two states: bulky, low density (super-cooled water); and high density, in which the molecules are packed more closely together.

The sixty-seven anomalies that water exhibits, listed by Chaplin, can be explained by the two states of water: for instance, liquid water is denser than in its solid phase, compared to other liquids that become denser in their solid phase, because their molecules pack closer together.

Liquid water can be cooled below its freezing point without becoming ice, but when it is heated, it shrinks instead of expanding. When under pressure water's maximum density point lowers, whereas with ordinary liquids it is raised.

WATER AS A SOLVENT

The simplicity of the water molecule makes its electromagnetic qualities more effective. The positive charge of the hydrogen atoms attracts negative ions from the substance with which it is in contact. Oxygen's double-negative charge in turn attracts the positive atoms of the substance. So, the combination of the positive and negative charges in the water that comes into contact with the substance will start to break down the substance's molecular structure.

In this way, water breaks down and dissolves a substance into its constituent parts. From the atmosphere it takes nitrogen, oxygen, and CO_2, while from rocks it absorbs potassium, sodium, calcium, and so on. It is constantly moving around the building blocks of life, taking from one source and depositing them elsewhere for new growth, in a manner that appears to be not entirely accidental.

Water carries, as solvents or solutes, substances that can be damaging to life, such as heavy metals or chemicals from household, agricultural, and industrial transfers; these can be substantially removed by physical filters. Nature also has her own way of dealing with them, which require rather more space, natural energies, and varying surfaces than are possible to introduce on a local scale.

WATER CONVEYS ENERGY

Water's primary biological role is to carry information and transfer energy, which is beneficial when balancing an organism's energy. It also retains the detrimental energy of toxic substances, which can be as damaging to human health as the actual physical substances.

Our modern lifestyle sullies many water supplies. Rivers, lakes, and underground water are frequently polluted with metals and chemicals that cannot be "purified" by filtering or adding chemical disinfectant. Wolfgang Ludwig, an internationally renowned microbiologist from the Technical University in Munich warns: After the water treatment has "purified" the water, as far as the "science of yesterday" is concerned, it still carries certain electrical frequencies, oscillations in specific wavelengths. By further analyses these can be tracked precisely to those detrimental substances that were physically detected in the water before treatment.

Certain electromagnetic frequencies of heavy-metal polluted water have been found in cancer tissue as well. Let us take the very low frequency of 1.8 hertz. We have been able to confirm that fresh water in a certain major German city carried this 1.8-hertz frequency, even though that water had been distilled twice before this measurement.[2]

WATER AND LIFE

Water is an essential part of two metabolic processes in the body:

- *Anabolism.* In condensation reactions the elements of water are yielded from the combining of smaller molecules to create larger ones (for instance, starches and proteins) for fuel storage, structural components, and information.
- *Catabolism.* Water is used to *break* bonds to make smaller molecules (glucose, fatty, and amino acids); for example, to produce energy.

Water is essential to photosynthesis, the basic energy-generating and building process of life through which plants use the sun's energy to separate hydrogen from oxygen in water. Hydrogen is then combined with CO_2 from air and water to produce simple sugars for the plant's growth and to release oxygen to nourish higher life-forms.

AN ANOMALOUS SUBSTANCE

Compared to any other known substance, water is pretty weird—it doesn't behave as it should, or in the same way as any other liquid. The fact that ice floats, for example, not only means that life can flourish below the frozen surface of water but also allows more reflection of sunlight from its lighter-colored surface than liquid water would allow. Most substances are much denser in solid than in liquid form, with more tightly packed molecules, but not water. Because of hydrogen bonding, the freezing point of water is much higher than expected, but the transition from liquid to solid is easier because ice has 15 percent fewer hydrogen bonds than the liquid state.

Other hydrogen-bonded liquids in the hydrides family have boiling points that relate to their molecular weight. If water's boiling point related to its molecular weight, it would boil at -80°C (-112°F) instead of 100°C (212°F). Other solvents and alcohols boil at much lower temperatures, between 38° and 80°C (100° to 176°F). The very high boiling point for water is due to the extensive hydrogen bonding of the molecules. It takes a lot more energy to break apart those tight bonds (see figure 3.1).

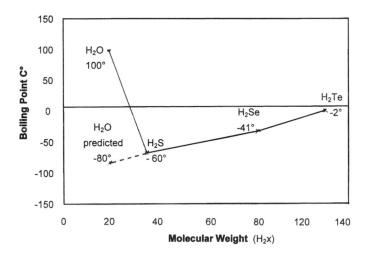

Figure 3.1. Hydrides boiling points. Water's boiling point is much higher than any other hydrogen compounds, making it fit for life. (Jill Granger)

The Celsius temperature scale is based on the freezing and boiling points of water because of water's familiarity, not its normality. It is the same with the measurement of specific heat (the ability to store heat), where water again is the benchmark. Once heated, it takes a long time to cool. Liquid water has the benchmark specific heat of one (one calorie of heat needed to raise one gram of water by 1°C). This is high compared to ice, which is 0.5; and to water vapor, which is 0.47.* Mammals could not survive without the heat storage capacity of their bodily fluids. Water is also a very efficient heat storage medium for buildings.

Water is much more responsive to changes in temperature and pressure than other liquids are. From 4°C (39°F) at its densest, water expands on cooling *or* heating. When cold water is heated, it shrinks; when hot water is further heated, it expands. With increasing pressure, hot water molecules move more slowly, but cold molecules move more quickly. It would not be an overstatement to say that life depends on the weirdness of water. Its high specific heat keeps the body warm in the cold, and the high latent heat of evaporation (that is, a lot of energy is needed to change water into a vapor) allows the body temperature to stay within healthy limits. A dog may not sweat like a human, but when he's hot, just watch his tongue and see how he expels water from his body.

In a large body of water, density-driven convection takes life-giving oxygen to the depths. The large heat capacity of the oceans means they can act as heat reservoirs, fluctuating far less than land, staying cooler in summer and warmer in winter, thus moderating the world's temperature. A coastal environment always has a more moderate climate than inland. Because water releases a lot of heat before it freezes, this has the effect of moving the planet's coldest zones toward the poles, extending the temperate habitable zone. The Gulf Stream's warm water gives western Europe a much more pleasant climate than it would have otherwise.

---

*Specific heat of other substances: ethyl alcohol 0.54, wood 0.42, aluminium 0.21, iron 0.12, glass 0.11, copper 0.9, silver 0.6, gold 0.3.

THE INTELLIGENCE OF WATER

Moving from the more conventional attributes of water to the more unorthodox, we use the term "intelligence" in connection with water because it optimizes the conditions for life by regulating environmental processes. At a temperature of 37°C (98.4°F), water requires the least kinetic energy input in order for its temperature to rise, allowing it to keep the blood in the human body at a constant temperature. Although the internal body temperature level is now considered to be healthy anywhere from 98°F to 99°F, depending on the individual and time of day, it should not depart significantly from that narrow range.

Another "intelligence" of water is that it takes a lot of energy to freeze or melt. A layer of ice formed on a water body's frozen surface slows down the deeper process of freezing. A large amount of heat is extracted from the water to allow it to freeze, which warms the environment and slows down the freezing process. Similarly, because water extracts huge amounts of heat from the air on evaporation (which is why perspiration is so effective), the hottest planetary zones are pushed back toward the equator.

The third intelligence of water is due to another of its anomalies— the huge amount of energy required to vaporize water (called the latent heat of evaporation). This stops the air from excessive heating, as water retains its heat before evaporation. If the air is cold, the condensing water releases heat into the air. This is a very effective balancer of climatic extremes. The warmer the air, the more water vapor it can hold, and the longer the temperature can remain constant.

Earth maintains a temperate climatic zone with optimum conditions for evolution of the human species through the interaction of these three properties of water. Certainly complex civilizations could not have evolved without the stability of moderate, stable climates.

This variety and complexity of the planet's regulatory systems are so extraordinary that it is difficult to believe that the manner in which they developed and stimulated evolution was purely accidental. Without these self-regulating systems, life could never have developed beyond the simplest forms (see box).

Earth's Self-regulating Systems

There have been breakdowns in climatic self-regulation that precipitated massive climate change and species' extinctions (for instance, during the Permian period 250 million years ago); but then perhaps another self-regulating system at a higher level took over, to allow an evolutionary jump to a higher level of complexity to take place. However, it may be that this is more connected with Earth's evolution, which will, in any case, stimulate Nature's evolution.

One of the most important functions of water is to facilitate cellular functions in the body. Because of its unusual hydrogen bonding, it has the unique ability through hydration to activate proteins and through its ionizing abilities to facilitate proton exchange and cell formation. Its particular ability to act as a solvent is essential in the action of salts and ionic compounds.

The degree to which water is the ideal substance to facilitate living processes begs the question: Did the unique properties of water facilitate evolutionary development in organisms? Neo-Darwinists proffer one explanation of this; in chapter 9 we shall examine a different possibility.

THE ANOMALY POINT OF WATER

The density of water is crucial to its behavior. At its densest—4°C (39°F)—it has its greatest energy content. This is the so-called anomaly point, which has a major influence on its quality. Schauberger called this water temperature "the state of indifference," meaning that when in its highest natural condition of health, vitality, and life-giving potential, water is at an internal state of energetic equilibrium and in a thermally and spatially neutral condition.

It was very convenient of Nature to arrange for mammals and other creatures to depend on blood for homeothermic balance. In the body the temperature of the blood (composed 90 percent of water) is almost exactly the same as that of water at its most stable temperature, 37°C (98.4°F). This means that our bodies are able to tolerate a wide range of ambient temperatures, for a great amount of heat or cold is required to change the temperature of water. But it also retains heat well, a quality that makes it well suited for both body temperature and domestic heating systems.

COHERENCE

Water appears to be a disorganized medium. The order created by its hydrogen-bonding networks seems to have a very local effect. In an effort to understand how water is able to display such an integrative role in organisms, scientists have searched with X-ray equipment for decades, hoping to find evidence of a more long-range order.

This principle may be similar to that of water clumping. Recently two chemists in South Korea discovered that, contrary to the laws of chemistry, when a solution is diluted, the water solutes bunch (clump) together, giving the water more coherence. This may be a key to the way homeopathy works (see chapters 11 and 15).[3]

Recent research using magnetic resonance imaging (MRI) has shown that salt dissolved in water quickly spreads throughout the entire water body. Dr. Masaru Emoto used a similar imaging technique in his research with ice crystals (see chapter 15).

It appears that this long-range order, or coherence, is a quantum effect. The problem for mainstream physics and chemistry is that the quantum domain has different laws from the classical Newtonian. Biochemists trained in Newtonian physics struggle to understand the molecular behavior of water, whereas quantum physicists traditionally study the submicroscopic world. However, Dr. Mae-Wan Ho, following research by Herbert Fröhlich and Fritz-Albert Popp, found that there are quantum coherence qualities in the organism, which are now being considered by a number of physicists.[4] We'll look further at this research in chapter 11.

Schauberger, an unorthodox researcher whose peers mocked him for insisting that water behaves like a living organism, established a wonderful picture of the behavior of water: he showed that vibrant, healthy water pulsates, twists, and spirals in a very specific way that maintains its vitality and purity, enabling it to fulfill its function as an energy channel and conveyor of nutrients and waste.

It is important to identify the difference between orthodox and unconventional ideas about energy. The orthodox perceives energy in water as the ability to do work; for example, the potential of a column of water to drive a turbine. The unconventional picture is of an electromagnetic energy with polarities, resonance, and the ability to transfer information from one state or order to another; we call these subtle, or dynamic, energies.

We can observe water's coherence in everyday situations. If we watch water streaming down an incline after a rain shower, or as a rivulet on a sloping beach, we will notice how it pushes down in a jerky rhythm, as pulsations. That is because water is alive, and its inherent nature is to pulsate, just as blood pulsates through the veins and arteries of the body. But the most extraordinary fact that Schauberger discovered is that water has the power of self-purification and can restore its generative properties in the same way that other living things can heal themselves.

PROPERTIES OF WATER

We will note different properties of water as we go along, but in general, there are properties connected with flowing water, such as turbulence, which may be either totally chaotic and destructive, or purposeful chaos. For example, a rock in a stream can create a train of longitudinal vortices that introduce higher energy into the stream body.

Another property, turbidity, stops overheating of the water body in mature streams and keeps the bottom water more active. Viscosity relates to the ability of water to flow—its degree of "thickness." Water of higher viscosity is found near springs (when the meniscus, or skin, is better formed); lower viscosity water is more wetting and more easily absorbed. Further properties that are taken into account by conventional hydrologists examine whether water has a tractive (pulling) or shear (sweeping) force, as well as its flow velocity and sediment load.

ICE

Ice, which has a stable structure that makes it easier to study, can be any of fifteen solid phases of water, depending on pressure and temperature.[5] The ice we commonly come into contact with is called I_h, which is crystalline and either bluish white or transparent. When liquid water or condensed water vapor is cooled below 0°C (32°F), it forms ice. It can also form directly from water vapor, as frost forming on any solid object, or as snowflakes or hail forming around a minute dust particle. It begins as snow crystals that collect on a frozen surface and gradually compact into ice globules.

We know so little about water, as yet. It is likely that, in time, at least as many types of water will be identified as there have been of ice.

> *Water is H_2O, hydrogen two parts, oxygen one, but there is also a third thing that makes it water and nobody knows what it is.*
>
> D. H. Lawrence (1885–1930)

FOUR

THE BLOOD
OF THE EARTH

Were water actually what hydrologists deem it to be—a chemically inert substance—then a long time ago there would already have been no water and no life on this Earth. I regard water as the blood of the Earth. Its internal process, while not identical to that of our blood, is nonetheless very similar. It is this process that gives water its movement.

VIKTOR SCHAUBERGER

WATER AND THE HEALTH OF THE EARTH

Water in the earth works like blood in the human body; it performs similar roles of nourishing, communicating, and recycling. Likewise, the health of water is as much an indication of the health of the whole organism as is blood to the body, as Schauberger and environmentalist Sir David Attenborough have both warned.

Earth's water domain is going through enormous changes brought about by global warming. Climate change is altering the behavior and distribution of rainfall, causing extreme weather, and melting the glaciers, which have been a valuable storehouse of fresh water and maintainer of river flow for the millennia of humanity's existence. The oceans are losing their ability to store CO_2, and their fauna are suffering stress, migration, and species loss.

THE WATER PLANET

Earth is known as the water planet. The wonderful blue color it presents from space derives from the abundant amount of water in its atmosphere (which optically screens out the red end of the spectrum) and from its surface being 70 percent covered by oceans. The atmosphere is composed of 78 percent nitrogen and 21 percent oxygen and a tiny amount of trace gases. Greenhouse gases, which act like a blanket preventing the planet from losing too much heat, are a tiny fraction of the total atmosphere, spatially limited mostly to the layer known as the troposphere. Water vapor accounts for 60 percent of the greenhouse effect, CO_2 for roughly 36 percent.

As the principal component of this planet's surface, water is constantly moving, circulating, and interchanging. In its vaporous state it swirls in great streams, moving heat and cold from one latitude to another, balancing the temperature.

Despite its ubiquitous presence, water prefers to play a mysterious role. Like the chorus in a Greek play, it stays in the background, yet it is the foundation of all processes. Its role is a dichotomy, on the one hand passive—for it does not in itself initiate processes, being the vehicle for change; on the other, active and facilitating. The outcome of energetic processes may be beneficial or catastrophic but water, in one of its three states, makes it all happen.

Our incomplete knowledge of water's role and function makes it hard to predict the processes of instability and change that we are experiencing today. Water magnifies and accelerates a process like that of climate change. The future of humanity on the planet will to some extent rest on our ability to understand that the critical points of the warming cycle are determined by positive feedback loops that depend on water. For example, we have only recently come to understand that the oceans are the largest store of CO_2. Teeming with life, they have stored enormous amounts of minerals and salts washed down from the continents over three billion years. They have their own complex circulatory system, which balances temperatures and nutrients (see p. 79). The landmasses receive most of their fresh water as precipitation derived from the oceans. Much of this finds its way into the surface of the earth, forming artesian basins and enormous inaccessible aquifers. But there are even greater amounts of ancient water locked up in rocks and volcanic material from the very formation of our planet, which may also be making new primary water. All of this water circulates, carrying energy.

The habitable mass of the oceans is hundreds of times greater than that of the land and the atmosphere just above it. Although it has been calculated that 90 percent of life is in the oceans, we still know much less about the oceans and their history than about the land. This study, however, is concerned with fresh water. Water, as the vehicle for life, may indeed have its own evolutionary journey.

DISTRIBUTION OF WATER

Ninety-seven percent of the world's water is in the oceans. The remaining 3 percent is fresh water, of which:

Ice sheets and glaciers	75 percent (much of which will be lost by global warming)
Very deep groundwater	14 percent (inaccessible)
Less deep groundwater	10 percent (for example, aquifers)
Lakes	0.3 percent
Rivers	0.3 percent
Soil	0.06 percent
Atmosphere	0.035 percent

ICE SHEETS AND GLACIERS

For the past three-thousand million years, our planet has switched to and fro between a world that basks in a greenhouse climate (90 percent of its existence) and one that is largely covered by ice. There have been at least four major ice ages. The most recent started about 1.8 million years ago and has still not ended, with vast ice sheets still covering Greenland and Antarctica. The ice started as snowflakes that consolidated into grains of ice with the weight of continually consolidating snow.

Earlier in the current ice age, continent-size ice sheets spread over North America and northwest Europe. Ice caps and glaciers ground down the bedrock, carving out huge valleys. Ice has had more impact on Man than any other environmental influence in the past two million years, principally because of its beneficial climatic effects.

Man evolved during the Pleistocene Ice Age, which had some four major advances interspersed with warm interglacial periods when the climate was sometimes warmer than now. In times of warming, glacial meltwater formed huge lakes that, when the dams that held them back were eroded, caused inundations on a continental scale.

Earth has some 30 million cubic km (nearly 19 million cubic miles) of ice, enough to cover the entire planet to an average depth of 60 meters (200 feet).[1] Ten percent of our landmass is snow and ice: 84.16 percent in Antarctica, 13.9 percent in Greenland, 0.77 percent Himalayas, 0.51 percent North America, 0.15 percent South America, and 0.06 percent Europe.[2] However, scientists are now predicting that enough of it will melt by the end of this century to flood most coastal cities and plains.

The Greenland ice cap has been experiencing unprecedented and accelerating melting in the past decade; the entire structure is becoming unstable. It is comprised of enough ice to raise sea level by six meters (twenty feet). Its rate of melting is accelerating, but it still occupies 80 percent of the island up to a depth of 3,000 kilometers and a volume of 3 million cubic kilometers. There is a risk that the freshwater melt flowing down either side of Cape Farewell (Greenland's southern point) could cause the beneficial Gulf Stream's motion to stop (see p. 79).

In the Arctic what has surprised scientists is how quickly the sea ice is melting. At the present rate there may be no summer sea ice by 2020. It has a strong albedo effect, reflecting the summer sun to keep the Arctic waters cool.* When this is lost, summer warming will accelerate.

The Antarctic ice cap covers 13 million square kilometers, one and a half times the area of the United States, and contains 30 million cubic kilometers (7.2 million cubic miles) of ice. It has an average thickness of approximately 2,000 meters (6,600 feet), in places reaching depths of 4,000 meters (13,000 feet) or more. The Antarctic summer (when the ice melts) has lengthened from sixty to ninety days since the 1970s. Since measurements began in the 1950s, the average temperature on the Antarctic peninsula has risen by approximately 2.5°C (4.5°F).[3]

The most dramatic sign of change in the Antarctic in 2002 was the sudden breaking off of the Ross Ice Shelf, 400-feet thick and roughly the size of Spain. As it had been floating on the sea, its melting has not much affected sea level.

Polar ice makes the temperate latitudes much more habitable. This cooling is amplified by the negative feedback of the white surface reflecting the sun's energy in summer. An unglaciated planet, without polar ice caps and a developed system of mountain glaciers, does not favor Man's evolutionary potential. It is becoming clear that without polar ice to balance tropical heat, Earth's climates will become more extreme. This changed environment will be hostile to our species and will almost certainly contribute to a rapid drop in the current world population.

The glaciers of the Himalayas and associated ranges function as a "third pole." Because they feed the giant rivers of Asia and support half of humanity, their disappearance will cause much deprivation, particularly for the people of China, India, and central Asia (see chapter 17).

If the glacial meltwater disappears from the lush and productive Kashmir valley (reclaimed from a primordial lake), there will be no

---

*Albedo is a secondary feedback effect of the bright surface of ice and snow, which reflect substantial amounts of the sun's heat back into space.

summer surface water in the valley. If the groundwater is not replenished by the melt, it will become desiccated and barren.

We live in transitional times. Theoretically, we are still in one of those exceptional periods favored by Nature for evolutionary accelerations, an ice age. Yet, clearly the environment is changing before our eyes, and the world will look very different by the end of this century. But the great water cycles will continue, with increasing potency.

DEEP GROUNDWATER

There is an enormous amount of water distributed through the deep crust of our planet. An aquifer is formed where it collects in a basin, absorbed by layers of permeable rock or sand. The upper limit may be the water table, or the layers may be many hundreds of meters below the surface and millions of years old. American, Australian, and Russian scientists have discovered substantial water resources in Earth's mantle. One of these is a body equal in volume to the Arctic Ocean beneath eastern Asia at a depth of roughly 1,000 kilometers (620 miles).

In total, these underground resources probably represent 90 percent of the fresh water on Earth. Only a small amount of this is accessible, and historically any drawing off has always been replenished by rainfall seepage. In the past century, industrial farming techniques and the growth of cities have created enormous demands for water that could be supplied only by exploiting the accessible aquifers far beyond their ability to be replenished.* As much as 80 percent of all fresh water is consumed by irrigation, much of which now comes unsustainably from aquifers.

There is, as yet, little understanding of how to gauge when extraction of resources from an aquifer is sustainable—that is, the refill balances the extraction. In fact, most of the world's aquifers are fast depleting (see box).

---

*For instance, the waters of the Sahara.

Aquifer Depeletion

Anything that obstructs natural replenishment can assist overexploitation, for example, land development and building, roads and parking lots, inappropriate crops (cotton) or trees (thirsty eucalyptus); swamps and wetlands drained for farming; accelerated water flow from straightened rivers and flood prevention—all prevent water from sinking into the ground.

When an aquifer beneath a city is drained, land subsidence follows (25 feet in Mexico City over the past one hundred years). When commercial plantations and urban fill replace natural ecosystems and small farms, flash floods will increase and urban pollution will con taminate the surface and groundwaters.

Countries importing amounts in excess of their own water supplies: Libya, 711percent; Saudi Arabia, 722 percent; United Arab Emirates, 1,553 percent, which does not include bottled drinking water. Imported quarts of bottled drinking water annually per person: France 154, Spain 145, Mexico 179, Italy 194 (reference: Caldecott, *Water: The Causes, Costs, and Future of a Global Crisis*).

The quality of the water varies considerably. The vast Artesian Basin of Australia has a high sodium content, making it unsuitable for crop irrigation. As a powerful solvent, water picks up and dissolves many chemicals and gases, such as sulfates, sodium, or the radioactive gas radon. In India serious groundwater contamination by arsenic and fluoride has led to bone deformities and crippling organic damage.

LAKES

Lakes contain the largest amount of accessible fresh water. Many are found in recently glaciated terrain where natural dams were formed by retreating ice sheets or glaciers (for example, the Great Lakes of North

America). The very deep ones are found in regions of tectonic movement or in rift valleys (Lake Baikal in Siberia, the African Rift Valley lakes, Loch Ness in Scotland); they are the oldest and are often still growing in depth and volume. Some form in volcanic craters (Crater Lake, Oregon), or under an ice sheet (the enormous Lake Vostok under Antarctica). Then there are salt lakes, which have no outlet (Caspian and Dead Seas).

Deep lakes tend to be layered so that the cold lower water is not disturbed. Nutrient-rich lakes have complex fauna and flora, sometimes with algal blooms and poor ecosystems due to lack of dissolved oxygen.

Many lakes are now severely polluted if they are fed by rivers from agricultural land or are near cities. Lake Baikal, the world's oldest, largest (in volume), and deepest lake contains about 1,700 species of plants and animals unique to the lake. It holds 27 percent of the world's surface fresh water, of pristine quality. This is now under threat from a planned uranium processing plant in the vicinity. Environmental protesters have been harassed by the Russian government.[4]

> *The river is everywhere at once, at the source and at the mouth, at the waterfall, at the ferry, at the rapids, in the sea, in the mountains, everywhere at once . . . there is only the present time for it, not the shadow of the past, nor the shadow of the future.*
>
> HERMANN HESSE, *SIDDHARTHA*

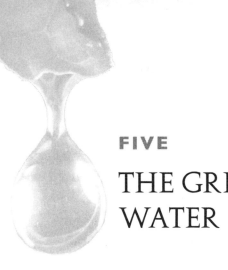

FIVE

THE GREAT
WATER CYCLES

The atmosphere is . . . not merely a biological product, but more probably a biological construction: not living, but, like cat's fur, an extension of a living system designed to maintain a chosen environment.

JAMES LOVELOCK, *GAIA*

Water is the engine and workhorse of the planet. It is always moving in cycles, great and small, slow and fast. Water is always circulating in an exchange between the deep, steam-heated water of Earth's magma and the deep groundwater above the mantle. In the slow cycle, groundwater is held in deep aquifers or glaciers for millennia, gradually seeping through to the surface through springs or from melting glaciers. The fast cycle lubricates the active parts of the atmosphere, with 500,000 cubic kilometers of water evaporating annually from the ocean and land as vapor, condensing into clouds and precipitating back to the surface. There are also the cycles of the circulation systems in organisms.

THE GREAT AERIAL OCEAN

The great aerial ocean is a term coined by Alfred Russel Wallace, cofounder with Charles Darwin of the theory of evolution by natural selection. It well describes the intimate relationship between the oceans and Earth's atmosphere, the sun driving the great water cycle. The heat received on Earth's surface is greatest at the equator, which leads to a transfer of heat from the equator toward the poles. Three-quarters of this heat is carried by water in the atmosphere, one-quarter in the ocean currents. This cycle is a fundamental role of water for the maintenance of life on this planet. The primary cycle is atmospheric; the atmosphere is warmed from below, while the oceans are heated at the surface. The surface winds drive the ocean currents, assisted by the spinning of Earth on its axis.

THE ATMOSPHERE

The atmosphere could be described as the front line of the water story. In its early days, Earth's atmosphere must have been very dark, hot, and thick, with a high percentage of CO_2, hydrogen, sulfides, and methane. This hostile mixture persisted for about two billion years, and then a remarkable thing happened. Cushion formations of bacteria, called "stromatholites," appeared—the first oxygen producers—and over the next billion years gradually built up enough oxygen in the atmosphere to prepare for the emergence of land-based animals, aided later by the photosynthesis of plants.

The atmosphere, for most of Earth's history, has been an unstable environment, disturbed by volcanic eruptions, cosmic collisions, and other unpredictable events. It was only when Earth calmed down sufficiently for life to become established on land that Gaia was able to develop climates necessary for the progress of evolution.

The geological record shows that there were times when climatic conditions were more balanced, more or less defined by geological periods, interrupted by violent earth changes. The violent periods were typified by tectonic shifts, volcanic activity, mountain formation, cosmic collisions, global warming and cooling, ice ages, species extinctions, and later, carbon dioxide shifts.

We don't know a great deal about the composition of the atmosphere in past geological eras. For the past 500 million years it must have been a mixture of simple gases, not dissimilar to ours today. The atmosphere is highly compressible, so that at 18,000 feet above the sea, it is only half as dense as at sea level. Ninety percent of all the atmospheric gases are found below fifteen kilometers (about nine miles) above sea level, yet the atmosphere extends up to one hundred kilometers (about sixty-two miles) above Earth's surface. The overall thickness of the atmosphere at the poles is half what it is at the equator. Earth's gravity is what prevents the thin atmosphere from escaping.

The atmosphere is now composed of 78 percent nitrogen, 20.9 percent oxygen, and .08 percent argon. The remaining .03 percent is trace gases. One is ozone, present in tiny amounts, which keeps us from going blind, getting sun-caused cancer, and so on. Then there are the greenhouse gases, of which water vapor comprises 60 percent; and most of the rest is CO_2, with a smattering of methane and CFCs (chlorofluorocarbons).

The amount of water in the atmosphere varies considerably, depending on the temperature (cold air can hold very little), but doesn't exceed 4 percent by volume. Nevertheless, it is water vapor that carries the heat and creates the weather, influenced by the amount of water carried (degree of humidity) and, of course, temperature.

Water vapor has a complex role in the atmosphere. We tend to think of CO_2 as the principal greenhouse gas, but water vapor absorbs about 70 percent of solar radiation, mainly in the stratosphere. The two gases act together, creating positive feedback loops. So a CO_2 concentration warming the atmosphere allows it to take up more moisture, which then further heats the atmosphere.

Without plants and algae to soak up our waste CO_2, we would soon run out of oxygen and suffocate in CO_2. This is a self-sustaining cycle that is the foundation for life on Earth. The amount of carbon in the cycle is prodigious. Living things account for a trillion tons, while the amount stored in the ground is several thousandfold greater, and the oceans contain more than fifty times what is found in the atmosphere.

Are the North and South Poles Changing Places?

The magnetic poles are not fixed but tend to shift in the course of a year. Quite recently their strength has shown a marked decrease, which may indicate that the north and south magnetic poles might soon change places. This gradual weakening, with magnetic eddies developing all over the planet until they concentrate at the opposite pole, occurs regularly every 500,000 years or so, and we are overdue. The effects would be a temporary loss of the magnetic shield that protects us from solar storms, occasional events that have in the past knocked out electricity networks and communication satellites. It would also, until the new poles were reestablished, result in worldwide displays of the aurorae. (Iain Stewart, *Earth: The Power of the Planet.*)

The Atmospheric Layers

The atmosphere can be divided into several well-marked layers (see figure 5.1). The lowest layer, the troposphere, is the zone of weather phenomena and turbulence. Water vapor represents 75 percent of the total gas mass of the troposphere. Temperature decreases with altitude up to its upper boundary, the tropopause, to a temperature that is just right for enough water to vaporize to produce the rains that continue the water cycle, irrigating the land. This varies in altitude from 17 kilometers (11 miles) at the equator to 11 kilometers (6.8 miles) at the poles. Above this height the temperature remains constant, then increases, causing a temperature inversion that stops the water vapor from escaping, ensuring the water cycle's reliability.

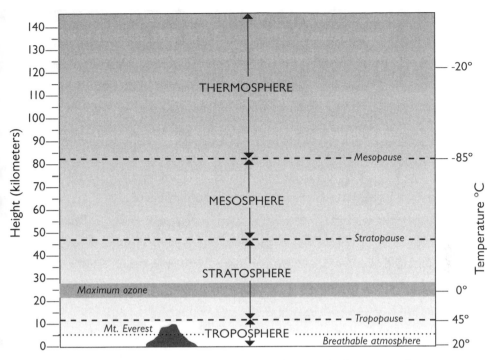

Figure 5.1. Cross-section of the atmosphere, showing the four major layers. It is composed of nitrogen (78 percent), oxygen (21 percent), and argon (1 percent). There is a tiny amount (0.000001 percent) of ozone gas, without which we would go blind and get skin cancer. Only a small amount is breathable air—at 77°F, water vapor makes up 3 percent of what we inhale. (Tim Flannery)

The second major division is the stratosphere, which extends from the tropopause to the stratopause at about fifty kilometers (thirty miles). Ozone, the gas that protects life from ultraviolet radiation, is formed at the stratopause and accumulates lower in the stratosphere. Modern jet aircraft fly in this level of the atmosphere.

Above this is the mesosphere, which has sufficient gas particles to burn up meteors, acting as a protection for Earth. There is just enough water here for noctilucent clouds to form. Above this is the thermosphere at eighty-five kilometers, the environment for the space shuttle and for the aurora borealis (see plate 9). This awe-inspiring phenomenon is thought to be caused by plasma particles from the

The Cold Trap

The tropopause is part of the greenhouse effect that keeps Earth's temperature just right for life. It is often called the Cold Trap because the temperature inversion stops air rising and holds in the water vapor, which is the most important greenhouse gas and the basic driver of Earth's water cycle (see figure 5.2). You might have been in the mountains on a cold winter's day and observed rising smoke forming a layer caused by such a temperature inversion.

The cause of this Cold Trap is not widely agreed upon. Peter Bunyard, the British meteorologist, believes it is caused by the reaction of oxygen (produced by plant photosynthesis) with ozone. This is a good example of the biosphere's self-regulation, supporting James Lovelock's Gaia theory. This ingenious system must have been in place two billion years ago when the first primitive organisms started producing oxygen.

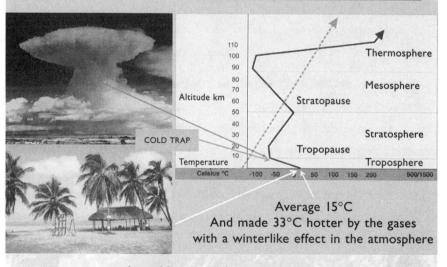

Stratification and inversion of the temperature in the lowest part of our atmosphere (the troposphere)

Thermosphere

Mesosphere

Stratopause

Altitude km

Stratosphere

COLD TRAP

Tropopause

Temperature

Troposphere

Celsius °C   -100   -50   50   100   150   200   500/1500

Average 15°C
And made 33°C hotter by the gases
with a winterlike effect in the atmosphere

Figure 5.2. The Cold Trap at the tropopause (Peter Bunyard)

sun being deflected toward the magnetic poles and colliding with air and water vapor molecules, surrendering their energy as photon emissions.[1]

CLIMATES

Balanced climates are vital to terrestrial life. Their present forms probably date from Caledonian times about 400 million years ago, when the first forests and land animals became established and high-quality water was an evolutionary requirement. Before this, climates were perhaps irrelevant. The atmosphere became an invaluable shield against harmful radiation and, with vegetation, was the indispensable thermostat to ensure the optimum environmental conditions for evolution to proceed.

There is insufficient awareness of how much of the sun's energy is reflected back to space by ice and snow (the albedo effect). The resultant cooling of the polar regions produces a larger climatic contrast between the tropics and the poles than in unglaciated times. The world's atmospheric and oceanic circulatory system balances these out, creating a climate fit for a complex species like Man to develop his enormous potential. The average world temperature is lower in glaciated times. As we have already noted, an unglaciated planet would not favor Man's evolutionary potential, unless the sun's energy continues to wane.

A climate derives from the specific way in which the given energy from the sun is affected by the local influences of moisture from the ocean, continental mass, temperature, and topography. It varies according to latitude and season. So, for example, the plains of India warm up in the summer, drawing in the damp maritime air from the tropical oceans. The mass of the Himalayas forces this damp air to rise and release deluges, known as the monsoon.

Continental masses tend to produce areas of high pressure. Climates are the result of many local factors, such as wind belts (jet stream, roaring forties, trade winds of the sub-equatorial region, El Niño, and so on). A climate is also affected by turbulence in the weather, so in temperate latitudes, where there is more mixing of different types of air masses (see the discussion of the Ferrel circulatory system on pp. 77–78), changeable weather patterns determine climatic variations. This is particularly true of a coastal environment, such as that of the British Isles. The El Niño effect, when the warm southern Pacific Ocean current changes its direction of flow, is at a maximum early in the second decade of the twenty-first century, which is likely to have adverse effects on worldwide weather.

Air masses play a large part in both climate and the resultant weather. An air mass that forms over the ocean will have high humidity, while a continental air mass generally has low humidity. The boundaries between air masses are called fronts, which tend to be the breeding grounds for storms and unsettled weather. People respond very differently to varying humidity, to the amount of sun, and to stormy conditions. The change in the seasons also affects people differently. This will often determine where one decides to work or settle.

The British Isles are interesting in that they don't have a climate of their own but are subjected to seven different climate types. No wonder the weather forecasters have a difficult time! The islands are at the crossroads of several air masses, demonstrating the way that huge differences in moisture content and temperature affect the resulting weather. The west side of Britain is influenced by the humidity of the ocean and by the warming Gulf Stream; the east comes under the influence of the continental climates; and northern air streams can have a great cooling effect.

There is also the powerful jet stream, favored by commercial aircraft flying eastward, which flows like a giant river at about 120 miles an hour at altitudes of about 30,000 feet. The jet stream can change its normal position from the ocean off Iceland to the south or southeast of Britain and can have a disruptive effect on British weather. In the summers of 2007 and 2008 it caused some areas to experience an average month's rainfall in a couple of hours, while torrid heat baked the Black Sea and the Mediterranean regions.

Land heats up more than water does but loses its heat more quickly (for instance, at night). Low pressure cells or depressions often come in a series, bred by weather fronts or perturbations in major wind streams.

WEATHER AND CLOUDS

We usually think of weather as variety. When I lived in the United States, where in summer the skies are often cloudless, I used to yearn for the fluffy clouds of home.

When we learn how special and magical water is, we might accept its gifts more graciously. Have you ever gone out in a light drizzle and tilted your head to let your face become refreshingly moistened? To walk barefoot on a dew-kissed lawn at dawn can be a most invigorating experience!

In winter, the weather can bring some astonishing effects, like the magic of a fresh snowfall, which produces a strange silence in the landscape and muffled sounds, or ice forming on tree branches or power and telephone cables.* The most magical of all is when fog freezes on a spider's web.

The atmosphere is largely invisible except for clouds, which are valuable in alerting us to changing weather. They can tell us when cold air is coming in or a warm front is approaching. There are three main families of clouds: cumulus, including the towering cumulo-nimbus thunder clouds; stratus, layer clouds of middle altitudes, which cover the whole sky; and cirrus, icy high clouds that spread across the heavens and portend a weather change. Clouds form when rising air expands and cools, allowing water vapor molecules to clump together and condense.

Water vapor forms when the sun evaporates moisture from the ocean's surface. It also collects through transpiration from plants, particularly from the equatorial rain forests. The vapor is mixed through the lower atmosphere (up to twelve kilometers) by turbulence. There is

---

*These ice formations can create major power failures.

very little water vapor or ice above this height.* The main role of water in the atmosphere is as a greenhouse gas, contributing up to 60 percent of the total greenhouse effect.

Clouds form from surplus moisture in fully saturated air. The saturation level is called the dew point, which depends on temperature. Warm air can hold two or three times the amount of moisture (and energy) as cool air, so you may get thunderstorms from warm, saturated air and only drizzle from cool.

Condensation in the air rarely happens without some impurity upon which the droplet can form. The air particles may be dust, smoke particles, salts, or other "wettable" nuclei. On land, condensation will form as dew on any object or plant, which means it is pure water. There is much folklore about the magical qualities of dew versus rain.

One of the most ancient techniques for retrieving moisture from the air was the creation of dew ponds. These are not connected to groundwater or designed to catch rainfall, yet they always contain some water, condensed from the night air. They were made typically on the downs of southern England, insulated so that they remained cooler than the sun-warmed earth. They were often 20 meters (70 feet) wide, and 1.2 meters (4 feet) deep.

The optical effects of light on water vapor and ice particles can be extraordinary. The most striking of these is the rainbow, caused by refraction of light, which functions in the same way as a glass prism. When the sun breaks out behind you during a shower, the water vapor breaks up the light into the colors of the spectrum

Other effects are rings around the moon or sun through high cloud, sometimes with a full-color spectrum. From a mountaintop in winter you may see the "glories"—a shadow of yourself projected by a low sun

---

*However, meteoric dust particles act as nuclei for ice crystals when traces of water vapor are carried upward by high-level convection caused by the vertical decrease of temperature to form noctilucent clouds. Noctilucent clouds generally form in summer at about eighty kilometers (fifty miles) altitude in high latitudes and often have a shimmering, opalescent quality. The aurorae are also created in high latitudes by ionizing effects on ice crystals above the mesopause.

onto the cloud below, with colored rings around your head. The better-known Brocken specter is similar but with a longer distance to the shadow. These coronae depend on ice crystals rather than liquid water.

I found that gliding, which depends on finding updrafts of warm air, taught me so much about atmospheric air movements. It is fascinating to see how layers of clouds of varying heights often move in different directions. Clearly there's a lot more going on in the atmosphere than meets the eye. It is a very complex system of air currents, with air masses of different temperatures and humidity that sometimes clash and produce dramatic weather.

ATMOSPHERIC CIRCULATION

The lower atmosphere acts rather like a gigantic heat engine constantly seeking to balance the temperature difference between the equator and the poles. Rising and descending air converts the heat energy into kinetic energy to provide the horizontal motion of the air streams within the troposphere (whose upper boundary is from nine to eighteen kilometers above Earth's surface).

The wind belts and jet streams circling the planet are steered by three cells—the Hadley, Ferrel, and polar cells (see figure 5.3 on p. 78)—which are separated by boundaries of calmer air. The Hadley cell is an active, closed loop system extending from the equator to latitudes 30°N and S, where the air descends, creating an area of high pressure. Some of this descending air moves along the surface, creating the trade winds. The Hadley cell moves farther north in the northern summer, and vice versa in the southern.

The polar cell is also a fairly simple system, with warm moist air rising at about 60° latitude up to the top of the troposphere, moving toward the pole and sinking down to create an area of high pressure and the polar easterly winds in the north and westerly winds near the southern pole.

Between these two circulatory systems is an area of more variable

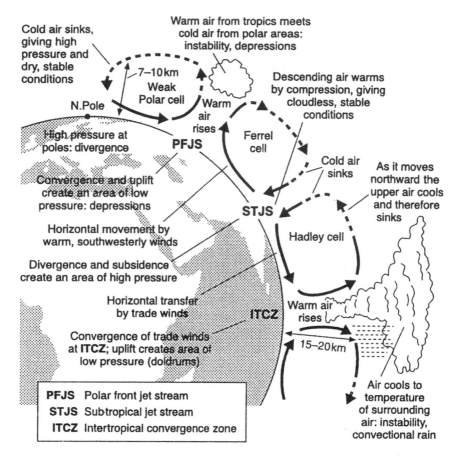

Cold air sinks, giving high pressure and dry, stable conditions

Warm air from tropics meets cold air from polar areas: instability, depressions

7–10 km Weak Polar cell

N.Pole

Descending air warms by compression, giving cloudless, stable conditions

Warm air rises

High pressure at poles: divergence

Ferrel cell

PFJS

Cold air sinks

As it moves northward the upper air cools and therefore sinks

Convergence and uplift create an area of low pressure: depressions

STJS

Horizontal movement by warm, southwesterly winds

Hadley cell

Divergence and subsidence create an area of high pressure

Horizontal transfer by trade winds

ITCZ

Warm air rises

Convergence of trade winds at ITCZ; uplift creates area of low pressure (doldrums)

15–20 km

PFJS   Polar front jet stream
STJS   Subtropical jet stream
ITCZ   Intertropical convergence zone

Air cools to temperature of surrounding air: instability, convectional rain

Figure 5.3. Ferrel atmospheric cells. Atmospheric circulation in the Northern Hemisphere. (Peter Bunyard)

circulation, called the Ferrel cell, which acts like a ball bearing between the other two systems. While the upper winds and the jet stream will be prevailing westerlies, the lower air masses are influenced by high- and low-pressure areas that can cause large variations in wind patterns.

The varying path of the polar front jet stream has a significant impact on the weather. Its usual path with southwesterly winds brings most of Britain's more miserable wet weather. When it shifts northward, Britain is bathed in hot, dry weather, while regions to the south are drenched in unseasonable rain.

CIRCULATION OF THE OCEANS

The oceans formed early in Earth's history, around three and a half billion years ago, probably achieving their present salinity level about one billion years ago. They were to become the womb of life, from about 1.3 billion years ago until Caledonian times, some 400 million years ago, when the first plants and animals appeared on land. The oceans soon became the principal absorber of CO_2 from the atmosphere, which helped the planet cool and prepare for the biodiversity of life. This ongoing role as a carbon sink has probably been its most important role in evolution. Marine life became abundant within a further 500 million years, absorbing CO_2 from the water. The oceans nurtured a complex evolutionary journey for sea life.

The oceans basically control the environment and the world's climate. They receive most of the sun's energy, as well as energy from the cosmos, and provide water vapor for the atmosphere. The fact that we know far more about the land than we do about the ocean is a serious deficiency.

The basic oceanic circulation is driven by surface winds and by the Coriolis effect of Earth's rotation, counterclockwise as viewed from above the North Pole. This deflects liquids to the east as they flow from the equator to the poles in the Northern Hemisphere and to the west in the Southern Hemisphere. It is initiated in the area of the Gulf of Mexico forming a strong current, the Gulf Stream, which flows up the eastern side of North America to Newfoundland and then crosses the Atlantic toward western Europe. The warmth of this current raises the temperature of the British Isles by about 4°C.

As it turns west to the south of Greenland, the Gulf Stream meets the cold, saltier waters coming down from the Arctic Ocean, which act like a pump pulling the stream into the deep. There it returns to the southern Atlantic and then into the Indian and Pacific Oceans as a slow bottom current. In the northern Pacific it wells up and returns as a surface flow, back through the Indian and (south) Atlantic Oceans to complete the thermohaline circulation system (a kind of conveyor belt in the ocean linking surface water with deep currents), with branches to the southern oceans. The complete circulation takes as much as one thousand years to complete (see plate 10).

There is much concern over recent research that shows the Gulf Stream's flow rate diminished 30 percent in the thirteen years between 1992 and 2005, caused by fresh meltwater from Greenland's ice cap, which is believed to interfere with planetary circulation by stopping the Gulf Stream's surface waters from sinking and making their way to the deeper currents.

It is thought that a slowing or shutting down of the Gulf Stream has happened a number of times in the historical past, bringing very cold conditions to western Europe and to the east coast of North America. These climatic changes can happen suddenly and may last for a century or more.

MONSOONS AND TSUNAMIS

A summer combination of strong evaporation from the ocean with land warming can draw in very humid air masses in the tropical and sub-tropical latitudes. The southern Asian summer monsoon is initiated by dry air rising from the warming Tibetan high plateau, which pulls the humid air in from the Indian Ocean. As we have seen earlier, the enormous Himalayan mountain range causes these moist air masses to rise and deposit vast amounts of rainfall.

Oceans can produce devastating damage to coastal regions with a long-range wave pattern called a *tsunami,* Japanese for "harbor wave," usually caused by underwater seismic activity. These wave systems can travel at speeds greater than 800 kph (500 mph) across thousands of miles of ocean, slowing as they approach land.[2] Historically, the damage caused when they hit a landmass was greatly lessened by forests of mangrove, coastal plants that can tolerate seawater and act as a shock absorber.

Technological Man does not understand their significance and has steadily replaced these safety barriers with profitable shrimp farms and rice paddies. The enormous loss of life in the December 2004 Indian Ocean tsunami, the 2008 Burmese typhoon, and Hurricane Katrina in

New Orleans in 2005 would have been mostly avoided with intact mangrove swamps.

THE TERRESTRIAL WATER CYCLE

The underground water cycle is a vital part of water's story, creating aquifers and huge storage systems that have remained, even beneath deserts, for many millions of years (until technological Man, without a thought for the future, began draining them unsustainably). Wells and springs are part of this system. The relationship between underground and surface water cycles is significant. Working together, they form a balanced system of fresh water of high enough quality to provide optimum conditions for biodiversity.

This combined cycle of water, minerals, and trace elements, kept active for millions of years by occasional orogeny, allowed nutrients to penetrate the banks of rivers, create fertile flood plains, and with the cooperation of plants and bacteria, gradually build up a soil profile, often many feet in thickness. From the onset of each episode of mountain building, it might take scores of millions of years to establish the soil fertility required for abundant growth and forests. The forest was Nature's brilliant innovation for the next surge of evolutionary expansion, at its most developed in the tropical rain forest.

Vegetation plays a crucial role in the water cycle. It creates a climate that allows life to evolve fruitfully with increasing complexity, biodiversity, and quality by producing oxygen through photosynthesis and highly energized water through transpiration.

Trees do this most efficiently, and the tropical rain forests have huge impact on the world's climates (see chapter 8). The greatest tragedy affecting the future of humanity is the collusion of world leaders with greedy commercial interests to destroy the rain forests. Of primary concern is the climate, without which species biodiversity cannot exist, but there is also tremendous loss of species, including valuable plants that have not yet been properly studied or collected.

THE FULL HYDROLOGICAL CYCLE

In the same way that blood flows through the arteries and veins of the human body, so does water flow through the lithosphere of our planetary body. The cyclical movement of water from subterranean regions to the atmosphere and back again is called the terrestrial water cycle.

The diagram opposite (figure 5.4) shows the full hydrological cycle. Fresh water evaporates from the sea, rises, condenses, and falls as rain. Some sinks into the earth and some drains away over the ground surface, depending on whether the ground is forested and what type of temperature gradient is active. In areas of natural forest where a positive temperature gradient normally prevails, about 85 percent of rainfall is retained; of this, 15 percent is used by vegetation and humus, and about 70 percent sinks to the groundwater aquifer and underground stream to recharge and pick up the negative energy charge of the earth.

In a natural forest mature trees with deep roots bring up this negatively charged water, along with vital minerals and trace elements from the deeper soils. Trees act as biocondensers, harmonizing positive energy from the sun with the negative energy of the earth (see chapter 8). As a result, the evapotranspiration from the leaves of the trees is a balanced, creative energy.

The forest, as a more dynamic living system, creates transpiration that carries the subtle energy (nonmaterial) imprint of all the resonances of the complex biosystem, including the subterranean elements. Rainfall generated from the forest carries this beneficial influence. The ocean, although it is recharged by undersea volcanic eruptions and exposure to the atmosphere, mainly consumes all it produces and therefore lacks these dynamic qualities. This is best explained in terms of homeopathic theory, in which the greater the dilution of a substance, the more powerful its energetic effect. This is an aspect of the water's ability to carry information, which we shall be exploring later.

The reduction in evapotranspiration from the dynamic forests substantially affects the quality of water vapor and its distribution in the atmosphere. Water vapor created by the natural forest has been bal-

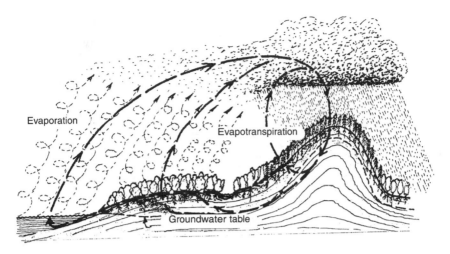

Figure 5.4. Full hydrological circulation. The full hydrological cycle links precipitation with groundwater circulation, bringing important energy exchange. (Callum Coats)

anced by fertile energies from the earth that bring with it the power to stimulate and heal. Water vapor from the oceans has more of the raw untamed energy of the sun, and global warming increases evaporation from the oceans. Without the forest's water there is a greater contrast between areas with abundant water vapor and those with almost none. This greatly disrupts weather patterns and causes an increase in violent storms, hurricanes, and serious flooding near coasts, while the areas away from coastal winds suffer drought and cold night temperatures.

THE HALF HYDROLOGICAL CYCLE

Man's clearing of trees and groundcover exposes the land surface, which allows the ground surface to overheat, causing a negative temperature gradient in the soil. This means that the cooler rain cannot penetrate into the warmer ground, and fast surface runoff in areas of heavy rainfall causes catastrophic floods. Recent floods in Central America, Colombia, Mozambique, Assam, and Bangladesh were all caused by deforestation on high ground.

This disruption of the natural water cycle, which Schauberger called the half hydrological cycle, is now prevalent almost worldwide and has contributed significantly to our present climate change. Notice the difference between figure 5.5, below, and figure 5.4, on page 83. The drawing below shows that in the absence of tree cover, the water table has sunk. Once the forest has been removed, the exposed ground heats up rapidly, all the more so if dry.

This type of evaporation, now lacking evapotranspiration from living things, has more destructive energies. If the rainfall is excessive, flooding inevitably occurs. In many hot countries denuded of vegetation, dry valleys and creeks can be suddenly engulfed by a wall of water, as terrifying flash floods sweep away everything in their paths.

In the absence of trees and groundcover to absorb it, rainwater spreads widely over the surface of the ground, resulting in massive abnormal reevaporation. The increase in water vapor in the atmosphere soon causes increased precipitation. One flood causes another, while in inland areas, droughts become more frequent. The only answer to this vicious cycle is a massive international campaign to plant trees, particularly in the warmer latitudes.

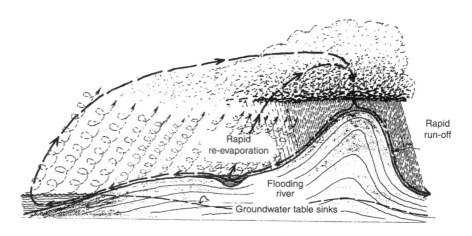

Figure 5.5. Half hydrological circulation. When the ground becomes warmer than the precipitation, through deforestation, it cannot absorb the nourishing rain. (Callum Coats)

The most serious result of the half cycle is that there is no replenishment of the groundwater. When the groundwater level drops, the supply of nutrients to vegetation is curtailed; the essential soil moisture, trace elements, and other nutrients that tree roots normally raise for the benefit of other plants sink below reach. Any water being evaporated into the atmosphere becomes virtually lifeless, lacking in the energy and qualities that groundwater acquires, and results in desertification, which is becoming prevalent in many tropical areas. Schauberger called this stalemate a "biological short circuit."

The limited circulation of the half cycle also increases the intensity of thunderstorms. These can raise the water vapor to levels far higher than normal. At altitudes of forty to eighty kilometers, vapor is exposed to much stronger ultraviolet and high-energy gamma radiation that breaks up the water molecule, separating the hydrogen and oxygen atoms. The hydrogen then rises because of its lower specific weight, the oxygen sinks, and that water becomes permanently lost. Although the atmosphere first warms up due to the greater amount of water vapor, some of this increase in heat is offset by the loss of water atoms at high altitudes.

SIX

SPRINGS AND RIVERS

When you drink the water, remember the spring.

CHINESE PROVERB

Before the advent of public water supplies, springs were the most valued—and sometimes only—sources of drinking water. Settlements were established around a spring that delivered high-quality water. Possibly because of the connection between living water and good health, some of the springs established a reputation for curative powers. Viktor Schauberger was convinced that the high-quality water produced by his springwater machine had healing qualities.

Springwater and mineral water are often said to be "pure," but what is meant is "good quality." The term *pure* should be reserved for H_2O, or virgin water, found in Nature only in evaporated form.

THE VENERATION OF SPRINGS

Springs have long been associated with folk medicine, ritual, and religion, frequently being reported as places of power. Springs thus endowed are often called "holy wells," which is confusing, because the word derives from the Anglo-Saxon for spring—*wella* (hence the expression "to well up")—not for its modern use as a shaft excavated to reach the underground water table. The tradition of venerated springs is found in all cultures and major religions, as far back as prehistoric times. The most common association is the bestowal of supernatural qualities, and more specifically, as the abode of spirits or deities, or linked with holy figures or saints. In Britain, in most cases, a saint named at a spring had no connection with the site, but the saint's qualities may have been associated with those previously ascribed to the spring by the pagan culture.

The waters of most sacred springs are credited with healing powers that bring about cures through immersion or drinking. In British lore the most common affliction to claim healing is infertility, followed by eye complaints. However, some springs are regarded as being so powerful—for example, Lourdes in France, or England's only thermal spring at Bath— that they are reputed to heal many diseases. Offerings (usually coins) are made to the pools served by the springs, either as part of the locally established ritual, or as a tithe for a wish to be granted. Throughout history, such fonts have been decorated with flowers, paintings, statues, or strips of colored cloth, a tradition found all over Europe, Asia, Africa, and Central America.

Natural springs were also valued because the quality and reliability of the water flow in times of drought might make the difference between life and death. It is not difficult to see why people invested these sites with magical powers, or saw them as inhabited by a living spirit who was guardian of the waters. It is likely that many of our forebears would empathize with Schauberger's vision of water as "the blood of the earth" when they saw the perfect nourishing liquid issuing mysteriously from the womb of the planet (see plate 11).

When the rationalism of the Enlightenment replaced the superstitions of an earlier age, some explanation had to be found for the curative powers of certain famous springs. This led, in the eighteenth century, to the birth of the spa culture. To give legitimacy to their spa water, doctors would examine any deposits left behind when they had boiled away the water, in order to identify this or that mineral as the true elixir. During the Protestant Reformation in England, and then with the decline of rural populations, many sacred springs fell into disuse until the nineteenth century, when they were rediscovered by Irish immigrants whose Celtic-based Catholicism still had strong pagan roots.

Today, with the revival of ancient rural traditions, many sacred springs are being restored in Britain and in continental Europe.

SEEPAGE SPRINGS

What is generally called a spring is actually not a true spring, but a seepage spring, which is the overflowing of surplus water from soil and rock strata of a limited depth. Rainwater that is warmer than the ground (a positive temperature gradient) soaks down until it reaches an impervious claylike layer, which channels it out as a spring at a lower level. Its movement is dictated by gravity. The temperature of the water is that of the strata from which it emerges, probably between 6°C (43°F) and 9°C (48°F). This water contains some trace elements, minerals, and dissolved salts but, generally speaking, in a narrower spectrum than that of true springs (see below). The seepage spring responds quickly to variations in precipitation, frequently drying up in a hot summer and flowing strongly after heavy rain.

TRUE SPRINGS

A true spring originates from much deeper strata (see figure 6.1). Water collects in ancient aquifers and retaining basins over many years, and the water emerging to the surface might be hundreds of years old, or even thousands in the case of certain therapeutic hot springs. Because of their vintage, such spa waters are extraordinarily rich in well-balanced minerals.

The rich waters of the Hunza Valley in Pakistan and the waters of the Caucasus Mountains, which in both instances are credited for the longevity of the local people, also originate in true springs. Their waters, augmented by rich "glacial milk," are teeming with minerals from the action of the aggressive mountain streams eroding the surface rocks.

Rainwater penetrates the ground surface under the influence of a positive temperature gradient in a way similar to that of a seepage spring, but in this case it is drawn much deeper into the earth, helped by the increasing pressure, so that it condenses and cools to around 4°C (39°F). Being immature water, it will absorb what it can, so it removes salts from the upper layers of the ground, depositing them later as the water condenses and cools with depth. This makes the upper layers more fertile, and the salts are now available to deep-rooted trees that have the ability to metabolize them, converting them to nutrients for more shallow-rooted plants.

Downward percolating rainwater increases pressure on the groundwater body, pressing the lowest layer into rocks that are affected by

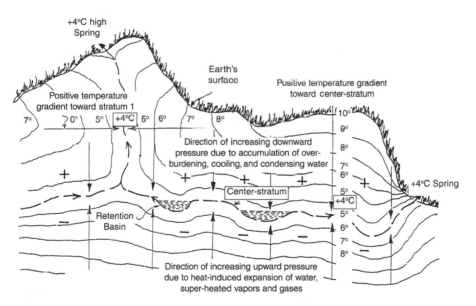

Figure 6.1. A true spring. True springs and high-altitude springs depend on the existence of the 4°C (39°F) denser water level that is called the "center stratum." This gets squeezed between the weight of water in the rocks above, and the water strata below. At 4°C (39°F) it will compress no more and must move vertically or laterally, eventually emerging as a spring. This is why true springs are normally very cold and can issue forth on mountaintops. (Callum Coats)

geothermal heat. This causes them to expand, compressing the layers above. But the 4°C (39°F) stratum water is already at its densest and virtually incompressible at this temperature, so all it can do is push out laterally, providing the springs with their flow. This action explains how springs can emerge at such cold temperatures from high mountain peaks, where there would be insufficient local collection for gravity.

Rain absorbs oxygen in its fall through the atmosphere. After it enters the ground and percolates through the soil, plant roots and organisms reduce its oxygen content. So when it eventually emerges as a true spring, the water is often oxygen deficient, though rich in carbonic acid. It is unwise to drink this water directly from the spring, because being hungry for oxygen, the water can steal it from susceptible organs, such as the stomach, causing great discomfort. If breathed directly, carbonic acid can damage the lungs. This is known by mountain folk as "damp-worm" and by miners as "choke damp" and can be fatal. However, within ten meters (about thirty feet) of the source the water has usually, through its active movement, absorbed sufficient oxygen to be quite safe to drink.

RIVERS AND HOW THEY FLOW

If we understood the importance of water for both the environment and for life, we would nurture and protect our rivers, which are Earth's great arteries. Healthy streams and rivers are water at its most active, powerful, and playful. In our ignorance of the way in which water needs to move, we restrict rivers with embankments and other unnatural constructions. We treat rivers as sewers for waste, and we extract the energy and spirit from their form in hydropower dynamos.

For scores of thousands of years, since people started to settle on the land, our forebears were aware that their prosperity depended on the river. Because soil is quickly depleted of its nutrients by agriculture, particularly if intensive, remineralization via regular flooding was vital to obtaining good crops. This allowed the great civilizations to grow and flourish in Mesopotamia and in the valleys of the Nile, Yellow River, and Indus, to name a few.

Today's technocrats have a need to control this apparently chaotic behavior of the natural river by steering the flow, sometimes behind high banks, and disregarding the ecosystem to the great loss of fertility of the surrounding fields. Artificial, inorganic NPK fertilizers (nitrogen, phosphorus, and potassium) cannot take the place of Nature's remineralization; in fact, they often cause great problems by creating imbalance and pollution.

STAGES OF A RIVER

A river has three stages of life. Its youthful stage energizes the water as the steep landscape puts it through vigorous tumbling, spinning, and intense vortical movements. The immature cold water is hungry, taking up minerals as it scours the rock, cutting gullies with the suspended gravel, and chiseling the sides of the valley, especially when it is in spate. It is oxygenated in rapids and waterfalls, and put through exercises that it will use well when it matures.

When the stream leaves the steep country, the flow slows and deposits some of the heavier rock matter it carried in suspension, which will be picked up again when the flow accelerates. The water is now mature, having absorbed minerals and generative energies, and if it is prevented from excessive warming by trees on its banks, the stream water is absorbed by the banks, recharging the groundwater of the surrounding countryside (see figure 6.2 on page 92). The richness of movement of the young stream is carried into the body of the meandering river. The water is creating its own form, which in turn regulates its flow.

On entering the plains, a river, left to its own devices, meanders across the flat country; where a bend twists back on itself, a shortcut will be created at flood time, leaving behind an oxbow crescent lake. It is mostly in the plains country that people try to manipulate the river, heavy with silt, by straight embankments that stop the river from spreading. If these

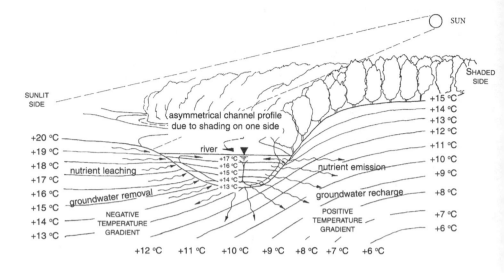

Figure 6.2. Asymmetrical river development. The bank exposed to the sun is warmed so that its groundwater leaches minerals into the stream. The shady side allows the cooler ground to absorb the mineral-rich water. (Callum Coats)

natural floods were permitted, they might not be particularly destructive and they would remineralize the soil, making it more productive.

However, technical Man believes he can control Nature. The old river is now typically forced to perch sometimes fifty feet above the surrounding countryside. If the river should burst its artificial banks at this stage, flooding is often catastrophic. Without the river's normal twisting movement and the positive temperature gradient that keeps silt in suspension, the silt is deposited, blocking the channel. Its natural path thus obstructed, the flow becomes angry and unpredictable. There are very few major rivers that are still allowed to flow naturally.

THE RIVERS ARE THE ARTERIES OF GAIA

If rivers are not allowed to operate as natural conveyors of energy and nutrients to the land through which they flow (for example, if they are disrupted by dams or artificial straightening), the fertility of the land is compromised. If we were really to take care of our rivers, protecting their banks from overheating and allowing them to flow sinuously as they want to, rather than making them follow straight lines, we would be taking important steps to give back to Nature her own power.

Do rivers have individual identity? Many people become attached to a great tree and feel its natural wisdom. Why not a great river? The tree is a column of water, spiraling upward during the day, and downward at night. A river is a horizontal column of water, spiraling and self-cleansing, bringing nourishment to the land through which it flows.

It would be good to befriend a river in your own land and experience the full span of birth, youthful joy, reaching maturity, and the serene meandering of its fullness as it nears its destination. You will learn how its energy changes with the seasons, with its rate of flow, or where a tributary joins the main stream.

It is easier to follow shorter rivers, like those of New England or parts of Europe. The identity of great rivers is also more complex and often compromised by pollution or overextraction. When you get to know a river in this way, it becomes your friend, and you will want to return and return, at different times in the year, revisiting your favorite spots.*

HOW THE RIVER PROTECTS ITSELF

Schauberger saw water as being conceived in the cool, dark cradle of the virgin forest. As it slowly rises from the depths, water matures by absorbing minerals and trace elements on its upward path. Only when it is ripe does it emerge as a spring. In the cool, scattered light of the forest, water begins its long journey down the valley as a lively, sparkling stream.

---

*The Australian dowser Alanna Moore describes a group pilgrimage down the Wimmera River in Victoria, teaching rivercare to the whole community, in her book *The Wisdom of Water*.

Water, when it is alive, spirals in a convoluting motion that helps to retain its coolness and maintain its vital inner energy and health. It is thus able to convey its vibrancy to the surrounding environment. Have you noticed how refreshing and enlivening it is to sit by a healthy, bubbling stream?

Naturally flowing water seeks to protect itself from the damaging direct light of the sun. Trees and shrubs grow along the banks of streams not because people planted them, but because the energies from the flowing stream facilitated their growth there, to shade the water. When a stream is able to maintain its energies, it will rarely overflow its banks. In its natural motion, the faster it flows, the greater its carrying capacity and scouring ability, and the more it deepens its bed.

Schauberger discovered the reason for this—that in-winding, longitudinal spiral vortices form down the central axis of the current, moving alternately clockwise and counterclockwise (see figure 6.3). The nature of inwardly spiraling vortical movement is to cool, so these complex water movements constantly cool and recool the water, maintaining it at a healthy temperature. This leads to a faster, more laminar spiral flow that ejects or neutralizes undesirable substances.

As the stream gets bigger, it is less able to protect itself from light and heat. It begins to lose its vitality and health, and with this, its ability to energize the environment through which it passes.

When it ultimately becomes a broad river, the water flows slug-

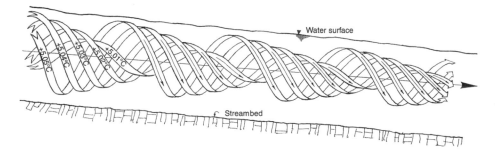

Figure 6.3. A longitudinal vortex showing the laminar flow of a river around the central axis where the water temperature is always coldest. (Callum Coats)

gishly and becomes more opaque with the increasing silt content. This, however, protects the lower strata from the heat of the sun; they remain cooler, retaining the spiral, vortical motion that is able to shift sediment of larger grain size (pebbles, gravel, and so on) from the center of the watercourse and keep down the risk of flooding. This motion also discourages the generation of harmful bacteria so that the water remains disease free.

TEMPERATURE GRADIENTS AND NUTRIENT SUPPLY

As we have seen, unless vegetation keeps the ground surface cooler than the falling rain, water will not easily penetrate the soil. The direction of the temperature gradient indicates the direction of movement. Energy or nutrient transfer is always from heat to cold, so a positive temperature gradient is also essential for nutrients to be able to rise up to the roots of the plants (see figures 6.4 and 6.5 on pages 96 and 97).

If the surface is well forested, the rainwater is warmer than the soil and penetrates to the lower strata, replenishing the groundwater body and the aquifers. The salts remain at a level where they cannot pollute the upper strata and harm those plants that are salt-sensitive. The groundwater hugs the configuration of the ground surface. The lower part of figure 6.4 shows how the salts in the ground rise near the surface, particularly on a hilltop, when part of the forest is cut down, leaving the ground exposed to sunlight.

Schauberger demonstrated that when light and air are absent well below the surface of the ground, minerals and salts are precipitated near the temperature horizon of 4°C (39°F). Warm ground will encourage evaporation of moisture near the surface, so that minerals and salts are deposited near the surface, lowering the fertility of the soil. If all the trees are removed, there will be no penetration of rainwater; the water table initially rises, due to the now uncompensated upward pressure from below described earlier, bringing up all the salts. Eventually, however, it

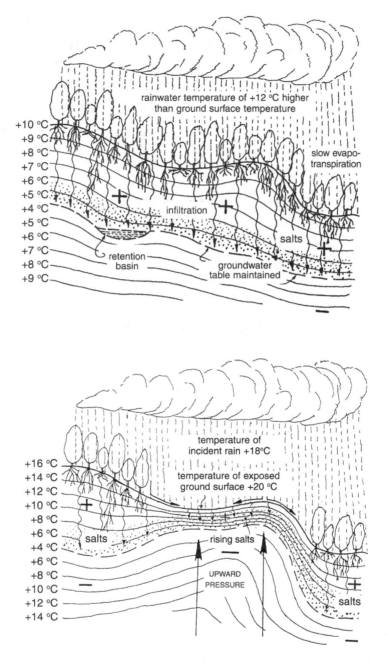

Figure 6.4. Temperature gradients. Upper: The warmer rain is absorbed into the cooler ground (positive temperature gradient), because it is protected by trees. Lower: The unprotected land surface sheds the cooler rain, causing the groundwater to rise, bringing with it unwanted salts. (Callum Coats)

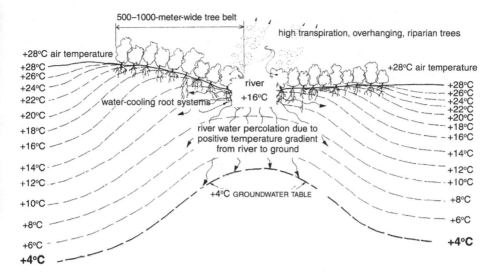

Figure 6.5. Groundwater recharge. Trees cool the ground like a refrigerator, allowing a positive gradient to draw water from the river to recharge the water table. (Callum Coats)

will sink or disappear altogether without the replenishment of rainwater. Fertility can be restored only through reforestation, which brings about the reestablishment of a positive temperature gradient.

Replanting must be initiated with salt-tolerating trees and other primitive plants, as only these would survive under such conditions. Later, due to the cooling of the ground by the shading of the pioneer trees, rainwater can penetrate the ground, taking the salts with it. Over time, as the soil climate improves, the pioneer trees die, because the improved soil conditions don't suit them. Other species of tree can replace them as the dynamic balance of Nature is restored.

Irrigation in hot climates aggravates the problem because ground temperatures cool during the night, allowing irrigation water to penetrate the upper, salt-containing strata. With the increase in temperature during the day, the infiltrated irrigation water with its acquired salts is drawn up, and upon exposure to light and heat the salts are deposited on the soil surface. The seriousness of the problem will vary with latitude, height, and season.

THE FORMATION OF VORTICES AND BENDS

We have seen that energy is always connected with movement. The natural movement of water is sinuous, convoluting, and vortical. Without such movement there is no polarity. Vortices, however, cannot form without the existence of polarities. Through the action of vortices come rhythms, the pulsations that act as a gateway—a breathing process that the river performs for the environment (see figure 6.6).

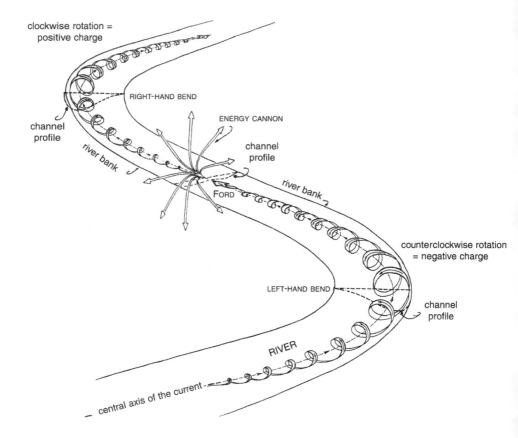

Figure 6.6. The energy cannon. Approaching a bend, the water forms a cooling counterclockwise longitudinal vortex (see figure 6.3 on page 94), grinding sediment and releasing nutrients into the river. After the bend the vortex slows down as the water warms in the shallower riverbed, releasing nutrients. Just before a new clockwise vortex forms anticipating the next bend, it releases energy into the environment. Schauberger called this the "energy cannon." (Callum Coats)

Schauberger invented a novel way of deflecting the flow to the center of the stream in order to form cooling longitudinal vortices.

HYDROELECTRIC POWER

Until the development of coal-fired steam engines, water wheels were an important source of power. With the arrival of electricity came an interest in water as a large-scale energy source, and dams were built to provide a higher level of kinetic energy. There are now tens of thousands of hydroelectric dams that collectively generate about 20 percent of the world's electricity. Although dams prevent downstream flooding and provide water for irrigation, they are controversial because the associated upstream flooding destroys valuable agricultural land, ecosystems, fish migration patterns, and communities that have been established for centuries. If there is any deforestation or agriculture upstream, an artificial lake can silt up quickly, rendering the entire project virtually useless. Hydroelectricity is often seen as a desirable source of power because it does not produce CO_2. However, the production of every ton of cement creates a ton of CO_2, and the steel materials and transport required for construction create a whole lot more.

Large dams, which are built primarily for the political and economic interest of central government and multinational companies, can have disastrous effects on rural populations. In India, notably, large dams have displaced between 16 and 38 million people.[1] The Three Gorges hydroelectric project on the Yellow River in China, completed in 2008, is particularly controversial. It has wiped out some of the most fertile land in central China. Here, 1.24 million people have had to be resettled, usually on poor-quality land. The river's fauna has been irretrievably damaged, archaeological treasures have been submerged, and already the enormous lake is filling with silt. All this is to satisfy the rapidly expanding and energy-hungry Chinese economy. It could become a catastrophe, particularly if the enormous dam were to be damaged by an earthquake, which is not entirely unlikely in this part of China. The Yellow River's energy dominates central China, and its interruption affects the entire country.

At present (2010), details have not yet been published on the proposed World Bank–financed River Congo dam, which is to be three times larger than Three Gorges. The health of the tropical rain forest is closely dependent on this main river system. If it is emasculated by a gigantic dam, the whole of central Africa will suffer irremediably.

The prevailing methods of hydroelectric power generation destroy the water, which is thrust down cylindrical pipes under enormous pressure. Upon leaving these, it is smashed to smithereens against steel turbine blades. The physical structure of the water is literally demolished and all the dissolved oxygen, and even some of the oxygen in the water molecule itself, is centrifuged out of the water.

This fragmented and largely oxygen-deficient water, a virtual skeleton of healthy water by the time it is forcibly expelled into the river, has disastrous consequences for fish and other aquatic life. Inevitably, certain species of fish disappear once these power stations are commissioned, and other forms of life survive with difficulty.

Smaller scale and microhydro are more environmentally friendly.[2] Some have even installed fish ladders so that the energy created by the stream that nourishes the valley is not completely destroyed. Schauberger and others produced plans for channeling water spirally so that its energy is not damaged by the generators.

> *The water that springs from the mountains is the blood that keeps those same mountains living and is the vein that is formed within and across them.*
>
> LEONARDO DA VINCI

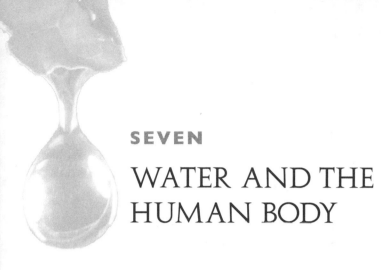

SEVEN

WATER AND THE HUMAN BODY

*Water is the bridge between the silent, unseen ocean of
electric and magnetic vibrations in which we are now
embedded, and the subtle, complex biochemical rhythms
that form the basis of all organic life.*

ALAN HALL, *WATER, ELECTRICITY, AND HEALTH*

Albert Szent-Gyorgyi, who discovered vitamin C, called water the
mother and matrix of all life. He said that water is so much a part of
life that we tend to ignore it and look elsewhere for the magic bullet,
secret herb, or nutrient that will increase health and energy and extend
life span.

BIOLOGICAL WATER

The human body is composed of 60 to 80 percent water, the actual
amount varying with age and the amount of fat. For example, in a
developing fetus water is about 90 percent of total weight. This drops
to about 74 percent for an infant, and to 60 percent for a child. Muscles
store fluid (75 percent of muscle tissue), so adult men tend to have
greater water content than women, but the amount of water gradually

drops with age, so that in the elderly it may drop to less than 50 percent. What is the function in the body of all this water?

- A significant proportion of it is "bulk water," found in the principal organs and having specific metabolic functions related to energy exchange.
- It drives the digestive system; it is the basis for the digestive juices and acids that break down our food.
- It drives the respiratory system; the lung and sinus systems depend on large quantities of water.
- It is essential to our circulatory system. Blood is 82 percent water; blood plasma is 92 percent water; blood cells, 60 percent. The kidneys, another water organ, regulate the composition of blood and produce urine.
- Water is essential for the liver's function of producing and converting nutrients from the digestive system, and particularly for detoxification.
- Because the brain has a high water content (70 percent or higher), adequate hydration is required for efficient brain activity.

Water's journey through the body involves a complex web of interdependent relationships. A list of the bodily fluids, all high in water content, numbers some thirty, each with its specific purpose (see box). Most of us do not drink a sufficient amount of good-quality water to maintain the metabolic action and flushing of wastes and toxins at an optimum level.

CELLULAR WATER

The greatest amount of biological water is extracellular. It is not pure water but has a saline content, which allows it to carry an electric charge, for it has the essential role of facilitating instant communication across the whole organism. Extracellular water also supplies nutrients and removes toxins.

Biological water: The evolution of water structures through the geological ages is demonstrated by the complexity of water forms found in human biological water today. There are approximately thirty forms, all of which are purpose-specific drivers of metabolic and physical processes in the body, all working in harmony.

Digestive—bile, chyle, chyme, mucus, saliva, vomit, feces

Intracellular—drives cellular metabolic processes

Extracellular—provides cells with nutrients and waste removal, lymph

Superficial—sweat, sebum, tears

Blood—plasma, serum, pus, urine

Cerebrospinal fluid—surrounding brain and spinal cord

Sexual and Reproductive—menses, amniotic fluid, breast milk

Synovial fluid—surrounding bone joints

Miscellaneous—pleural fluid, cerumen (earwax), aqueous humor (eyes).[1]

One of the most important functions of intracellular water is to facilitate cellular functions in the body. Because of its unusual hydrogen bonding it has the unique ability through hydration to activate proteins and through its ionizing abilities to facilitate proton exchange and cell formation. Its particular ability to act as a solvent is essential in the action of salts and ionic compounds.

HUMAN BLOOD

The composition of human blood is comparable to that of sea water, except that the ocean's principal salt is potassium, whereas the blood's is sodium. Scientific intuitives Johann Wolfgang von Goethe, Rudolf Steiner, and Viktor Schauberger all believed that blood behaves like an organ.

It is common for those who use the ancient practice of observing the breath when they meditate to experience the strange sensation of "being breathed" as part of a "greater breathing." In a similar vein, Schauberger would often insist that a bird "is flown" and a fish "is swum." On many occasions he said that the heart is not a pump, but that it "is pumped." He saw the heart not as a pump, but as a regulator of blood flow. The spurts of blood that the heart produces during contraction are more like an automatic reaction to having been full, similar to the out-breath from the lungs.

THE HUMORS—VARIATIONS OF BIOLOGICAL WATER

The notion that health was controlled by the four humors dominated European and Arab medicine for 1,800 years, from the time of Hippocrates (fifth century BCE) until the mid-nineteenth century, when medicine moved away from the study of the body as a whole. The humors were the bodily fluids associated with specific organs: phlegm with brain and lungs, yellow bile with the gallbladder, black bile with digestion and spleen, and blood with the heart.

The humors have correspondences: winter (wet and cold) is associated with phlegm and the element of water; spring with blood (wet and hot) and air; summer (dry and hot) with yellow bile and fire; autumn (dry and cold) with black bile and earth. They were also associated with different temperaments: phlegmatic (conservative, compassionate); sanguine (optimistic, impulsive); choleric (ambitious, passionate); and melancholic (creative, depressive).

It was essentially a holistic theory. Illness occurred when the humors were out of balance, and balance (health) was restored by eating the right foods or removing the excess of one humor. Bloodletting was common, as blood was thought to contain the other three humors. Vomiting was induced for someone suffering from a choleric complaint; diarrhea for melancholy.

The humors were a complex and sophisticated system, especially after being revived by Galen in the second century CE. It suggested correspondences with temperament, astrology, climate, latitude, and environment. There were variations—as few as five or as many as twelve humors—but the four primary ones remained the most referenced. This system of studying human behavior based on physiological origins continues today. A number of modern researchers have based their analysis of temperaments and psychological types on the humors.

THE BODY'S SKIN

The skin of any organism performs a number of important functions. As the outside layer, it defines the integrity and coherence of the organism and protects its vulnerability to physical assault and infection. It is the vital heat-balancing organ for most animals, excess heat being discharged by evaporation through sweat glands. Sweating can also be a sign of stress; lie detector tests measure any sudden increase in water content of the skin (see chapter 14).

The skin is porous. It can absorb fluids therapeutically, as with aromatherapy or herbal salves, as well as creams to make it more supple. While protecting against invasion by harmful substances, it is also sensitive to them and can provide a useful advance warning system.

It is full of tiny sensors; in some animals these represent their main "antennae" for picking up information from the surrounding environment. In humans, this function has become less important—although blind people depend on it—but we can still receive impressions with the whole of our body (for instance, in dowsing) or intuitively. Have you ever met someone and had the feeling that the person "made my skin crawl"? The body is also an antenna for receiving deeper cosmic, volcanic, or earth energies. The skin's health is important for effectively performing these functions.

WATER IN THE BODY

Water is an excellent solvent and suspension medium. In the blood it combines with a small part of the oxygen you inhale to form a solution that will carry oxygen to body cells. It also dissolves some of the CO_2 that is carried to the lungs to be exhaled. Water moistens the air sacs in the lungs to allow inhaled oxygen to be dissolved and then distributed to different parts of the body.

In recent years research has demonstrated the importance of adequate body hydration. Processed and adulterated foods, a dearth of fresh fruits and vegetables, too much sugar (or artificial sweeteners) and salt, commercial fizzy drinks with questionable ingredients, and too much tea and coffee (both diuretics or biological water reducers) can all lead to imbalances in the body, one of the results of which is dehydration.

Many of the body's primary organs depend on plentiful, good-quality water for their efficient functioning, especially the brain, lungs, kidneys, and liver. The kidney and liver cycles are the two principal energy cycles in the body. If the kidneys suffer dehydration, for example as a result of chronic diarrhea, the lungs are affected and breathlessness can become a problem, which can then affect the heart. Liver function is later affected, and its function of feeding energy into the blood is further compromised by dehydration. Unless prompt action is taken, dehydration in these circumstances can result in kidney and liver damage. We can survive weeks without food but will soon die without water. (In dire situations, survivors can keep going a bit longer by recycling their urine.)

Oncologist Karol Sikora writes: "The commonest cause of death is not cancer, stroke, heart disease, or earthquakes, but dehydration caused by diarrhea disease in 15 million children a year. Investing £10 [$15] a life could solve the problem."[2]

Avoiding Dehydration

It is clear that water plays a major part in balancing the health of the body, and both our kidneys and bladder are essential water organs. In any stress situation, fluid is ejected. When we have a cold, we sniffle; with a fever or excessive heat, we sweat; when distressed or our eyes are irritated, we weep. The lungs must be lubricated with water to function. Next time you have a head cold, observe how much imbalance there is in your head fluids. Or, after a busy bladder night, see how much rehydration you need.

We all know how dependent our mouths are on water. It is the same with all animals. If the mouth is not constantly well lubricated, the whole body is eventually affected. Anxiety or tension can dry the mouth, as can a lot of talking. Speakers often keep water handy during a presentation.

There has been a big change in public awareness of the need for hydration, and this perception is even changing social conventions. In Britain, while it is still a cup of tea or glass of beer for refreshment, more and more people take a small bottle of water everywhere. In France bottled water is replacing wine, and in the United States many people drink water in place of soft drinks. The greatly increased level of toxins in our environment has increased the body's need for the flushing action of water.

We are urged to drink lots of water for our health, up to eight glasses a day. While it is true that we lose on average about 1.5 liters (about three pints) a day through perspiration, breath, and urine, we also absorb water as part of our food intake, particularly from fruits and vegetables. When we eat plant foods, their carbohydrates are broken down into glucose and glycogen. The glucose is available for immediate energy needs, while the glycogen, which holds a lot of water, is stored in the liver and muscles to be released when sugar is needed for exertion.

This water needs to be converted into cellular water, which is easy enough when you are young and healthy, but it becomes more difficult when you age or are unwell, a time when it is particularly important to drink more and better quality water. Kidney shrinkage makes dehydration a common problem among the elderly, as one of the problems older people often face is the shrinkage of their kidneys. The charity Action on Elder Abuse, arguing for stronger guidance on malnutrition, finds that the elderly are more vulnerable to infections, dizziness, confusion, and falls as a result of dehydration. In care homes in Suffolk, England, where residents are encouraged to drink eight to ten glasses of water a day, the number of falls has diminished sharply.[3]

PATRICK FLANAGAN'S WATER RESEARCH

Patrick Flanagan's specialty was the liquid crystal structure of water. At the age of seventeen he was named in *Life* magazine as one of America's top ten scientists. A protégé of Dr Henri Coanda, "the father of fluid dynamics," he researched for clues to the longevity found in mountain communities like the Hunza and Caucasus previously mentioned, and Vilcabamba in Ecuador. People who live in these regions and drink local water are known to live long, healthy, active lives; many live to age one hundred or older.

For ages, Man has made pilgrimages to these remote regions in order to drink their healing waters, the chief constituent of which seems to be a rare form of colloidal silica. Flanagan discovered that this water came from glacial melt and had very distinct physical properties of viscosity, heat, and energy potential. Normal water depends for its cohesion on ionization. Hunza water does not; it is similar to intercellular water with a liquid crystal structure that is loose enough to easily transport both toxins and nutrients, saving the system from clogging.

Flanagan researched for decades how to replicate this water and in 1982 finally came up with "microcluster silica," which has electromagnetic properties that encourage water molecules to separate, making the water "wetter," or more easily absorbed by the body. (A similar effect can be obtained by placing a magnetic pad under a water container.) The surface tension is lower, facilitating hydration, nutrient uptake, and toxin removal. It is also claimed to adjust pH in whichever direction you need. He markets this special water as Crystal Energy.

The seeds of this crystalline structure are colloids—particles in suspension or solution that are too small to be seen with an ordinary microscope—charged with energy to attract disorganized water molecules. The water cannot retain its colloidal structure without an electric charge, which is easily dissipated.

Flanagan was particularly interested in biological water and found that it contained a much higher percentage of structured water because the colloids had their electrical charge protected by a coating of collagen, albumin, or gelatin.

From Theodor Schwenk's research (see chapter 13), Flanagan knew that all flowing water, though appearing to be a uniform mass, is made up of layers. Turbulence in water produces a more complex laminar structure, generating an electrical charge difference between the layers. He wanted to see if he could reproduce the effect of fast-flowing glacial torrents by constructing an artificial vortex, realizing that it was the stream's vortices that charged the particles, allowing them to become colloids.

To view the intricate structure of the vortex, it helps to add a little glycerin or a few drops of food coloring. This makes it apparent that it has a life of its own—the diameter of the structure shrinks as the point plunges to the bottom of the vessel, then expands as the point rises up and the structure diminishes. There is a rhythmic pulsation, like breathing, that is the mark of a living vortex; the formative inner layers spin more rapidly than the outer layers, which develop corkscrew forms that resemble the spirals inside conch shells.

In 1983 Flanagan decided to use an ellipsoid shape for his vortex generator and was able to produce a surface tension of 38 dynes/cm.* By adding an ounce of this mixture to a gallon of distilled water he created a product with a surface tension of between 55 and 65 that he felt was close to the quality of Hunza water.

Surface tension (ST) is the ability of water to stick to itself, to form a sphere. This is the form with the least surface area for its volume,

---

*The dyne per centimeter is the unit traditionally associated with measuring surface tension. For example, the surface tension of distilled water is 72 dyn/cm at 25°C (77°F).

requiring the least amount of energy to maintain itself. Ordinary tap water has an ST of about 75 dynes/cm, while Hunza water shows a much lower (less sticky) 68 dynes/cm. Washing machine detergents have an ST of about 45. Flanagan was able to produce with his "vortex tangential amplifier" an ST of 26 (as low as ethyl alcohol) but settled on one of 38, which has greater stability. He had notable success giving the treated water to several sick animals that quickly responded to the treatment. While strict double-blind tests may not yet have been attempted, these biological and structural tests have yielded impressive results.

Flanagan points out that mercury, cadmium, and lead are commonly found in drinking water. These heavy metals are a major source of cancer, and it is important to use a filter to remove them. He claims that his product is a good chelator of toxins, causing them to bind for easier elimination.

Dehydration is a much greater health problem in the United States than is generally acknowledged. Flanagan estimates 75 percent of Americans are chronically dehydrated, due to high consumption of colas, caffeine, and alcohol; climate-controlled environments (both heated and air conditioned); and excessive exercise. He claims that a loss of only 2 percent of body water causes impaired physiological and mental performance, that mild dehydration slows the metabolism by as much as 3 percent, and that insufficient water is the main trigger of daytime fatigue. Other factors are confusion of thirst with hunger and a decrease in the body's ability to make cell water as we age.

THE HEALING POWER OF WATER

F. Batmanghelidj, a London-trained doctor imprisoned in Persia (now Iran) during the 1979 revolution, was pardoned because he healed several hundreds of fellow prisoners suffering from acute, stress-induced, and life-threatening peptic ulcers by giving them glasses of tap water instead of the medication sometimes available.

Following on the success of this therapy he introduced new treatments to reduce dehydration that is often mistaken for ordinary illnesses and for which medication is usually prescribed. Instead, he found that many of these conditions could be cured by adequate hydration. He believes that conventional medical training does not address the complex functions of water in the body. His book, *Your Body's Many Cries for Water,* is an international bestseller.

Batmanghelidj describes five mistaken assumptions of modern medicine: First, that dry mouth is the only reliable sign of dehydration; he claims it is one of the last signs. Second, medical practitioners see dehydration symptoms as diseases of toxicity requiring medication, rather than as internal, localized droughts. Third is the mistake of thinking that water's function is only life-sustaining, thus dismissing its more important role of giving life. The fourth is that the body can regulate its water intake throughout the person's life span; as we grow older, we lose our perception of thirst and fail to drink adequately. Finally, many doctors believe that any fluid can replace the water needs of the body. In fact, tea, coffee, alcohol, and many manufactured beverages can dehydrate and make the body more toxic.

BRAIN GYM

Inefficient hydration can seriously affect brain function and integrity. Dyslexia can be helped by drinking more water, and many forms of autism are being ameliorated in this way. The varied forms of brain dysfunction, or lack of integration, are being looked at though a system known as Brain Gym.

Educators Paul and Gail Dennison, seeking to help children with learning disabilities, formed Brain Gym in the 1970s, building on research by developmental specialists who had been experimenting with physical movement to enhance learning ability.

Today Brain Gym supports people of widely varying abilities in improving their mental functioning, through thousands of public and private schools and in corporate, performing arts, and athletic train-ing programs. The system is comprised of twenty-six targeted exercises designed to integrate body and mind to bring about rapid and often dramatic improvements in concentration, memory, reading, writing, organizing, listening, physical coordination, and more.

In *Smart Moves,* Carla Hannaford's authoritative manual for Brain Gym teachers, she states that our bodies are very much a part of learn-ing, that learning is not an isolated brain function. Every nerve and cell is part of a network that contributes to our intelligence and learning capability.

A key element of the Brain Gym system is drinking water before and during any mental activity to "grease the wheels." Drinking water is also very important before any stressful situation, because we tend to perspire under stress, and dehydration can negatively affect concentra-tion. Many schools routinely advise students to drink plenty of water before exams.

WATER BIRTH

The amniotic fluid surrounding the fetus in the womb is similar in composition to that of sea water. Traditionally, many women living near the sea have given birth in the ocean, which offers a natural transition for the baby. Indigenous peoples have also used streams and lakes as birthing environments.

Water birthing has become relatively common, and for births that have low risk of complications it's usually quite safe. It's possible to lease a portable pool, but some hospitals in both the United States and United Kingdom offer water birth facilities. It's estimated that more than two-thirds of American birth centers now have this option.

In a water birth, both baby and mother are immersed, which allows the baby a gentle transition from the mother's womb to her arms. Water birth reduces gravitational distress, relaxes the mother, and eliminates stress for the baby. What could be more lovely?

URINE THERAPY

A recognized medical therapy in South Asia is to drink one's own urine to combat infection. It is a form of homeopathy wherein a dilution of one's illness is being used to counter its symptoms. If you avoid the first flush after a night's sleep, this is not as unpleasant as you might imagine. External application of urine is often suggested to treat snakebite and skin ailments, and it is also not uncommon for Glaswegian construction workers to rinse their hands in their urine when they come off a building site.[4] Apparently this keeps their hands from getting sore.

> *The amazing organizing properties of water are becoming more and more evident, which will go a long way toward explaining the detailed organization of molecules in cells and their biological functions.*
>
> MAE-WAN HO (SiS *NEW AGE OF WATER* SERIES)

EIGHT

WATER CIRCULATION IN PLANTS

We may ask why all trees and bushes—or at least most of them—unfold a flower in a five-sided pattern, with five petals. Some botanist might well examine the sap of plants to see if any difference there corresponds to the shape of their flowers.

JOHANNES KEPLER,
ASTRONOMER AND MATHEMATICIAN

THE GREATEST MIRACLE

For all living organisms, hydration equals life; dehydration equals life withdrawn. As any cactus grower can tell you, the way to stimulate flowering is to let a plant dry out and then water it profusely.

Have you ever been in a desert environment after months of drought followed by a downpour of rain, when suddenly sprouts of new life start appearing all over the barren ground? Before long, if the rain continues, there is a verdant carpet of green. Or you may have seen this happen in a natural history movie. It happens in hot climates at the beginning of the rainy season.

It really is miraculous to think that there are many trillions of dormant seeds in the ground waiting—maybe for decades—for the chance to burst into life. Which ones will awaken? If they don't now, will they awaken the next time? Maybe it's similar to the billions of souls said to be waiting on the eternal planes for an opportunity to incarnate.

What if there are seeds of life all over the universe, like sleeping beauties waiting for the water prince to come and kiss them into life? There is always this potential for life, just as there is potential in all of our lives for new creativity to break forth when the time and circumstances are right, or when given the right stimulus.

When I was a child, there were tight flower buds made of paper (Japanese, I think), which, if you laid them on a water surface, would gradually open into a beautiful petaled flower. Nature works much more magically. The desert's irrigating water carries information that reminds the sleeping potentiality that it can actually come to life according to its own template. The water's kiss of life is a reminder to the seed of its potential to become a plant according to universal cosmic laws. (See chapter 13.)

The more primitive life-forms—bacteria, algae, and worms—were early colonizers of our planet and built the foundations for more complex life-forms. But it was the arrival of the plant kingdom late in Earth's history that accelerated evolutionary development. Plants had the exceptional role of creating an oxygen-rich atmosphere and the base of the food chain that higher life-forms required.

The aristocrat of the plant kingdom is the tree. We hear much about the important role of the equatorial forests for storing CO_2, but their role in creating beneficial climates and fresh water are seldom acknowledged and little understood.

PHOTOSYNTHESIS

This was undoubtedly the most important process introduced by evolving Nature, for it allowed life to take an enormous stride toward greater complexity and higher levels of energy. Photosynthesis is the process by which organisms, higher plants as well as phytoplankton, algae, and bacteria, convert the sun's energy into chemical energy. This respiration involves inhaling carbon dioxide, exhaling oxygen, and storing glucose.

This marvelous alchemy transforms the basic, plentiful substance of CO_2 into essential food. Water is the medium, or engine, for this process. The roots bring up water replete with mineral nourishment for the plant. Photosynthesis converts CO_2 and H_2O into carbohydrates and oxygen. The breaking down of carbohydrates produces water of greater volume and higher quality than the water that was taken up, to be transpired by the leaves.

In this way forests actually create water. Richard St. Barbe Baker, founder of Men of the Trees, an international movement to advance tree planting and conservation, demonstrated that planting the right kind of trees can transform desert landscapes into productive forests that both produce new water and attract rainfall.

There is another, more subtle way in which water mediates energy through trees. In order to evolve and sustain itself, life on earth depends on a balance between the positive energy of the sun and the negative energy of Earth. Water acts a bit like sperm, as the fertilizing agent in this process.* The tree, as the highest form of the plant, has the vital role of balancing this energy for the benefit of the whole biosphere.

EVOLUTION OF THE FOREST

Viktor Schauberger believed that only people who love the forest should be its caretakers. "Those who view the forest merely as an object of speculation do it and all other living creatures great harm," he said, "for the forest is the cradle of water. If the forest dies, the springs will dry up, meadows will become barren, and many countries will inevitably be seized by unrest of such a kind that it will bode ill for every one of us."[1]

---

*Schauberger identified subtle energies of the fourth and fifth dimensions (see chapter 10) as responsible for this alchemical process. He named them "dynagens," the primal male (sun) energies, which initiate growth; "fructigens," the feminine (Earth) energies, which symbolize fruitfulness; and "qualigens," which determine the quality of life.

Schauberger's core belief was that healthy forests are the main source of high-quality water, but that they also ensure that rainfall is available in continental regions that would otherwise become arid. As equatorial deforestation has greatly accelerated since he died, it might be useful to summarize the effects of this devastation.

Plants have been around for 420 million years, which is only 9 percent of Earth's history. Without plants there could have been no higher life, for plants are the essential link for converting the sun's energy into food. Trees are the highest form of the plant and the most efficient exchangers of energy between Earth and the sun. The forests are the main source of oxygen, an essential building block of life; they are the planet's "lungs" but also are vital to producing equable climates.

The establishment of forests was the essential prerequisite for the evolution of higher animals. Trees were also necessary to establish stable landscapes, allowing rivers to channel permanent watercourses and rivers instead of the chaotic migration of alluvial flows and mud delta meanders that had been the norm (and what is found on Mars).

There have been four periods when forests have flourished: in the Carboniferous age 350 million years ago, when land vertebrates became established; in the Jurassic age, the time of the dinosaurs, 170 million years ago; in the Eocene, 60 million years ago, when primitive mammals first appeared; and in the past 500,000 years, during which the cultures of modern Man developed (see figure 2.1 on p. 37). Perhaps in each case the forests delivered a boost in the oxygen content of the atmosphere, which may have been a trigger for an evolutionary explosion of life-forms.

These extensive forests developed in the equatorial regions where heat was plentiful to prime a remarkable engine for moderating extremes of temperature and often-chaotic climates. In the first case they were evergreen forests, interspersed with enormous swamps. In the Jurassic era they were more diverse. In the Eocene, when the current great mountain ranges were rising, there were large tropical jungles, perhaps not too different from our contemporary ones but with less biodiversity, that flourished on all the continents until the late nineteenth century.

Earth's restless periods—volcanic eruptions and mountain building—often led to the establishment of forests, with mighty rivers providing nutrients for the plants. The forests built up a soil profile for the establishment of biodiversity, the essential conditions for evolutionary progress. Forests were the natural cover of probably three-quarters of the planet's land surface during these periods of evolutionary expansion.

DESTRUCTION OF THE FORESTS

Over the possibly half a million or so years of human history, our species has been responsible for reduction of the forest cover to about 25 percent of its optimum extent. Early agriculturists burned clearings to grow their crops, then moved on to allow replenishment of fertility. Early civilizations, some well documented and others passed down in story, felled vast tracts of forest.

Many of these lands became desertified, becoming the Gobi, Sind, Arabian, Mesopotamian, North African, and Kalahari Deserts—probably through a combination of deforestation and climate change. Whole societies were uprooted and forced to migrate in their search for subsistence. The same is likely to happen today where great swaths of rich equatorial forest have been cleared. In those days there was somewhere else for the displaced to go, because the world's population was still relatively small. Today, however, because of overpopulation and an unsustainable birth rate, any climate changes that produce crop failure can mean only disease, starvation, and the decimation of life.

Ten thousand years ago the land bordering the Mediterranean was covered with forests, mainly oak and conifer. The forests of Lebanon provided timber for the Phoenician empire and their exploring ships in the third century BCE (see box). Two thousand years ago North Africa was so fertile that the Romans called it "the breadbasket" of the Mediterranean; a combination of deforestation and climate change have turned it into arid desert. A thousand years ago 80 percent of Europe was forested; today it is about 20 percent, much of which is monocultured industrial woodland, which lacks the biodiversity and energy of natural forest. In North America, before the arrival of European settlers, the forest extended from the Atlantic to beyond the Mississippi River, and of course west of the Rocky Mountains.

Deforestation Promotes Drought and Erosion

Writing 2,300 years ago in his *Critias*, Plato described how Attica's mountains a century or two before had been covered in verdant forest, and her fertile plains had deep soil that, by his day, had become stony shingle. The rainfall and the soil had disappeared because the forests had been cut down.

Even then the forests were sometimes exploited to provide fast economic expansion, regardless of the cost to future generations. In order to outfit a navy capable of ruling the seas, in the early sixteenth century King Henry VIII ordered the felling of a million mature oak trees, virtually denuding England of its finest oaks.

The proportion of the world's surface covered by forest was reduced from about 75 percent at its optimum to about 50 percent in medieval times. By 1900 it had dropped to about 35 percent. In the frantic rush to get rich quick, regardless of the consequences, the figure has dropped further to 25 percent, and every year we continue to lose equatorial forest the size of Belgium. It has been calculated that 20 percent of all global warming CO_2 emissions results from destruction of the equatorial forest.[2]

Today unstable social conditions worldwide and irresponsible political leadership favor greedy opportunists anxious to make their fortunes, often illegally, by logging many of the finest stands of prime forest on every continent. This destruction will be seen in the future as dangerous planetary vandalism, because it will bring more extreme weather, loss of soil, and increased desertification.

Crucially, though still little understood, forests create the environment for the propagation of water, the "firstborn" of the energies of life, as Schauberger put it; they moderate the climate, making it cooler in summer and warmer in winter. They are also responsible for the mineralization and fertilization of the surface soils, essential for the nutrition of higher life-forms. Most important of all, forests create rich humus and bacterial life, the foundation of a rich biodiversity, which stores and recycles vast amounts of rainfall, preventing floods on lower land.

Scientist James Lovelock believes recent deforestation to be the cause of global warming, because forests are the principal regulator of climate. In his book, *The Vanishing Face of Gaia,* he puts the case that global warming is now unstoppable and that Earth's capacity to sustain humanity by the end of this century could be as low as one billion people (see box). They would be limited to those environments remaining habitable, such as northern Europe, Siberia, Canada, Japan, and southern South America.

Chaos: Gateway to Evolution

Lovelock comments: "Over the last million years, several climatic events brought decimation of numbers of the human species, yet each trauma seemed to herald an evolutionary advance; e.g., between the ice ages, sea level rose 120 meters, flooding the plains, but *Homo sapiens* emerged."[3] (See chapter 11 for more about the way that chaos introduces higher energies.) Lovelock believes that humanity should benefit from the coming population collapse.

MONOCULTURE AND BIODIVERSITY

A typical conifer plantation is impenetrable, dark, and feels dead—a veritable green desert. No birds sing nor animals scurry, and there is little opportunity for any other plants to grow. Those that do are removed on the theory that they take away nourishment from the trees. In fact, their absence increases the competition. The individual trees are all of the same age and species; they vie with each other for space and nutrients, for all their roots go down to the same level, creating a hardpan of salts, which prevents access to the valuable minerals and energized groundwater below. There is only a certain amount of each element and chemical compound available that is suitable for that species, and all the trees whose existence is wholly dependent on them must compete to get it.

Plantations of young, fast-growing trees are thirsty and dry out the soil. These young trees are then clear-felled, leaving a scene of devastation with the valuable soil vulnerable to erosion. It is hardly surprising that the wood from such a plantation is of very poor quality.

A natural, undisturbed forest has rich diversity in color, form, and vitality that brings a sense of inner tranquillity and peace. In addition, old-growth forests with mature trees that have deep taproots and minimal growth are superb for water catchment. Water is central to the quality of life. By degrading the quality of water and limiting the conditions required for the evolution of biodiversity, we put at risk the health of the whole biosphere.

There is a threat of worldwide famine resulting from the wheat stem rust fungus, which is resistant to all fungicides. Wheat suffers, as does the potato, from genetic monoculture through agronomy's plant-breeding techniques. There is a similar problem with rice. The urgent need is to restore the genetic diversity of native species of all basic foods in order to protect our future food supplies.

TROPICAL RAIN FORESTS

The Prince of Wales has proposed a new partnership with Brazil, Indonesia, and the Congo to launch better integrated rural development programs to halt deforestation. He has emphasized the irreplaceable roles of the rain forest in providing an air-conditioning system for the entire planet and producing 20 billion tons of fresh water every day.[4]

It would cost £50 (nearly $80) a ton to sequester carbon with new technologies being proposed. The rain forests do it for free and more effectively. The "Stern Review," a 2006 report on the economics of climate change, put the cost of halving deforestation at $15–20 billion. Prince Charles estimated a cost of $30 billion to stop deforestation, less than 1 percent of worldwide annual insurance premiums. He is encouraging multinational businesses to commit funds to this purpose and has personally approached heads of governments with some promising results.

One huge obstacle is the collusion of government with international agribusiness: for ranching and to grow biofuels, mining, and logging interests. The latest madness—the creation of enormous plantations to grow biofuel crops that will satisfy modern Man's insatiable dependence on the automobile—removes land from productive food production that is already down because of changes in rainfall patterns and increased costs of agriculture. Multinational corporations have cynically attacked and disabled courageous campaigns by Brazilian (and international) environmentalists over several decades.

One of the richest natural experiences is to visit a tropical rain forest, one of the priceless jewels of our ecosystem. They are vital not just for the incredible richness and variety of their fauna and flora (Amazonia contains about 30 percent of all terrestrial biological material) but in substantially modifying the world's climate, making temperate regions more productive (see plate 12). They were formerly on four continents, but now cover only about half their extent of 500 years ago. The South American is the most complete, at about 75 percent of its original size; the Southeast Asian, from India to Indonesia and Australia, is about a third of what it was; and in Africa, it is about 40 percent of its original size. The Central American rain forest has been virtually eradicated.

More than twice as much of the sun's energy reaches Earth's surface at the tropics as in high latitudes, where the sun's angle above the horizon is very low. The tropical rain forests of the world act as heat pumps, transferring to higher latitudes some of the enormous energy they generate, thus balancing the temperature difference. Without them, the equatorial regions would be much hotter and the higher latitudes much colder. The larger the mass of a tropical rain forest, the more effectively it functions as a heat pump.

A gigantic, irreplaceable water pump, the Amazon rain forest is an essential part of the planetary circulation system, whereby a drop of water evaporated from the Atlantic is recycled six times on its way to the Andes (see figure 8.1 on p. 125). Masses of humid air energy move from the Amazon basin to temperate and higher latitudes. The airflow then splits into three: the southern part is deflected as far as Patagonia; the central part flows over the Andes into the Pacific, continuing west as the trade winds; the northern airflow crosses the Caribbean and helps to drive the Gulf Stream northeastward to Europe. Argentina, thousands of miles from the Amazon, gets half its rainfall from the South American jet stream, powered by the Amazon water pump. The Midwest of the United States—the golden corn belt—depends on rain brought to it from the Amazon basin in spring and early summer.

Rain forests act as regulators and balancers of atmospheric and oceanic systems. A new theory, based on the concept of rain forests as organic rather than mechanistic thermodynamic systems, shows how they not only regulate the world's climates but can also manage their own environment (see box on p. 124).

Now that we have a study of the Amazon rain forest showing how the heat pump works, it is possible to conjecture that the African continent would not have been nearly as dry as it is today if its rain forest was large enough to pump moisture northward. In Southeast Asia rain forest destruction has reached cataclysmic proportions, with a free-for-all between corrupt local interests and greedy multinational companies, particularly in Borneo, where most of the virgin forests, theoretically protected, are likely to disappear within a decade. Courageous projects are being attempted. A conservation group

Forests Are Biotic Pumps

Two Russian physicists, Anastassia Makarieva and Victor Gorshkov, have challenged the prevailing mechanistic theory of a thermodynamic driver of air mass circulation with a new theory of a biotic pump driven by the prolific tropical vegetation. The enormous area of leaf coverage in the forest produces a prodigious amount of evaporation, condensation, and convection, which draws in saturated air from the ocean to give rise to the trade winds. If the natural forest is replaced by grassland or crops that cannot provide the high level of evapotranspiration necessary to draw in the moist sea air, a reverse air flow from land to sea will dry up the soil. Without the rain forest to recycle rain, precipitation will disappear from one coast to the other, creating a desert as dry as the Negev in Israel. Makarieva and Gorshkov's thesis implies that the world cannot do without its rain forests. Instead of quibbling over how much should be conserved, we must ensure that no more forest is destroyed. Forests are not just carbon sinks or havens of biodiversity; they have an essential and irreplaceable hydrological role in Earth's climate. They can even anticipate approaching drought by increasing evapotranspiration through advanced leaf production.

Makarieva and Gorshkov say that biotic regulation of the water cycle also takes place in undisturbed temperate and boreal forests in the spring and summer months when the pressure gradient runs from ocean to land. (See also Peter Bunyard, "The Real Importance of the Amazon Rain Forest," www.Schauberger.co.uk/articles.)

trying to save the last remaining orangutans has replanted a parcel of the cleared forest and managed to increase the number of primates in that region.[5]

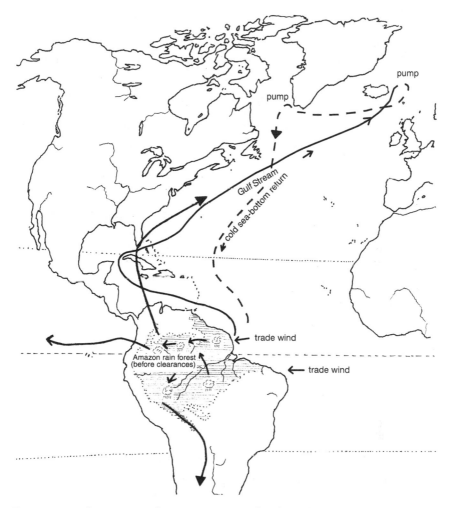

Figure 8.1. The Amazon heat engine transfers heat from the tropics to cooler latitudes, moderating the world's climates. Intense evapotranspiration from the leaf surfaces sucks in the trade winds that bring the rain. Deforestation will cause these winds to falter, eventually reducing the forest to desert. Accelerated melting of the Greenland ice cap may cause the saltwater pumps that keep the Gulf Stream flowing to fail, causing rapid cooling of northwest Europe. (A. Bartholomew)

TEMPERATE RAIN FORESTS

Temperate forests, though a fraction of their former spread, still cover a large part of planet Earth, but temperate rain forests occur in only a few regions where there is abundant rainfall precipitated by onshore winds on coastal mountains.*

The most prolific temperate rain forest, where in places the rainfall exceeds three meters (ten feet) a year, is the Great Bear Rainforest, which runs from Vancouver Island in British Columbia up through the Alaska panhandle. This magnificent virgin wilderness is richer in species than most tropical rain forests and is now the focus of an important conservation project by ForestEthics, Greenpeace, Sierra Club Canada, and British Columbian pressure groups.

This rain forest is very fertile. Its rivers are also the cleanest in the world, as the water is filtered by the tree roots and transpired by the trees in a cycle that produces the purest new water.

It is home to hundreds of species of mammals, including bear, wolves, and cougar, as well as various species of Pacific salmon, half a billion of which make the perilous journey every summer up the rivers of their birth to spawn. These salmon are the primary diet of the bears and dozens of other animals. They do not return to the ocean as Atlantic salmon do, but die where they spawn. They have not fed in the fresh water, so they bring the energy of the ocean up to the mountain pastures. Their rotting bodies also feed the trees, providing 80 percent of the nitrogen that helps the coast redwood, Douglas fir, Sitka spruce, western hemlock, and red cedar to grow so tall and prolifically.[6]

THE CREATION OF WATER

Through their transpiration, trees actually create water. Old-growth trees grow little but have deep tap roots that raise the water table and create a healthy water catchment area. Although same-age plantations in hotter countries may dry out the land, there is much evidence that even in arid or desert conditions, appropriate species' tree planting brings an

---

*The northwest coast of North America, the southwest of South America, small segments in northwest Europe, Japan, southeast Australia, and the west coast of South Island, New Zealand.

increase in rainfall. This may be due to chemicals produced by photo-synthesis, which help to generate clouds.[7]

Only when the ground surface is colder than the air (that is, it has a positive temperature gradient) is rainwater able to penetrate the soil, a fact not generally recognized by mainstream science. Rainwater releases its free oxygen into the surrounding soil, activating microorganisms in the soil's upper layers. Sinking deeper into the substrata, the rainwater continues to release surplus oxygen. As it cools toward the 4°C anomaly point (39°F), the remaining hydrogen combines with the now passive oxygen, creating new water molecules.

MATURATION OF WATER

Pure, immature water is created at the temperature when its density is highest, about 4°C (39°F). It sets out on a return journey from the deepest levels, becoming transformed from a hungry "taking" substance into a mature state that is ready to nourish living systems.

The water rises through strata from which it takes different subtle energies, becoming warmer and absorbing minerals and trace elements. These inorganic nutrients cannot be absorbed by plants and microorganisms, but on their upward journey the molecules become ionized; they take on an electric charge that allows them to recombine as organic, ionized elements, which the microorganisms and plants can absorb.

The water molecule carries the energy of the trace elements it absorbed in the roots right up into the tree's crown. From the leaves' minute stomata it is transpired into the atmosphere. On reaching its energy and temperature anomaly point at an altitude of about 3,000 meters (10,000 feet) above the earth, it is once more in receiving mode, ready to absorb the finer and more spiritual energies from the sun and the cosmos. Over time this continuous water cycle feeds the processes that drive evolution.

During the night the descending phloem plays another important role. It interacts with suspended positively charged xylem, and because

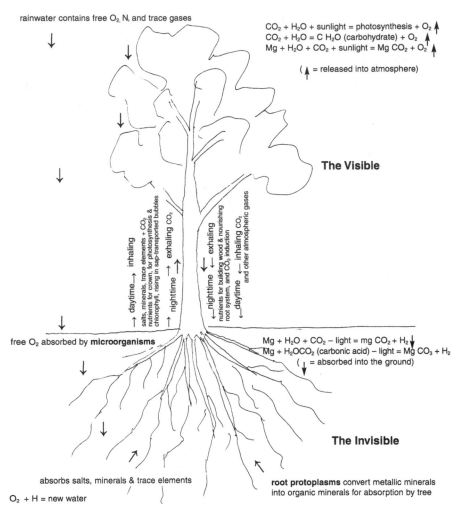

rainwater contains free O_2, N, and trace gases

$CO_2 + H_2O + \text{sunlight} = \text{photosynthesis} + O_2$ ↑
$CO_2 + H_2O = C H_2O \text{ (carbohydrate)} + O_2$ ↑
$Mg + H_2O + CO_2 + \text{sunlight} = Mg CO_2 + O_2$ ↑

(↑ = released into atmosphere)

The Visible

daytime → inhaling
salts, minerals, trace elements + CO_2
nutrients for crown, for photosynthesis &
chlorophyll, rising in sap-transported bubbles
nighttime ↑ exhaling CO_2

nighttime ↓ exhaling
nutrients for building wood & nourishing
root system, and CO_2 induction
daytime ↓ inhaling CO_2
and other atmospheric gases

free O_2 absorbed by **microorganisms**

$Mg + H_2O + CO_2 - \text{light} = mg CO_2 + H_2$ ↓
$Mg + H_2OCO_2 \text{ (carbonic acid)} - \text{light} = Mg CO_3 + H_2$
(↓ = absorbed into the ground)

The Invisible

absorbs salts, minerals & trace elements
O_2 + H = new water

root protoplasms convert metallic minerals
into organic minerals for absorption by tree

Figure 8.2. Tree metabolism. The vital exchange between yang solar and yin earth energies for the production of photosynthesis, chlorophyll, and carbohydrates and its role in the creation of water. (A. Bartholomew)

of the prevailing positive temperature gradient (see figure 8.2 above) is drawn toward the exterior of the trunk. This produces new wood growth that becomes denser and harder with winter cold, forming an annual ring.

On a commercial plantation, a shade-demanding tree grows more branches in order to protect itself from direct sunlight. The sap is therefore diverted from its normal progress up the trunk to nourish the spurious branches, twisting around the extra knots in the trunk.

SOIL AND NUTRITION

Cooling was the key to water making its appearance on the surface of the earth. As the groundcover spread, the lowering temperature affected the deeper ground, allowing the water table to rise, bringing minerals, trace elements, and nutritional substances nearer to the surface. This created the conditions for higher quality plants to evolve. These higher plants had deeper root systems that brought up minerals from a different horizon.

The more evolved plants held the soil together, trapping moisture that helped to attract microbacterial activity to break down the mineral particles into finer dust, the first step toward the humus that is necessary for higher plant forms. The root systems became more complex, interweaving at different levels so that they could not easily be disentangled. Greater fertility brought a richer soil, too rich for the pioneer plants, which now disappeared. A more favorable microclimate in the higher soil levels increased the diversity of bacteria, which encouraged more complex root systems.

This process of soil formation took several million years before larger plants, such as small bushes and trees, were able to gain a hold; and they had to go through thousands of years of evolution before a forest could develop. The forest is the most productive environment for the accumulation of soil and fertile humus. It is self-fertilizing and self-sustaining. The great forests were able, over thousands of years, to build up twenty feet or more of soil depth. With our heedless disrespect for Nature's bounty, in one century we have allowed these great soil banks to be eroded and destroyed, first through deforestation and then by careless tilling of the unprotected soil surface.

The web of life that evolves in a natural forest is so complex and sensitive that the removal of key species can cause a depletion of the

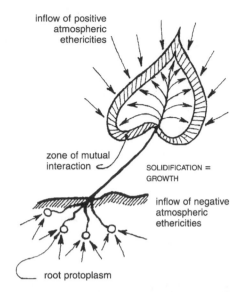

Figure 8.3. Energy exchange. Schauberger's diagram illustrates the way in which a plant is a biocondenser of positive atmospheric and negative geospheric energies. (Callum Coats)

energy and lead to a progressive decline of the system, as more species fail for want of the sustenance that was provided by the missing species. A hole is created in the complex root network that is the interconnecting link between deeper ground and surface. Because the root system raises the water table, the disappearance of a species creates a hole in the water system that supplies the nutrients. Over time, a shortage of nutrients puts more plants under stress, leading to more species extinction.

It is clear that there is much lacking in our present understanding of the needs of plants, especially trees. Our agricultural and forestry policies are extractive rather than sustaining. There is a close relationship between trees and growing food, the next stop on our journey.

> *Did the farmer know how important the forest is, he would cherish it as he would life itself.*
>
> Viktor Schauberger, *Fertile Earth*

NINE

THE EVOLUTION CONTROVERSY

A cell's life is controlled by the physical and energetic environment and not by its genes. Genes are simply molecular blueprints used in the construction of cells, tissues, and organs.

BRUCE LIPTON, *THE BIOLOGY OF BELIEF*

Do you believe that the extraordinary qualities of water we have discussed (for example, in chapter 3) could have developed through a mechanical, accidental process? We have proposed a somewhat heretical hypothesis—that water is the creator and "stage manager" of life, a key player in the process of evolution. It might, therefore, be pertinent to look briefly at the current debate about evolution.

EVOLUTIONARY THEORIES

Darwin's theory of evolution rests on the assumption that life has evolved through a series of biological changes brought about by a combination of random mutations and natural selection. Those species that are able to adapt most successfully to changing conditions in their environment will supersede those less successful; in other words, "survival of the fittest."

No serious student of science will deny that the evolution of species is a verifiable natural process. However, the enormous publicity given the 2009 bicentenary of Darwin's birth demonstrated that an ideology can be built around one man's work, no matter how many researchers before and particularly after have followed similar paths of inquiry. It also shows the way in which a pioneer's zealous followers can distort a theory, making of it almost holy writ.[1]

Over a long period, the Darwinians say, one species gradually evolved into another. Sea creatures adapted to being amphibians, which became reptiles; reptiles evolved into birds, which metamorphosed into mammals. This theory has been taught as if it were a law for well over a century (and still is), in spite of the fact that it has never been validated.

The difficulty is that the fossil record, which is the most accepted form of proof, has not revealed the transitional organisms, the intermediate forms between major groups. There exist, for example, an abundance of fossils of early primates, hominids, Neanderthals, and *Homo sapiens,* but no definitive link has been found between the ape and Man. The same problem appears with plants: no intermediate fossils have been found between primitive nonflowering plants and the sudden appearance of flowering plants. Many species seem to have just appeared, without apparent links to earlier species. This is a real conundrum—a mystery. Many scientists don't like mysteries!

There is also a problem with the other cornerstone of Darwin's theory, and it concerns genetic mutation. Geneticists have long accepted that mutations are usually mistakes that result from DNA failing to replicate correct information. Natural selection as a process for raising quality and effectiveness would need a mechanism much more reliable and predictable than genetic mutation based on chance.

There is some evidence that Charles Darwin was rather less dogmatic than many of his subsequent followers, particularly the neo-Darwinists. He was well aware of the shortcomings of his theory and described the origin of flowering plants as "an abominable mystery." He observed, "The number of intermediate varieties that formerly existed on earth must be truly enormous. Why, then, is not every geological formation and every stratum full of such intermediate links? Geology assuredly does not reveal any such finely graduated organic chain; and this, perhaps is the most obvious and gravest objection that can be urged against my theory."[2]

Another problem for his theory is that it was proposed when the prevailing theory of geological change was uniformitarianism—that geological change is very slow, a theory that, due to Darwin's influence, some scholars still doggedly embrace—which would allow for gradual mutation of species. However, most geologists now accept that the big changes happen cataclysmically (the catastrophism theory), bringing with them mass extinctions of species followed by the sudden appearance of something completely new, at a higher order of complexity.

The crux of the difficulty for evolutionary theory lies in the discovery of the enormous complexity of organic processes, and particularly in the intricately linked interdependencies of biodiversity. It is difficult to believe that this miracle of vibrant life working in complete synergy could have evolved in a random manner or by chance.

Nevertheless, Darwin's theory of evolution is a pivotal part of the current scientific orthodoxy of reductionism, which sees Nature's processes as mechanical, rather than organic. To this day, a scientist who challenges it risks his career.

It is evident that a natural process of evolution of species does take place. Outside scientific circles, there is little awareness about the problems associated with the Darwinian theory. Many have heard about the war between creationists and evolutionists as a replay of the battle between religion and science, which the Scopes trial brought into sharp focus nearly a century ago.*

It may not be a coincidence that great advances in evolutionary complexity have coincided with great periods of Earth restlessness—

---

*In 1925 John Scopes, a high school biology teacher, legally challenged his right to teach evolution in the classroom, in defiance of a Tennessee law.

the four principal mountain-building movements. New species suddenly appeared, without precedent. How this could have occurred is an enigma. You can take your pick from competing theories: happenstance, intelligent design, divine intervention, extraterrestrial genetic experiments, or purposeful evolution.

What I am proposing here is not creationism in disguise, but an initiative of the intelligence of Nature in her search for greater complexity, biodiversity, and "consciousness" in life-forms. With each burst of new life-forms, a stage higher than the last is attained in terms of finer energy or consciousness. I see this form of evolution as spontaneous steps emerging out of a catastrophic situation initiated by Earth herself in the process of her evolution—sweeping away the old forms, so that something more meaningful can develop. In chapter 12 we suggest that chaos is the prior requirement for a positive energy shift. We sometimes hear the term "divine chaos" used to describe our present uncertain times.

Evolution needs an agent to apply the evolutionary imperative to the natural order. This agent has to be water, because only water has the sensitivity; can produce the templates, forms, and patterns; and can convey consciousness to organisms (see chapter 14).

Most natural history films aired on television give the impression that competition between species is the engine of evolution. However, if natural systems are perceived organically, then it soon becomes apparent that cooperation between species is more of the norm than competition. Lynn Margulis, biologist and cofounder of the Gaia hypothesis, insists that the survival of any environmentally interdependent organism shows that cooperation or symbiosis is far more important for evolution than is competition. This is more of a "quantum" idea than a reductionist one.

THE GENETIC CHALLENGE TO NEO-DARWINISM

Jean Baptiste de Lamarck (1744–1829) anticipated Charles Darwin's (1809–1882) theory of natural selection by fifty years. Darwin accepted

Lamarck's belief that acquired characteristics could be inherited, but modern neo-Darwinists refuse to acknowledge any Larmarckian influence, insisting that natural selection is completely random in Nature.

In a curious way, scientific and religious fundamentalism have much in common.[3] After James Watson, Francis Crick, and Maurice Wilkins were awarded their Nobel prize for solving the mechanism of DNA, Crick issued a "central dogma" of molecular biology, which stated that organisms are hardwired in their genetic structure and that the environment and life experiences have little effect on the gene.

This is closely related to the neo-Darwinian theory that claims natural selection favors the strong genes of the powerful by making them more prolific, while the weak genes of the dispossessed are weeded out. These claims, which support the status quo and the rich, carry more than a hint of eugenics.

Toward the end of his life Darwin had reservations, which his followers seem to be unwilling to acknowledge, about the genes and DNA within the cells controlling our biology. He acknowledged, "When I wrote the *Origin,* and for some years afterwards, I could find little good evidence of the direct action of the environment; now there is a large body of evidence."[4]

EPIGENETICS

The conventional concept of genetic theory—genetic determinism—holds that all characteristics are passed down by one's genes and that we cannot pass on any influences experienced in our lifetime. That has now been challenged by the discipline of *epi*genetics (outside genetics), which argues that environmental influences are more important than genes. The argument is known as "nature versus nurture."

Biochemistry and medicine have been more or less untouched by the revolution of the past one hundred years, which has transformed the physicist's worldview from reductionism to one of interconnections. Western medicine, still dominated by deterministic principles, treats symptoms as if they are unrelated to other parts of the organism.

Pioneers of the new biology have recognized the extraordinary damage inflicted on the long-term health of the general population as a direct result of these misunderstandings, and particularly the growth of iatrogenic illnesses (inadvertently caused by physicians), which were reported in 2001 as the biggest single source of death in the United States.[5] It is time for an organically based system of treatment, which would save many lives and enormous costs.*

The real causes of illness are social and environmental, and there is an urgent need to correct the mistaken dogma that our genes control our biology. The mainstream model in which genes determine health and well-being is incorrect. Rather, a person's thoughts and attitude, and particularly early upbringing, primarily determine health.

At about the time the Human Genome Project was making headlines in the 1980s, a group of scientists initiated the new field of epigenetics, which has profoundly changed our understanding of how life is controlled. It is the science of the way in which environmental signals select, modify, and regulate gene activity. In the 1990s, epigenetic research established that the DNA blueprints transmitted by our genes are not fixed at birth. The genes are constantly being modified by external influences (quality of nutrition, pollutants, social rituals, sexual cues) and by our inner environment (emotions, biochemical and mental processes, sense of the spiritual, and so on, even in the womb) without affecting the basic blueprint.

The most controversial finding was that our beliefs affect our genes, and therefore, our health. We all grow up with scripts or teachings about survival. In a nurturing environment these can be good and helpful, but a dysfunctional family life can produce damaging scripts. We are all, usually as children, subjected to criticism in our

---

*Mae-Wan Ho identifies the antiquated and destructive worldview that dominates medicine, biology, economic, and social/political systems with the contraction "domo," meaning "dominating model"; the powerful, controlling, and seductive antilife tool of the world seen as machine.

upbringing and education, which generates self-limiting messages that may damage our prospects and our health. The hope is that at some point we may be motivated to reject our false beliefs and reclaim our real potential.

There is a therapy known as Emotional Freedom Technique (EFT) that works on the principle that a disruption of the body's energy system caused by trauma or negative emotions can be corrected by tapping with the fingertips on specific acupuncture points, with appropriate visualization. Many of these points are on water meridians, which is relevant to our theme, because water is the medium of memory and association.

EFT practitioners believe they are communicating with cellular intelligence on a holistic level, rather than in the more limited mental mode. It has long been recognized that the body records every experience, storing memories in the morphic fields (see p. 211), not the brain. With the advent of epigenetics it is now clear that the cells have an overall intelligence and wisdom that can be accessed through the water meridian.

The help of a practitioner is advised for deeper questions, but EFT is a technique that can be self-administered and used in an immediate situation, such as difficulty getting to sleep, or getting over a block about learning a new language. It can also be effective for conditions that may not seem to have an emotional trigger, such as arteriosclerosis. It has implications for radical understanding of the individual human dilemma that most therapies don't easily reach.[6] We *can* change our lives through having a positive attitude and thoughts.

Epigenetics has created a profound shift in thinking about the human predicament. The old biology sees the human individual as a victim limited by a specific genetic situation. The new biology emphasizes self-empowerment and optimizing innate gifts, validating principles of the human potential movement of the 1970s.

THE CELLS

Single-celled organisms appeared six hundred million years after Earth's formation. Two and three-quarter billion years later they evolved into multicellular organisms that would eventually contain up to trillions in number.

The cell is an intelligent entity that can survive on its own. Researcher Bruce Lipton claims that cells show intention and purpose when they actively seek environments that support their survival and avoid hostile ones.* They are capable of learning through these environmental experiences and of creating an antibody blueprint for a specific virus (for example, measles). They pass on their environmental experience to their offspring, who retain the genetic "memory" of its antibody protein developed to cope with an invading virus.

Cell biology is an excellent example of the holistic principle of fractals, one of the principal techniques for evolutionary advance. A fractal is a design or pattern repeating itself at different magnitudes (see pp. 211–12). The "primitive" single-cell organism was the template for the evolution of highly complex evolved organisms of trillions of cells, only there is specialization of function to optimize efficiency and survival.

The more that cells are in touch with their environment, the better the organism's chances of survival. Epigenetics shows that genes are the physical (biochemical) memory of an organism's learned experience. In the new biology, evolution becomes survival of the fittest *group,* not the individual (cooperation, not competition). While DNA is the blueprint of a person's potentialities (perhaps analogous to a birth chart?), the genes are the material the organism has to work with, which are modified by experience (see box).

---

*In *The Biology of Belief,* Bruce Lipton presents an insightful introduction to the new biology that is inspired by epigenetic theory. Lipton is an award-winning cell biologist who taught in medical schools for twenty years.

Your Birth Chart and Your DNA Are Only Blueprints

The comparison of DNA with a birth chart is apposite. Many (for instance, the tabloid newspapers) regard your sun sign (and other aspects of your chart) deterministically, as "old biology" does the DNA. To the serious astrologer, however, the birth chart is a blueprint that can be transcended, in the same way that epigenetics shows how the genetic templates of DNA can be transcended.

Although humans are made up of trillions of cells, there is no function in our bodies that is not already expressed in a single cell; each cell has the functional equivalent of nervous, digestive, respiratory, excretory, endocrine, muscle, skeletal, circulatory, skin, reproductive, and even immune systems.

Epigenetics recognizes two mechanisms by which organisms pass on hereditary information: nature (through the genes) and nurture (epigenetic). If you focus only on blueprints (the old biology), environment seems totally irrelevant.

Old Biology versus New Biology

Old Biology

- The mechanisms of our physical body can be understood by dissecting cells down to their building blocks (reductionism).
- The linear flow of information is one-way—from DNA (long-term memory) to RNA (template for synthesizing protein) to protein.
- Our genes are fixed—we are lucky to have good genes, and unlucky if we don't. It's a chancy business. All characteristics are passed down by our genes; we cannot pass on any influences experienced in our lifetime.
- Watson and Crick proposed that DNA controls its own replication and serves as the blueprint for the body's proteins. DNA "rules," according to the central dogma.

- The primacy of DNA provides the logic for the age of genetic determinism.
- The Human Genome Project spent billions on the assumption that our biology is controlled by our genes. Only 25,000 genes were discovered—one-sixth of what was expected, no more than a humble worm possesses (it was a very poor investment).

New Biology

- The new biology emphasizes that coherence on all levels—cellular, molecular, atomic, and organic—governs all life processes.
- Quantum physics, with its view of the interconnections between all life-forms, demonstrates that our DNA is controlled from signals outside the cells, including our personal scripts—messages from positive and negative thoughts, from the environment, and from the experiences of the whole organism.
- Epigenetics is often called "the science of self-empowerment." The chief implication of this is that, as organisms, we can choose to influence our own evolution because our thoughts and experiences strongly influence our futures. "Mind over matter" is a reality. Conversely, people's lives are frequently stunted or destroyed through holding on to false or disempowering beliefs.
- The flow of information is multidirectional—a complex network of paths created by resonance interactions (each on its own wavelength). The new biology is superbly holistic.
- To quote Bruce Lipton: "Biomedicine doesn't recognize the massive complexity of inter-communication between physical parts and the energy field that make up the whole. Cellular constituents are woven into a complex web of crosstalk, feedback, and feed-forward communication loops. A biological dysfunction may arise from a miscommunication along any of the routes of information flow."*

---

*One example is the effects of harmful medication that can cause iatrogenic illness (or the possible side effects listed on the leaflet that comes with your prescription), which is now the main source of death in the United States (>300,000 per year: see Bruce Lipton's study of U.S. Government 2003 statistics).

The cell membrane (one-millionth of a millimeter thick and discovered in the 1950s with the electron microscope), a three-layered skin holding cytoplasm together, is the cell's "brain" (with a function similar to that of a silicone chip with its memory—"a liquid crystal semiconductor with gates and channels"). The nucleus is not the cell's brain (old biology).

Embedded in the hydrophobic middle layer are receptors (IMPs, or integral membrane proteins)—the equivalent of sensory nerves—that monitor specific external and internal signals; and effectors—the equivalent of action-generating motor nerves—that resonate to specific vibrational frequencies or by shape and electric charge locking on to a histamine molecule, for example. As on a modern computer, IMPs are programmable from outside; they are effectively a biocomputer.

I believe this is a similar water signal mechanism to that of Cleve Backster's biocommunication experiments (see pp. 201–208). Mae-Wan Ho points out that this is because of the innate coherence of the organism, both within and without, which makes it responsive to everything around it.[7]

It's not the quality of the human genetic makeup but the experience of the whole organism that can then be passed on to successive generations, usually selective within the same sex. In another epigenetics study, groundbreaking research at the Institute of Child Health, University College, London, demonstrated how young boys' experiences could affect not only their own health in later life but also the health of their sons and grandsons.[8]

INTELLIGENT DESIGN OR PURPOSEFUL EVOLUTION?

The biblical creationists' simplistic belief in the origins of life discourages credibility. The intelligent design theory, a trend in American Christian education with creationist roots, claims that life somehow assembled itself out of organic molecules.

Another theory, which has yet to be elaborated upon, is that knowledge of edible grains was somehow passed from an earlier, developed-but-forgotten civilization. A more recent theory, the interventionist theory, insists that life-forms were introduced by extraterrestrial civilizations; needless to say, this theory has no orthodox support.

Linked to the catastrophism position—and perhaps the most interesting—is the theory of continuous creation, which is in direct opposition to the now generally accepted big bang theory; it satisfies religious groups that believe in a single primordial act of creation by God. This new theory is proposed by physicist Paul LaViolette, who believes that the purpose of the relatively rare cosmic event of the galactic superwave caused by massive explosions at the galactic core (see below) is to create matter from the etheric flux that invisibly pervades the entire universe.[9]

The last occurrence of such explosions may have been about fifteen thousand years ago. The Vostock ice cores in Antarctica show a peak of cosmic radiation and a sharp increase in temperature at that time. LaViolette claims that this actual event could account for the classical Greek writer Ovid's description of a scorched earth phenomenon as well as for some eighty different indigenous societies' flood myths.

Why don't the more realistic theories of evolution get attention? Probably because the emotional polarization between the two extremes of neo-Darwinism and creationism creates a din that drowns out more moderate concepts. The way people hold to one point of view or another is both unscientific and irrational. There is much evidence for evolution, and the possibility of a creation plan is also difficult to completely discount. What is so wrong about being openminded and allowing room for both? Taking a dogmatic position does not help to reveal the truth.

The concept of an etheric substratum from which matter is created, which originated in Hindu metaphysics, has attracted considerable scientific credence over the years. It was more recently revived by the late physicist David Bohm, who saw the universe as part of something far vaster, ineffable, and essentially conscious.

My proposal holds a similar view of consciousness at all levels of life, but seen at the earth rather than the cosmic level, as a mechanism of intelligent Nature searching for greater complexity, biodiversity, and consciousness in life-forms. The quantum, or etheric, field may be seen as the ground of consciousness, with water as the vehicle for transmission and communication.

The evidence shows that, with each burst of new life-forms, a stage higher than the last was attained in terms of complexity and biodiversity. The great evolutionary advances always seemed to follow cataclysms of some kind I see this form of evolution as spontaneous steps emerging out of a catastrophic situation initiated by Earth herself in the process of her evolution, a theory quite dissimilar to any of those described above. We might call it "purposeful evolution."

CONSCIOUSNESS, MEANING, AND COHERENCE

Some may object to the concept of consciousness being introduced into evolutionary theory, but I believe it's as reasonable as part of the increased complexity and interconnectedness that evolution presents—consciousness defined as "a level of perception of relatedness on a hierarchical scale." It is the companion of spiritual meaning favored by those who take the wider worldview. Some of the scientific pioneers, such as Albert Einstein, Sir James Jeans, or Carl Gustav Jung, espoused a spiritual worldview.

Dr. Mae-Wan Ho equates the idea of organic coherence with the notion of consciousness.

Quantum coherent organisms invariably become entangled with one another. A quantum world is a world of universal mutual entanglement, the prerequisite for universal love and ethics. Because we are all entangled, and each being is implicit in every other, the best way to benefit oneself is to benefit the other. That's why we can really love our neighbour as ourselves. It is heartfelt and sincere. We are ethical and care about our neighbours and all of creation, because they are literally as dear to us as our own self.[10]

A TELEOLOGICAL DISCUSSION

In recent years there has been a rapprochement between esoteric theories of the evolution of life and some more holistic scientific ideas. Quantum physics entertains the possibility of unifying concepts, going so far as to suggest a sense of purpose in evolution. Earth has been empowered with a level of intelligence through creation myths and Eastern esotericism, and this has been mirrored by contemporary scientists, such as James Lovelock and Lynn Margulis. Their Gaia hypothesis (1979) holds that the biosphere is a self-regulating entity that keeps the environment constant and comfortable for living organisms. (As a geochemist, Lovelock's principal concern was the constitution and homoeostasis of the atmosphere, rather than the origin and evolution of life itself.)[11]

Taking the self-regulating concept of Earth a step further brings up the theory of our planet as an intelligent organism on its own evolutionary path, with Nature's evolution as a dependent part of the system. At this point there enters a spiritual dimension. In esoteric and spiritual traditions, Nature is called "the mirror of the divine," which could also be identified as a level of being of a more evolved Earth, manifesting complexities of life-forms in response to Earth's own evolution. The evolutionary imperative of Nature in these traditions seems to be toward greater complexity and biodiversity and toward higher levels of purpose.

WATER AND EVOLUTION

We have seen how evolution and biodiversity are dependent on water and how water's complexity changes with the demand of evolutionary blueprints. In the previous chapter we saw that water is responsible for driving climate change. It is clear that future prospects for life on this planet will depend on water. We would do well to try to communicate with water's consciousness, for this might give us clues about our options for the future.

We have, up to this point, been reviewing the role of water as it is generally understood by mainstream science. In the next chapter we'll consider the contribution that Viktor Schauberger, a pioneer of the science of Nature, has made in opening up science to a more holistic view of how Nature works, for in part 2 we shall be discussing new insights about water as the source of life.

> *The majority believes that everything hard to comprehend must be very profound. This is incorrect. What is hard to understand is what is immature, unclear, and often false. The highest wisdom is simple and passes through the brain directly into the heart.*
>
> VIKTOR SCHAUBERGER

TEN

THE WATER WIZARD

Water in the environment is like blood in the body, and ours is diseased. The arteries and veins of our countryside, its rivers and wetlands, are suffering from the equivalent of low blood pressure and blood poisoning. The condition has developed over many years and the need for treatment is now urgent.

Sir David Attenborough

We cannot progress in our study of water without going into more detail about the groundbreaking research of Viktor Schauberger (1885–1958), a genius whose ideas were way ahead of his time. He challenged conventional thinking about natural processes, and probably more than anyone else, his extraordinary insights into water have compelled us to think outside the box.

What was extraordinary about Schauberger was his ability to live in two separate worlds. He was at heart an intuitive, practical man with inherent engineering skills, from a family with a long tradition of caring for the forest. But he could also see that modern education was stifling the psychic sensitivity that had enabled his predecessors to work in tune with Nature. The man known as the water wizard was a curious combination of ingenious inventor and intuitive shaman. He was also a scholar in the habit of staying up late at night to study esoteric texts, much to his wife's dismay.

As a young man he left university to work as a "forest master" in the Austrian Alps when they were still a true wilderness, an experience that was to influence his entire life's work. From his precise observations of natural phenomena, Schauberger pioneered a completely new understanding of the nature of water as the most important life-giving and energy-empowering substance on the planet.

SCHAUBERGER'S INSIGHTS ON WATER

Schauberger, a holistic scientist who saw water as a living organism, intuited both the nature of living water and its importance for life processes, as well as the natural conditions required for its manifestation. He perceived that the necessary conditions involve water's innate tendency to move in a spiraling, centripetal (in-winding) manner that cools it and increases its density, encouraging life-forms to flourish.*

In Schauberger's vision, water is a pulsating, living substance that energizes all of life, both organic and inorganic. Whether in the form of water, blood, or sap, he believed it is the indispensable constituent of all life-forms, and its quality and temperature are fundamental to health. When it is healthy it has a complex structure that enables it to communicate information; carry subtle energy, nutrients, and healing; and self-cleanse and discharge wastes.

The water wizard believed that our disrespect for water, the bringer of life, contributes to the disintegration of our culture. He observed that we use inappropriate technologies to deliver into our homes poor, effectively lifeless water that has lost its dynamic energy and ability to pulsate. This dead water delivers inadequate nutrition, and Schauberger posited that its regressive energies are responsible for cancer and other degenerative diseases, for lowering human intelligence, and for communal disharmony.

---

*See the principal qualities essential for living water in appendix 1: Water and Health.

Natural forests (not the monoculture plantations of today) are the cradle of water and also the main source of oxygen for the planet. Their precipitate destruction, Schauberger predicted, would result in climate change, severe water shortage, and the creation of deserts. He made brilliant observations of the way in which trees in a natural, diversified environment create water and are biocondensers of subtle energy (accumulating, storing, and exchanging energy from both sun and earth), and how the groundwater brings the earth energy up into the trees to balance their intake of solar energy.

The most radical of Schauberger's discoveries were as follows.

Motion

He discovered that all life and growth are shaped through vibration and movement. There are two forms of flow or motion in Nature: outward moving, expanding (centrifugal), which Nature uses to break down and decompose; and inward moving, contracting (centripetal), which Nature uses to build and energize. Our current technology has it backward.

Our machines and processing methods channel agents such as air, water, other liquids, and gases into negative centrifugal motion. As a consequence, these substances are devitalized and debilitated, which affects their surroundings. The dynamic energy produced by our technology is harmful because in strengthening those subtle energies that break down structures and degrade quality, it causes deterioration in the environment. At the same time, it suppresses the dynamic energies that support the health of plants and animals.

This can dangerously affect the vital biodiversity and balance in our ecosystems. Our mechanical, technological systems of motion are nearly all heat- and friction-inducing, which makes them noisy and inefficient; this is how we generate our power, and in the process, contribute significantly to global warming through entropy (waste heat).

Nature uses the opposite, centripetal form of motion (moving from the outside inward with increasing velocity), which acts to cool, condense, and structure, assisting the emergence of living systems of higher

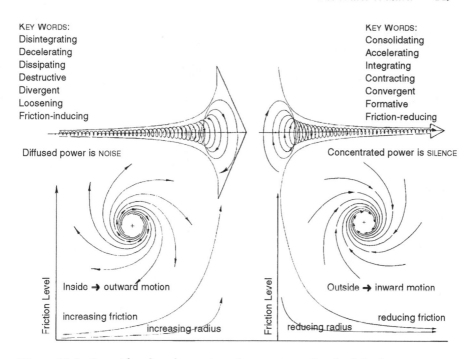

KEY WORDS:
Disintegrating
Decelerating
Dissipating
Destructive
Divergent
Loosening
Friction-inducing

Diffused power is NOISE

KEY WORDS:
Consolidating
Accelerating
Integrating
Contracting
Convergent
Formative
Friction-reducing

Concentrated power is SILENCE

Inside → outward motion

increasing friction

increasing radius

Friction Level

Outside → inward motion

reducing friction

reducing radius

Friction Level

Figure 10.1. Centrifugal and centripetal movement. On the left, the system our current technology uses (axial>radial—inside>outward). On the right, Nature's way of generating energy (radial>axial—outside>inward). (Callum Coats)

quality and greater complexity. Using his knowledge of the way that Nature energizes and purifies water, Schauberger was able to develop a springwater machine that transformed poor-quality water.

Most of us are aware of the polluting effects of chemicals in the body and in the soil, the dangers of radioactive waste, and the risks of biotechnology. But Schauberger was also concerned with something much more basically wrong with our technology. As a practical man, he observed the profligate squandering of resources and was appalled that the internal combustion and steam engines on which our civilization depended were not even 50 percent efficient. He saw that energy that is not turned into power or motion is wasted and heats up the atmosphere, adding to what we now call the greenhouse effect. From his observations of Nature came the answer: that we use the wrong form of motion.

Temperature

We are familiar with the principle that the normal temperature of blood in the human body is approximately 37°C (98.4°F). Any slight change from an individual's usual base temperature indicates imbalance. It is the same with water and with sap. One of Schauberger's most important discoveries was to show how small variations of temperature are as crucial to the healthy movement of water and sap as they are for human blood. As a thermodynamic principle, heat always moves toward cold. We know that humans must live within a certain temperature range in order to survive, but few realize how narrow this range is for all that is living.

Schauberger insisted that temperature change is the most important catalyst in Nature. He identified two modes—a rising gradient to break down and decompose (the negative gradient); and a falling gradient approaching the anomaly point of 4°C (39.2°F) to build (the positive gradient).

Having learned from his family about the importance of water temperature, Schauberger decided to do a demonstration for the world-renowned hydraulicist Philipp Forchheimer. He had colleagues heat 100 liters of water (26 gallons) that they poured into a large stream some distance above a stretch of rapids, 500 meters (1,640 feet) higher than where he stood observing a trout. The heated water caused the trout to become agitated and unable to hold its position in the fast-flowing stream, and it was swept down the rapids. The minute rise in the average temperature of the water had caused a loss of coherence in the water and interfered with the trout's hovering ability. Forchheimer was astonished; mainstream science did not accept that such small changes in temperature can make a dramatic difference to the water environment.

In the natural process of synthesis and decomposition in all water, trees, and other living organisms, both the rising and falling temperature gradients are active. Each form of gradient has its special function in Nature's great production; the positive (cooling) temperature gradient must play the principal role if evolution is to unfold creatively.

This important factor influences all the features of a river, such as flow velocity, tractive (pulling) force, sediment load, turbidity, and viscosity, as well as storage and transport through pipes. It is because modern hydrologists do not recognize the temperature gradient that they are unable to prevent flooding or deliver better quality water to our homes.

Flowing water behaves according to whichever temperature gradient is active. The positive temperature gradient builds up living systems by cooling, concentrating, and energizing as it approaches 4°C (39°F). The key to this process of healthy growth and development is that the ionized substances are drawn together into intimate and productive contact, and the contained oxygen becomes passive and easily bound by the cool carbones, the building blocks of life.* The increasing warming of the negative temperature gradient, however, reduces the cohering energy, loosening the structure of an organism, and the forms start disintegrating. The oxygen becomes increasingly aggressive and instead of helping to build structures, pulls them apart, risking pathogenic disease.

Polarity

Nature is founded far more on cooperation than on competition, because it is only through harmonious interplay that physical formation can occur and structures can be built. At the heart of the creative process in Nature are polarities, such as positive and negative, chaos and order, quantity and quality, gravitation and levitation, electricity and magnetism. In every case, for any natural process to be harmonious, one polarity cannot be present without the other, and each needs the other to make up the whole. As Schauberger describes it, creative evolution requires that the polarities not be fifty-fifty, which would result in atrophy, but unevenly balanced toward the yin, or negative.

Schauberger studied biomagnetism and bioelectricity, which are

---

*The extra "e" in "carbone" enlarges the usual range of elements used in forming the physical structures of life, excluding oxygen and hydrogen. (Schauberger also classified the elements as *yin* or *yang* (feminine or masculine).

complementary qualities. These always operate simultaneously, because everything is bipolar. The catalytic role of dual polarity starts with the positive charge of the sun and the negative of the earth but is an essential component for all biological processes.

The Memory of Water

Water's reputation as a powerful solvent derives from its electromagnetic qualities. Positive hydrogen atoms in the water molecule attract to themselves negative ions from the substance they are in contact with, while the oxygen atom with a double-negative charge joins up with positive ions, so that balance is maintained. In this way, water breaks down and dissolves substances into their constituent parts, taking oxygen, nitrogen, and carbon dioxide from the air; and calcium, potassium, sodium, manganese, and so on from the rocks. Water continually collects substances from one source and deposits them, usually as building blocks for new growth, somewhere else.

When water is flowing energetically in spirals and vortices as its nature dictates, it creates the structure necessary for it to carry constructive information. This structure comprises microclusters of vibrating energy centers, constantly receiving and transmuting energy from every contact the water body makes. Despite water's fluidity and its ability to change its state constantly, the molecules, if conditions permit, generally organize themselves into structures, or clusters.

The clusters can store vibrational impressions, or imprints. If these are beneficial they may be able to restore healthy resonance in the human body, functioning in a way similar to homeopathy. However, when water is treated with disrespect or ignorant handling, instead of bringing life and vitality, it takes on the imprint of toxins or disease and becomes anti-life, facilitating pathogenic processes that initiate physical decay and eventually bring death.

Water has a memory; we may think we have purified water of the chemicals and hormones that were added in an effort to make it drinkable, but the energy of these contaminants remains, polluting our energy bodies in the same way that chemicals affect our physical bodies. This was one of Schauberger's more controversial discoveries, that water that has lost its coherence takes on negative energy that precipitates moral, mental, and spiritual deterioration in the human being.

There was little support for Schauberger's insights about water, and it was not until the development of chaos theory in the late 1970s that hydrology, together with the discoveries of quantum mechanics, started to catch up with Schauberger's research.

> *Everything flows, floats, and moves. There is no state of equilibrium—there is no state of rest.*
> VIKTOR SCHAUBERGER, *NATURE AS TEACHER*

PART TWO

WATER AS THE SOURCE OF LIFE

ELEVEN

THE ORGANISM AND QUANTUM WATER

I think we are beginning to perceive nature in Earth in exactly the opposite way we viewed it in classical physics. We no longer conceive of nature as a passive object. . . . I see us as nearer to a Taoist view, in which we are embedded in a universe that is not foreign to us.

SCIENTIST ILYA PRIGOGINE

THE QUANTUM FIELD AND THE ETHER

Quantum physics gives us a scientific framework for understanding the interconnectedness of all life, including our physical, emotional, and mental experience. The idea that we are part of a dynamic energy field is not exactly new, but a rediscovery. Vedic philosophy postulated three thousand years ago that matter is created from the ether that surrounds us in space, and similar theories are found in the traditions of many early civilizations. However, the idea of the ether lost its credibility to the materialist worldview in the latter part of the nineteenth century. Our technological revolution owes its success to the supremacy of the concept of the world as a mechanism and Man as a competitive survival machine. According to Newtonian and Cartesian understanding, which still informs contemporary biology, biochemistry, physics, and medicine—indeed our whole worldview—everything works predictably.

A few early pioneers of quantum physics in the early twentieth century sensed that their discoveries would revolutionize our understanding of biology and cosmology, but it has taken a new generation since World War II to discover that quanta fill the macro environment as well as the microscopic, creating an enormous web of interconnected dynamic energy that seems to continue infinitely through space—a kind of communication system.

Einstein's Nobel prize–winning protégé, David Bohm (1917–1994), proposed that creation is aware of itself and its oneness in "continuous creation," meaning that all of space is filled with a dynamic energy he called the "etheric flux" (presumably an older term for the quantum field). The domain of the ether, or quantum field, is more refined than the physical.

METAPHYSICAL SCIENCE

The ancient sciences had a more holistic understanding of the world than we have today. However, we do use language that differentiates among different qualities of energy. We speak of a person having "coarse" or "refined energy." A product is considered tasteful or beautiful when it has an integral harmony and balance, but we don't use a scale of refinement.

Theosophy has a helpful schema for understanding energy.* It postulates a hierarchy of being or consciousness, from lower to higher frequencies, in terms of domains or dimensions, each separated by a "veil" that renders the higher level inaccessible. The higher frequency is aware

---

*Theosophy is a metaphysical philosophy that originated with the Russian philosopher Helena Petrovna Blavatsky in 1875. Theosophists trace its ancient origin to the universal striving for spiritual knowledge that has existed in all cultures. They believe that all religions are attempts by spiritual masters to help humanity evolve to a higher level of consciousness. It has strong links to esoteric Buddhism.

of the lower, but the lower frequency cannot apprehend the higher.

Our normal awareness is the domain of the third dimension, the physical, which has its own laws. We can have glimpses of the fourth (time) and fifth (thought) dimensions, through intuition or inspiration. All subtle dimensions are present on Earth, interpenetrating the third dimension, though we are not normally conscious of them. Many other animals or humans with raised consciousness have a wider range of perception. A close relationship with a dog, cat, or horse often reveals instances where the animal is aware of a nonphysical presence that is beyond our own awareness, or which may even be a spirit presence.[1]

If our consciousness is lowered, we feel less ability to control our own lives. If our three components of consciousness (physical, emotional, and mental) are being fully used, then we can experience the full potential of being human and having free will.

QUANTUM ENERGY

David Bohm, who was part of the renaissance of quantum physics in the post-war years, suggested a holographic model of the universe in his book, *Wholeness and the Implicate Order*.[2] In holography, a special plate exposed to a laser beam (coherent light) produces a three-dimensional image of the subject. If the holographic plate is smashed into a thousand pieces, each fragment will reproduce the whole picture.

According to Bohm, the vast reality that lies beyond our senses is an undivided and coherent whole, which he calls "implicate" or "implied." He insists that every element in everyday material reality—explicit, manifest—contains all the information of the implicit order. He saw the boundary between the two orders like the veil (*maya*) of the ancient Vedic tradition that needs to be pulled aside to reveal the full nature of reality. This was practiced by the ancient spiritual traditions through meditation and mystical trances. Their science studied the unseen as well as the manifest—it was a holistic system.

The study of fractals is based on a similar holographic principle. They are a mathematical description of biological self-repeating cycles, a vital part of the evolutionary process (see pp. 211–12). These beautiful organic-looking structures are found in fern development, in the branching patterns of trees, in blood vessels, and in the larger environment—in weather systems and coastline features.

Traditional conventional Western science and quantum physics are worlds apart in their understanding of how the organism functions. The Newtonian model visualizes central control by the brain and nervous system, with energy dissipation according to the second law of thermodynamics;* and the neo-Darwinian model holds to the competitive, random nature of life systems.

Quantum physics, on the other hand, describes the organism's main feature as that of wholeness based on intense intercommunication of all its parts, resulting in cooperation and reciprocity; local freedom and cohesion of the whole. Mae-Wan Ho (see below) likens the mechanistic view of matter to dead matter, while the holistic view studies the living fabric of life.[3]

THE WEIRDNESS OF WATER

Strangely, you will find almost nothing about the role of water as an organism in biology and biochemistry textbooks. That it behaves like an organism is one of the weirder ideas about water. Schauberger, whose theories about water have proved to be remarkably prescient, called water an organism. But as an intuitive, he did not expand on this very clearly.

Conventionally, an organism has the ability to reproduce. However, Mae-Wan Ho (see box on p. 160), who specializes in the study of the organism, is more interested in other important indications of an organism's aliveness—its sensitivity to cues from the environment, the

---

*The second law of thermodynamics states that all self-contained systems must degenerate into a condition of entropy unless there is a further input of energy.

efficiency with which it transmits dynamic energy within its bounds—both of which water demonstrates. An organism operates with long-range order and coordination, as does water in certain (quantum) conditions. Water departs from Ho's qualifications for being alive in that it does not have individuality or independence; however, it shows a certain wholeness and coherence in the manner in which it imparts these to what we normally consider to be organisms.

Holistic Challenge to Reductionist Thinking

Mae-Wan Ho, who has a world reputation in the new science of the organism, resigned from the Open University in protest at its increasing dependence on corporate funding for biological research (especially in genetics). Recognizing the need for transparency and open debate on public issues, in 1999 she and her husband founded the Institute of Science in Society, which publishes a bimonthly magazine. Ho is a genuine polymath and an outspoken and tireless campaigner who challenges the mainstream mechanistic and reductionist scientific worldview (see Links and Resources).

The key to the quantum qualities of water, Ho suggests, is the proposition that water comes in two states: bulky, low density (super-cooled water); and high density, when the molecules are packed more closely together.[4] In its dense state, it seems to have more long-range coherence and exhibit quantum qualities (memory, high dynamic energy, communication, self-refining, and so on). The form we are most familiar with is low-density water. Ho's research demonstrates that an organism functions by all its parts working together coherently, which is governed by the essential cohesion of the water medium.

BIOLOGICAL WATER

Most of our biological water is part of the intercellular matrix that governs metabolic functioning and chemical reactions. It is often called intercellular water, but what does it actually do? This water is in a crystalline state called the "liquid crystalline continuum," in which all the molecules are macroscopically aligned to form a network linking the whole body. This continuum is diffused through the connective tissues, the extracellular matrix, and into every single cell. All the molecules, including the water, are moving coherently together as a whole, even when the body is at rest.

This pattern is in the realm of quantum physics, which operates under different principles from those of Newtonian physics, the main feature of the quanta being how they interconnect all life-forms into a coherent whole. This operates from the micro to the macro level and is very much what makes an organism tick. Conventional physics, on the other hand, focuses more on individual molecules and is less able to see the larger picture.

Ho pioneered this exciting research using a polarizing microscope with special settings that enable it to film the behavior of the molecular structure of organisms. Her Institute of Science in Society has produced a video, *Quantum Jazz,* featuring the daphnia, a fruitfly larva (it could just as well be us) in glorious technicolor, with molecules dancing around as if part of a ballet (see plate 13).* Usually we're restricted to studying the interior of organisms when they are dead. This technology displays the changing subtle energy effects in the watery domains of a living organism. This effect has been filmed and everyone can see it on a simple DVD. It is electrifying and demonstrates quite vividly how living organisms operate with remarkable coherence.

---

*See Ho's background article "Quantum Jazz—the Tao of Life" on www.i-sis.org.uk. The science behind this research is contained in her remarkable book *The Rainbow and the Worm: The Physics of Organisms,* more popular presentations of which are her "New Age of Water" series of articles found on the institute's website.

WHAT IS LIFE?

As Ho recounts:

> To see it for the first time was a stunning, breathtaking experience, even though I have yet to lose my fascination for it, having seen it many, many times subsequently. The larva, all of one millimeter in length and perfectly formed in every minute detail, comes into focus on the color TV monitor as though straight out of a dream.
>
> As it crawls along, it weaves its head from side to side, flashing jaw muscles in blue and orange stripes on a magenta background. The segmental muscle bands switch from brilliant turquoise to bright vermilion, tracking waves of contraction along its body. The contracting body wall turns from magenta to purple, through iridescent shades of green, orange, and yellow. The egg yolk, trapped in the alimentary canal, shimmers a dull chartreuse as it gurgles back and forth in the commotion.
>
> A pair of pale orange tracheal tracts run from just behind the head down the sides, terminating in yellow spiracles at the posterior extremity. Within the posterior abdomen, fluorescent yellow malpighian tubules come in and out of focus like decorative ostrich feathers. And when highlighted, white nerve fibers can be seen radiating from the ventral nerve cords.
>
> Rotating the microscope stage 90° caused nearly all the colors of the worm instantly to take on their complementary hues. It is difficult to remember that these colors have physical meaning concerning the shape and arrangements of all the molecules making up the different tissues.
>
> It was some time before we realized that we had made a new discovery. The technique depends on using the polarizing microscope unconventionally, so as to optimize the detection of small birefringences or coherently aligned anisotropies in the molecular structures of the tissue.
>
> There is no conductor or choreographer. The organism is creating

and re-creating herself afresh with each passing moment, recoding and rewriting the genes in her cells in an intricate dance of life that enables the organism to survive and thrive. The dance is written as it is performed; every movement is new, as it is shaped by what has gone before. The organism never ceases to experience its environment, registering its experience for future reference.[5]

The coordination required for [humans to achieve] simultaneous multiple tasks and perform the most extraordinary feats depends on a special state of being whole, the ideal description for which is "quantum coherence." Quantum coherence is a paradoxical state that maximizes both local freedom and global cohesion.[6]

QUANTUM COHERENCE

Quantum entanglement is the term used for a high order of coherence or integrity. It is easiest to recognize in a school of fish or a flight of birds that suddenly changes direction at breakneck speed without colliding, behaving as a single organism, one part in complete harmony with every other part.

The Institute of Science in Society has pioneered research into how organisms actually work. Ho explains why Nature does not recognize the second law of thermodynamics. Natural systems work like wheels within wheels.

The perfect coordination required for simultaneous multiple tasks in everyday life and in performing the most extraordinary feats both depend on a special state of being whole, best described as "quantum coherence." Quantum coherence is a paradoxical state of wholeness that is anything but uniform. It is infinitely diverse and multiplex, it maximizes both local freedom and global cohesion.

The quantum coherent organism . . . is a domain of coherent energy storage that accumulates no waste or entropy within, because it mobilizes energy most efficiently and rapidly to grow and develop and reproduce. Not only does it not accumulate entropy, but the waste or entropy exported is also minimized.

Part of the secret for quantum coherence is that the life cycle itself contains many cycles of activities within. These cycles of different sizes are all coupled together so that activities yielding energy transfer the energy directly to activities requiring energy, losing little or nothing in the process (see box). If you look inside each small cycle that makes up the whole life cycle, you will see the same picture as the whole; and you can do this many times over until you come to the smallest cycle.[7]

Conservation of Energy in Organisms and Organizations

Ho's simple diagram of the conservation of energy in organisms is also a model for the successful working of any organization. If this were applied to the nation's financial policy we would not have seen the appalling hemorrhaging of money and resources, which have resulted in entropy and waste. It could also transform the way our communities are run and our energy and food is produced. It is the key to a sustainable human society and to living lightly on the earth. Ho has published a very telling example of new concepts of food production, which depend on the recycling of energy from one part of a model farm to another (diverse crops and animals, composting, aquaculture, worms, mushrooms, biogas and hydrogen production, and so on). See "Dream Farm," *SiS*, no. 38.

The organism's molecules are embedded in a water medium, which maintains them in a dynamic crystalline state, their electrical polarities forming a continuum that links the whole body. All the molecules are dancing together, and the more coherent their movement, the brighter their colors.

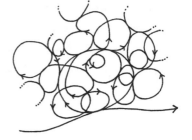

Figure 11.1. Cycles within cycles. Mae-Wan Ho's representation of the way in which an organism's energy continually recycles.

The high degree of coherence is dependent on the liquid crystalline nature of the water medium, which makes up about 70 percent of the total weight of a living organism. This allows all the molecules to inter-communicate and synchronize with each other. In Ho's words:

> I call the totality of these activities "quantum jazz" to emphasize the immense diversity and multiplicity of players on all scales, the complexity and coherence of the performance, and most importantly, the freedom and spontaneity of it all.

Quantum jazz is played out by the whole organism, in every nerve and sinew, every muscle, every single cell, molecule, atom, and elementary particle, emitting light and sound with wavelengths from nanometers to meters and kilometers; spanning a musical range of seventy octaves or more, each improvising spontaneously and freely, yet keeping in tune and in step with the whole.

Quantum jazz is written as it is performed; every movement is new, shaped by what has gone before—though not quite. The organism never ceases to experience her environment and take it in for future reference, modifying her liquid crystalline matrix and neural circuits, recoding and rewriting her genes.

Quantum jazz is why ordinary folks can talk and think at the same time, while our breakfast is being processed to give us energy. It is why top athletes can run a mile in less than four minutes, and kung fu masters can move with lightning speed and fly effortlessly through the air.

It is possible that this quality of quantum coherence could be the explanation for the way the human mind can influence events (outcomes). It might also account for the accomplishments of Hindu fakirs or even for the miracles of Jesus. It would depend upon which level you are able to access. Healers work on the quantum level, which has different laws that govern outcomes. It is generally understood in their profession that they might lose their gift if they give in to the temptations of the ego. By doing so they would lose coherence with their client. This could also be stated as: In order to work successfully with fifth dimensional energies, it is necessary to have integrity and a willingness to work within spiritual laws.

It has been suggested that humanity may have this gift of coherently visualizing outcomes as part of the free will package. If coherence can be equated with consciousness, then the future of humanity on Earth must be connected with the raising of consciousness of a significant number of people (a spiritual revival).

INTERFACIAL WATER AND WATER'S SKIN

All organisms have a skin that performs a number of important functions. As the outside layer, it defines the integrity and coherence of the organism and limits its vulnerability to physical assault and infection. It is the vital heat-balancing organ for most animals and is full of tiny sensors; in some animals these represent their main antennae for picking up information from the surrounding environment.

Earth, because of its individuality or independence, probably fulfils more completely than water Mae-Wan Ho's criteria for an organism. Its skin is the biosphere.

Water also has a skin. The surface in contact with the atmosphere is called the meniscus (from the Greek for "crescent"); it relates to the interaction of the water molecules, and it is this that allows water bugs to sit on its surface. The meniscus is pulled up at the edge of a glass of water by cohesion; water and glass have similar molecules, so the glass attracts the water molecules, forming a concave surface. But if you spread a hydrophobic (water repelling) oily layer on the glass, the water particles stick together and a convex boundary forms instead. Dr. Gerald Pollack, at the University of Washington, Seattle, calls this skin or part of a water body in contact with another medium surface the "interfacial water," or an "exclusion zone" (EZ), because it seems to be able to exclude solutes that are found in the main water body.[8]

A stream also has a skin where it contacts the streambed, and it contains the integrity of the whole. The water molecules next to the skin usually have a concentration of active oxygen, which acts as a neutralizer of elements that are out of balance in the water body. The water body can retain its freshness by circulating its flow, concentrating the higher quality in the center.

Water's skin, just like the skin of any other organism, is sensitive to both terrestrial and cosmic energies. The meniscus has a high surface tension (ST), which is the ability of water to stick to itself. It is ST that makes water want to form a sphere—the form with the least surface area for its volume, requiring the least amount of energy to maintain itself.

Just like cell water, exclusion zone water—water in contact with another surface—has complex ordered layers that sometimes are called liquid crystals. Mae-Wan Ho discovered that cells and organisms are liquid crystalline in structure.[9]

What Ho found is that this EZ water forms at every face of the water body, so that it is indeed like a skin preserving the water body's integrity. So perhaps the river's skin can not only absorb but also project subtle energy from the water body into the banks and bed of the river. Could it be that water's skin acts as an antenna to receive and transmit subtle energy, as the skin does with a more usual organism?

A link can be made to the restructuring of the water filaments in a stream by the action of the longitudinal vortex as described by Schauberger (see p. 94), who said that this complex water structure enabled the water body to absorb higher energies and healing qualities, for the different layers of the water structure act like skins.

An electrical field will improve water's stiffness and crystalline nature by perfecting the alignment of its molecules. Ho demonstrated this strikingly on her kitchen table by putting two nearly full beakers of water almost touching, then inserting a positive electrode from a power pack into one beaker and a negative into the other. In this experiment, a bridge of stiff water will form, connecting the two beakers and conducting electricity. Moving the beakers several centimeters apart will still maintain this bridge.[10]

BRAIN CONSCIOUSNESS VERSUS BODY CONSCIOUSNESS

The brain controls the central nervous system through the cranial nerves and spinal cord, as well as the peripheral nervous system. Biology traditionally identifies the brain as regulating virtually all human activity, including involuntary actions, such as heart rate, respiration, and digestion. This is a mechanistic view of the human body systems, which also assumes that the brain is the seat of consciousness, but brain science does not have an easy answer for how the brain is able to operate as an integrated whole. Is this not really the same question as how the organism operates as a coherent whole?

Biologists have long wondered how an organism like a bear or a human is able to respond so quickly to outside stimuli. For years it was assumed that the body's nervous system was responsible for passing messages from eyes to brain to hands or other parts. But careful measurements show that nervous energy paths can take large fractions of a second, too long for the instantaneous response that is usually the case.

It is a well-attested fact in the practice of aromatherapy that nutrients applied to the skin are very quickly conveyed throughout the body. An herbalist friend rubbed a clove of garlic on the sole of his baby's foot and was amazed to detect the smell of garlic on the baby's breath half a minute later! This is possible only through the link chains of water's magical crystalline structure.

Ho gives the example of the accomplished pianist's hand-eye coordination: "There simply isn't time enough, from one musical phrase to the next, for inputs to be sent to the brain, there to be integrated, and coordinated outputs to be sent back to the hands."[11]

COLLAGEN AND COLLOID CRYSTALS

One exciting discovery in recent years has been the strange role that water plays in biological communication. It has come to light that collagen, the connective tissue that makes up the bulk of all multicellular animals, is crucial to the integrity of the organism. It is composed of a crystalline matrix of collagen proteins embedded in water that is 60 to 70 percent by weight. This, suggests Ho, makes the connective tissues the ideal medium for communication. This water is specially structured in chains along the collagen fibers and has the ability to self-organize.[12]

Tests by Gary Fullerton at Texas University, San Antonio, suggest that water associated with collagen exhibits a high degree of quantum order, being structured in regular chains along the collagen fibers.[13] This would facilitate a process called "jump-conduction of protons" that would enable instant communication to take place between different parts of the body—essential for perfect coordination.

Ho believes this would enable water associated with collagen to become superconductive, an ideal medium for instantaneous intercommunication for coordination of all cellular activities. She believes that this liquid crystal continuum constitutes a "body consciousness" that may well have evolved before the nervous system but which today works both in partnership with, and also independently of, the nervous system. "This body consciousness is the basis of sentience, the prerequisite for conscious experience that involves the participation of the intercommunicating whole of the energy storage domain."[14] The body's energy, she points out, does not follow the conventional laws of thermodynamics but is able through quantum coherence to be stored dynamically in a closed system, to be available at a moment's notice.

Ho suggests that the acupuncture meridians of Chinese medicine may be structured water lines aligned with collagen, and that chi energy may be the positive bioelectric currents carried by the jump-conduction of protons through the hydrogen bonds of water molecules.

Another area where water can produce a high degree of order is in colloid crystallization. Colloids (suspensions made up of minute nanoparticles) were always thought to be homogeneous. Japanese researcher Norio Ise was able to create significant crystal forms in polymer solutions. The outcome of this research has been the development of a wide range of industrial applications in electronic and photon chips.

TRANSPLANTS

We tend to think of the organs of the body in the same way as engine parts that can be replaced when they wear out. Indeed, many lives have been saved by organ transplants from one body to another. Besides vital organs, bone marrow and blood are also transplanted or transfused.

But there is a downside to this practice. The human body is not just the sum of its parts. It is an organism that acts as a complete unity. The heart and blood are as individual as a person's brain, and unforeseen consequences may result from a blood transfusion.

Viktor Schauberger regarded blood (which is largely water) as an organ. There is anecdotal evidence of personality change in someone who has had his blood supply replaced by another's. Blood is similar to water in its ability to carry information, and perhaps also has memory. Perceived in this light, it is not surprising that some religions regard blood transfusions as unethical.

TWELVE

SPIRALS, THE VORTEX, AND THE ETHERIC

In the beginning was the vortex.

DEMOCRITUS (460–370 BCE)

We live on a planet that is hurtling through space at a breathtaking speed while spinning on its axis, and we are also subject to gravitational and magnetic forces. Earth's fluids are particularly affected by its spinning. As water is the most important constituent of life, the way it moves, its rhythms and pulsations, are at the heart of all life's processes.

SELF-ORGANIZING SYSTEMS

The linear system of Newtonian physics that has dominated the natural sciences for three centuries studies only predictable phenomena, which is why we still know so little about water. Newton did not recognize that living systems behave in what seems like a random, unpredictable way.

The idea that organisms are self-organizing was first suggested by the research of Boris Belousov, a Soviet chemist. In 1959 his crucial experiment was to prepare a solution of some thirty chemical substances, from colorless liquid to one with brilliant colors, which, to his surprise, organized itself into regular patterns of spirals and vortices. These self-organizing oscillations in water demonstrated that its chemical reactions are unpredictable. Belousov's research was not taken seriously, and eleven years elapsed before a young chemist called Anatoly Zhabotinsky repeated the older man's experiment, which then became known as the Belousov-Zhabotinsky reaction. Their findings were a challenge to the law of entropy, showing that from a disordered state spiral-forms emerge creating stable, oscillating patterns—order spontaneously emerges from chaos.

Ilya Prigogine (1917–2003), winner of the Nobel Prize for Chemistry in 1977, believed that organisms, though stable, are always striving toward greater equilibrium.* He saw organisms in a state of constant change, responding to other organisms in order to achieve harmonious balance. He acknowledged that his ideas were inspired by the Chinese tradition of fluctuation between yin and yang, tending toward harmony of the Tao, the ancient Chinese path of wisdom. Nature's imperative is to follow patterns that lead to equilibrium. This principle is also at the heart of Schauberger's work with polarities.

An organism is not a fixed entity. As Mae-Wan Ho shows in her *Quantum Jazz* (see p. 165), organisms are in a state of constant flux, with a tendency to cooperate with other organisms to create an ordered reality and higher symmetry.

ORDER FROM CHAOS

The principle has been recognized by the philosophers of all the great civilizations—that change can come only from the failure of the status quo. Put another way: order must be preceded by chaos; the two are inseparable partners (see box). In the Chinese *Tao Te Ching*, the hexagram for "crisis" is the same as that for "opportunity."†

---

*Ilya Prigogine's pioneering research in self-organizing systems, based on his dissipative systems theory, became a cornerstone of quantum physics.

†A hexagram is a six-line symbol that helps to discern both the energy in a particular situation and the best way to work with it.

Chaos Precedes Order

Author Callum Coats gives a helpful explanation of dialectic thinking, which he insists is imperative for comprehension of the whole. Thus, yin is balanced by yang (yin x yang = 1), magnetism by electricism, frequency by wavelength, spirit by matter, and so on. Thus also, chaos x order = 1, or wholeness. Without chaos (undifferentiated, unstructured matter or energy; or unordered, unmetamorphosed unconditional love), there could be no basis for the creation of order (differentiated, harmonically structured matter or energy). Therefore, the foundation for order is chaos.[*]

---

*In order to comprehend the whole, German philosopher G. W. F. Hegel (1770–1831) insisted that it is imperative to consider opposites as: "such contradictions that are seen to merge themselves into a higher truth that comprehends them." This is termed *dialectic thinking*. (Oxford English Dictionary)

Water stage-manages life, but water itself is a disorganized medium. It seems to thrive on paradoxes. The asymmetry of its molecule is responsible for many of the strange anomalies that make it fit for life. This imperfect symmetry holds the secret of matter's very existence, for instability and imperfect symmetry are the guiding laws of the universe.

Evolutionary initiatives seem to have a tentativeness about them, which translate as instability. It is the restlessness of water that gives living systems the ability to become ever more complex and to strive toward the perfection they can never attain. As the driver of evolution, water is a model for our own striving. It is the changeability and restlessness of water that drives evolution, for it allows life, by fits and starts, to become ever more complex. Organisms are self-organizing closed energy systems, but they also allow energy to pass through them.

We love to disparage meteorologists for getting their forecasts wrong, but weather systems are complex and nonlinear, and the watery domain, gaseous or liquid, is essentially unpredictable. Organisms based on water are in constant flux. They communicate with other organisms, as the overriding imperative in Nature is to bring about balance and higher order.

THE AMBIGUITY OF PATTERN, UNCERTAINTY, AND CHAOS

The Newtonian/Cartesian mechanistic worldview prefers processes to be predictable. But Euclidian geometry, straight lines, and boxed containers are alien to Nature. Yet Nature is not entirely unpredictable.

Classical societies identified patterns in the formation of natural organic systems, which they codified as natural laws, applying to them mathematical values out of which grew sacred geometry (see pp. 177–78). Nature works harmoniously, with every living thing participating in a vast ballet or orchestra, which Mae-Wan Ho vividly described in the previous chapter. Nature's intercommunication system is truly miraculous.

Mainstream science usually sees evolution as a meaningless random process, while, as we investigated in chapter 9, we can see patterns and trends in evolution that suggest a purpose.

Uncertainty is a fundamental principle of quantum mechanics. Restlessness is one of the primary features of water due, as we saw in chapter 3, to its unsymmetrical hydrogen bonds. It is constantly opening to new impressions, and consolidating them through turbulence, then chaos and restructuring.

The key to this new order is the fractal, the self-repeating structure that conveys to the smallest scale of life the patterns of the macro universe, through the action of the quantum field working through water.

Computers and abstract mathematics, working with the broader view of quantum physics, have given us a deeper understanding of chaotic systems. Contrary to what conventional physics might expect, this apparently random chaos is actually a precondition of higher order and intelligence.

You can extrapolate this idea into life in general. Any artist will tell you that inspiration does not arise out of the predictable but from the unexpected, the disturbing situation. A routine, predictable life lacks the creative spark that enables one to discover the best opportunities for growth.

Recognizing this can transform the distress of a relationship breakup or loss of one's job into an opportunity for creative change. The ancient Chinese saying "Breakdown brings opportunity" is really quite apposite. This is what water teaches us, as turbulence allows water to transform toward increased complexity and higher order. Going with the flow means having faith that the life process has a wisdom about balance and growth. Are we able consciously to allow Nature to break down our collapsing and unsustainable human organizations with the belief that new, positive structures will evolve?*

THE VORTEX

Earth's rotation causes all fluids and gases to move in spirals. Water's spiraling is most familiar because it is so visible. But it can be observed in smoke, mist, or a fog as it rolls up a valley. Spirals are a basic form of motion in Nature, but back in the 1930s, Schauberger recognized the vortex as the principal creative movement system in the universe, making it the core of his ecotechnology. The condition required to produce the vortex is turbulence, or chaotic motion. Turbulence increases with a small rise in the temperature of the water, which will disturb a fish and make it more likely to go for the fisherman's bait. Turbulence is the precursor to chaotic restructuring of the water.

The vortex we see as bathwater swirls down the drain is comparable to the structure of whirlpools, cyclones, DNA, magnetic force fields, and galaxies (see plate 14). It is a concentration of spiraling and dynamically increasing energy. A healer's subtle energy projects from his hands as a vortex of concentrated energy. A tornado's energy increases with the

---

*One such candidate might be the Transition Movement (see chapter 19), which seems to have a fractal way of multiplying. (Also see appendix 3: Ben Okri on "The Bankruptcy of Our Civilization.")

narrowing of the cone down to the point, where the tornado's destruction is greatest.

It was a Belfast physicist, Lord Kelvin (William Thomson, 1824–1907), who first proposed that atomic motion is vortical. This was picked up by James Clerk Maxwell (1831–1879), a Scottish theoretical physicist; and by Sir Joseph J. Thomson (1856–1940), the British physicist and Nobel Prize winner who discovered the electron.*

The idea fell into disfavor when the concept of the ether was discredited (the theory that atoms required a substance in which to move). The concept of wave motion took over, and the atom was demoted from its position as the smallest unit of matter.

It took the emergence of string theory in the 1970s and '80s to bring back the idea of atomic movement in spirals. It describes how dynamic energy can create what looks like static matter by conceiving a ball of string composed of countless short threads, each forming spirals intertwined with left- and right-hand spins, echoing the electromagnetic polarities found throughout the universe. The vortex was rediscovered by quantum theory.

DNA is probably the most famous spiral in Nature. It is also the battleground between neo-Darwinists, who explain evolution through random mistakes in replication of DNA, and those who interpret evolution as an imperative process of Nature's intelligence.

Science writer James Gleick, who popularized the ideas of chaos theory in the early 1980s, pointed out that life is created from chaos. Fluids are the ideal media of chaos because of their unpredictable and turbulent behavior. Water turbulence creates vortices and spirals in an energetic stream, with the flow direction constantly changing from left to right.

From the tornado to a growing plant, the vortex is Nature's mechanism for increasing the quality of energy, raising it from a lower to a

---

*James Clerk Maxwell synthesized previously unrelated theories to formulate electromagnetic theory. He challenged the omnipotence of the second law of thermodynamics with his Maxwell's Demon proposition in 1871, thus anticipating the basis of quantum physics.

higher level. It is a powerful tool for evolution, and perhaps water's most constructive role is to use the vortex for this purpose.

Ilya Prigogine saw that disorder creates simultaneously stable and unstable oscillating systems that are spiral-form in structure leading to order. This oscillation enables a dynamic homoeostasis (stability) to exist and to increase complexity and energy levels. This mirrors Schauberger's practical research into the way a stream raises energy levels, which he applied to his ecotechnological applications. Prigogine sees the vortex as energy dissipating, in line with Schauberger's view.

The vortex is a window between different qualities or levels of energy. Black holes can be thought of as vortices, gateways linking different parts of our universe, or even different universes. For Schauberger, the vortex and spiral were the key to all creative movement. As we shall demonstrate later, the vortex is most clearly seen with water, which uses vortical motion to purify and energize itself, introducing finer etheric energies to wipe the water clean of any negative energies from previous misuse.

One could use the image of a musty room that feels stale and unwelcoming. Once sunlight and fresh air are allowed to penetrate, the unpleasant atmosphere is quickly transformed. It is a natural principle that more refined energy always prevails over coarse. As Schauberger demonstrated, Nature's evolutionary purpose is to continually refine and create greater complexity and diversity, the vortex being the key process in this endeavor.

EGGS AND VORTICES

Until relatively recent times, scientists and philosophers recognized the creative energy of Nature as sacred. They viewed Nature's patterns and complex interdependences, often expressed in very specific shapes that could be described in geometric terms and ratios, as proof of God as architect of creation. Thus, they called these correspondences "sacred numbers" and "sacred geometry" (see plate 16).

Artists and architects sought true balance, perfect proportion, an aesthetically pleasing shape. The square seemed too mechanical, a long rectangle too awkward. The shape that seemed just right was the square rectangle with the proportions of 5:8, called the "golden mean," usually described by the Greek letter *phi* (φ). This turns out to be the magical proportion favored by Nature in her designs. It is also the key to the shape of the egg.[2]*

Schauberger was well aware that Nature uses the egg shape for creating and maintaining the dynamic energy of biological water. In *Fertile Earth* he wrote: "Every force . . . unfolds itself and springs forth from the original form of life, the egg."

He also understood the importance of the electromagnetic polarity being activated in water. For example, when generating vortices in egg-shaped vessels as a way of developing powerful energies in heating and cooling applications and for high-potency drinking water, he placed the pointy end in an upward direction. This produced a negative, yin subtle energy, like the in-drawing of breath. When he used eggs for potentizing natural fertilizers, he placed the pointy end down, producing an out-breathing, yang subtle energy. He did not, as far as we know, experiment with two eggs used together, but he demonstrated that an egg with the pointy end down generates dynamic energy; whereas point up, it gathers, condenses, and concentrates energy.[†]

Ralf Roessner, a German anthroposophical scientist, produced a model that ingeniously separates the yin and yang parts of the process, illustrating clearly what takes place. His process uses two glass eggs joined at their pointy ends by a short collar to produce high-quality drinking water (see plate 15). It is an ingenious system: the upper egg produces a fine vortex where the water accelerates and chaoticizes as it passes through the narrow neck. When it falls into the lower egg as turbulent and chaotic myriads of tiny electromagnetically polarized cyclones, liquid crystalline chains form and natural clustering takes

---

*Callum Coats clarifies the relationship between phi and the egg shape in *Living Energies*. The numerical value of phi is 1:1.6187, or 5:8 (a $\sqrt{3}$ rectangle).

†This is why pointy end up is the best way to store eggs.

place, which rebuilds the internal structure of the water at a higher dynamic energy level. The surfaces of the many layers in this laminar structure act like skins, or antennae, to absorb higher energy.

This dual system elegantly combines the energy-dissipating function of the vortex with the energy-enhancing mode of chaos in the lower egg. The natural egg shape (see above) in each case encourages the water body to circulate efficiently as a coherent whole. The natural coherence of water is amplified by the egg shape, helping it break through into the quantum domain, from which it can absorb higher quality subtle energies. Quantum coherence is much more dynamic than normal physical coherence.

Roessner spent ten years developing this double-egg system, with beautiful handblown eggs created individually by skilled glass craftsmen, to produce quantum water for domestic use.[3] He points out that through this very personal, hands-on way of energizing water, we can communicate with the water being energized. As we are essentially quantum water, our own biological water is involved with the process of spinning the water in the eggs.*

FLOWFORMS

We haven't talked much about the rhythm of water. In the flow of a healthy stream there is a natural rhythm of movement from side to side, which keeps the electromagnetic charge of the stream in balance. In order to create this rhythm in an artificial stream, it is necessary to understand the mathematics of flow in relation to form.

While still a sculpture student, John Wilkes was introduced to projective geometry by the anthroposophist George Adams, a colleague of Theodor Schwenk, whose pioneering research we will discuss in the next chapter. He believed that the quality of water may be dependent on the rhythms of that water moving across a specific surface. From this

---

*Schauberger believed that a water body (for instance, a stream) can communicate with our own water body (chapter 10). Cleve Backster's research suggests this might even happen at a distance (chapter 14).

theory emerged his idea of the flowform, which consists of a series of heart-shaped basins that introduce rhythmic movement into the water in a series of figure eights. It is usually built as a cascade of bowls, in a wide variety of shapes and in various materials, often in preformed concrete (see plate 17).

More than one thousand flowform projects have been set up in more than thirty countries. Their ability to invigorate the environment has made them popular in town centers, with large businesses, in parks, and in gardens (see plate 18). Their most practical use is in conjunction with water treatment plants, where they play a crucial role at the end of the purification process. They are also used in biological treatment systems, fish farms, and reed bed sewage systems.

THE GROUND OF ALL BEING

Goethe called water "the ground of all being." The "being" he referred to is more than manifest life; it is also the ground of Bohm's "implicate order." By the law of polarity, all systems have a dual aspect (see p. 289). Thus, it is reasonable to suppose that cosmic principles and forms are conveyed to organic life as a partnership between water (yin) and the quantum field, or etheric (yang).

Both are media for the transmission of subtle energies. Whereas the etheric may have to do more with the mental level, water is perhaps the medium for communicating formative information. It seems that they work together in harmonious balance.

I suspect that the quantum field may be related to electromagnetic energies as they are generally understood, but on a higher dimensional level (see p. 157), and therefore subject to different laws; for example, while normal electromagnetic waves are interrupted by lead shielding or a Faraday cage, the etheric may not be blocked.

These are still early days of understanding the etheric field and its interaction with the water domain.

THIRTEEN

WATER'S COSMIC ROLE

Like all living things, water is a self-organizing system: a drop of water is a universe unto itself, containing substances and living creatures, generating and responding to vibrations, perpetuating the same patterns and sequences that we find on a larger scale in our own bodies, in the Earth, indeed throughout the entire universe. [This drop of] water is the smallest, yet also the most all-encompassing and immanent of universes.

PAOLO CONSIGLI

THE COSMIC CONNECTION

From earliest times Man has believed that the heavens influence life on Earth. Over time the study of cosmology developed; science and religion became inseparable, and both were regarded as skills of the priesthood. The famous maxim "As above, so below," attributed to Hermes Trismegistus, the mysterious founder of alchemy, refers to the theory of correspondences: "That which is in the lesser world (the microcosm) reflects that of the greater world or universe (the macrocosm)."

The poetic phrase "harmony of the spheres" recognizes a natural order in the motion of the planets in the solar system and of stars in their constellations. All life is motion. Natural movement comes not in straight lines but as spirals, the shape taken by fluid energy evolving from chaos. Patterns and rhythms are the heartbeat of the universe, giving it design and structure. Nothing can come into being without a design or template. How are these templates or patterns for growth and harmony conveyed to the physical Earth environment?

Ancient cultures recognized mathematics and geometry as tools for understanding patterns in Nature and in the universe. It was from such relationships that the Pythagorean canon of proportions (mathematical proportions of the human body) was created. The basics of musical harmony depend on intervals created by these divine proportions. Canons of architecture, painting, and musical harmony were taught in medieval mystery schools and partly revived during the Renaissance. Understanding the mystery of these forms is a whole science in itself (sacred geometry).

Perhaps water's most important function is to be a transducer between the cosmic and earthly realms. Earth has a vast circulation system within its crust (nearly one-third of its fresh water is very deep underground). Earth's surface is penetrated by rain that is charged with cosmic energy, which joins this circulation to be charged with minerals and with the mother energy of the interior.

Cosmic energy is also absorbed into the water system by plants and directly by the land. This requires antennae, such as bud forms, seeds, egg shapes, and tree leaves (especially pine needles), or certain points in the landscape (for example, powerful hills or mountains).

In addition to carrying energy and supplying nutrients, water carries information that is the very basis of the web of life. The quality and amount of information carried depends on the structure of the water.

RESONANCE

All matter, though it may look solid and stationary, is based on subatomic particles in perpetual motion. The velocity of this motion determines its vibrational rate; this and the type and size of the object contribute to its vibrational or resonant frequency.

Life-forms in Nature respond to each other by means of resonance; Schauberger called it "Gaia's glue." It is the language of communication and response, the law of attraction bringing the bee to the lemon blossom and the moss to the damp earth. Resonance is similar to Mae-Wan Ho's concept of coherence (see chapter 11).

Sound is probably the most ancient form of resonance in human experience. Jericho was reputedly destroyed by destructive sound resonances. A piano tuner uses resonance. Music itself is more than a paradigm of the forces behind Nature. For millennia people have sung and played music to their crops, streams, lovers, children, and animals. The resonance and vibrational rate of water is at the heart of natural medicine (especially homeopathy), biocommunication, and husbandry, through sap and blood. The quality of the water affects both recharging and cleansing.

When we experience a sense of the sublime on listening to a musical composition of great integrity, we come into a state of resonance with the particular dynamic energy pattern of that composition. The same can happen with the thrill of watching the aurora borealis or similar natural phenomena—one's whole body resonates with that particular energy.

Of course you can resonate with degraded energy, too, particularly if your own dynamic energy is degraded.

COSMIC INFLUENCES: RUDOLF STEINER AND THEODOR SCHWENK

One of the best philosophical sources for understanding the greater cosmic system, or consciousness, is the body of knowledge called "anthroposophy" established by Rudolf Steiner (1861–1925). Steiner was an inspired polymath who relentlessly sought spiritual insight into the relationship between Man and the cosmos. He made no secret of being overlighted* by spiritual beings. He was influenced by Goethe,

*The term *overlighted* refers to a person who is a receiver of spiritual soul guidance, as opposed to direct psychic communication.

who believed Earth to be an intelligent organism, as did astronomer Johannes Kepler.

Also a practical reformer, Steiner was a pioneer: of holistic education for children, of a radical type of homeopathy, and of a new style of Christian worship. He was deeply involved in biodynamic farming (see p. 276), a type of horticulture that treats the land and crops as a self-nourishing system, which is now widely practiced in parts of Australia, New Zealand, North America, and Europe.

What concerns us in this study is his interest in planetary influences on organic life and agriculture, in sacred geometry, and in correspondences between the cosmos and living organisms. Steiner believed that our various organs have different roles from one another as receptors of cosmic or planetary energy.*

We have established that water quite probably exists throughout the universe. Its role, says Steiner, is to transfer information necessary for any particular part of the web of life for its growth, development, and connectedness to the whole, conveying to Earth's biosphere patterns of the cosmos, its rhythms and resonances.

Before the mechanization of Nature imposed by the dominant Western scientific model from the late seventeenth century, most of the people inhabiting our planet paced their lives upon cosmic rhythms. These influenced sowing and planting, irrigation, fertilizing, harvesting of crops, and the siting of buildings. The word *rhythm* comes from the Greek for "to flow" and suggests the need to "go with the flow."

Many highly qualified scientists were influenced by Steiner's vision and made original contributions in their fields: geology, holistic biology, botany, anthropology, hydrology, bioresonance, and sacred geometry.

While Steiner was very interested in the rhythms of the cosmos, Theodor Schwenk (1910–1986), who was inspired by both Steiner and

---

*The mystic George Gurdjieff said that our brains are principal receivers of cosmic energy.

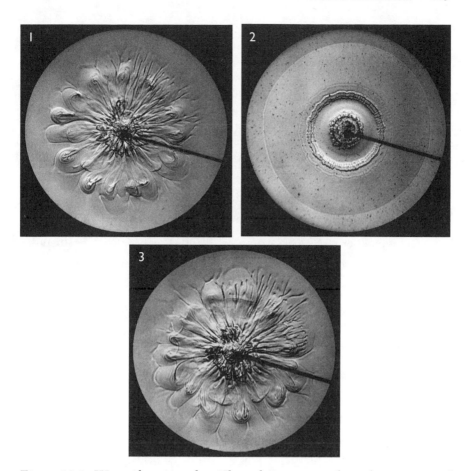

Figure 13.1. Water drop samples. These drop pictures show the structure of water samples. The first is of living spring water with its structure complete; the second, taken downstream after the inflow of domestic sewage and industrial effluents, with a trace of rudimentary development; a third, taken still farther downstream, shows how the stream has, through its naturally spiraling movement, rebuilt the water's structure. (Institut für Strömungswissenschaften)

Goethe, studied how these are mirrored in water. Schwenk founded the Institut für Strömungswissenschaften (Institute for Flow Sciences) in Herrischried, Germany. He pioneered research on the flow of water and gases and developed a method of analyzing the quality of water, called the water drop technique.

THE ROLE OF WATER

What we are proposing is that the etheric and water are conveyors of the cosmic intelligence we call "consciousness," which has put together the intricate interconnections of the web of life but which has required water to be self-regulating and self-evolving from the instincts of wholeness, perhaps preprogrammed before the beginning of time.

Remarking that the wisdom we find working in the smallest organism or tiny organ is the same wisdom that underlies the whole environment of life, which comes from the regulating element of water, Schwenk describes water as Nature's central organ, its "heart"—the pulsing, oscillating drop that allows the whole universe to pass through it. Just as the human heart mediates between all the other organs, so water mediates and balances the energy transfer between organisms. Ninety-nine percent of all chemical and other changes depend on water. As the heart balances the upper and lower functions in the human body, so water balances the cosmic and earth energies—the spiritual and material manifestations—in the Earth organism: "It acts as the small eccentricity of Nature, and through this, results in life."

The vortex is a structure complete in itself, with its own rhythms and movement that resemble that of the planets around the sun. It follows Kepler's second law of planetary movement, in that the speed of rotation is higher near the center of the vortex than it is on the outside. There is another cosmic connection that Schwenk observed: when a small piece of wood shaped like a pencil stub is immersed in the vortex, it will always point in the same direction, as the axes of planets do, circling the sun.

Schwenk's book, *Sensitive Chaos*—a title derived from the eighteenth-century German mystic and philosopher Novalis—is one of the most original in the study of water behavior. It offers an inspiring collection of photographs and drawings illustrating how our organs and bone structure often mimic water flow patterns, giving support to the idea that water carries the template for every form of life to develop as its blueprint demands.

Steiner died before Schauberger really hit his stride, and there is no evidence they met, but they had a common vision of the pivotal role water plays in the development of life. However, Schauberger's ideas must have influenced Schwenk; although the Schauberger books did not appear until after Schwenk's death, he published numerous articles in magazines, such as *Implosion,* which Schwenk is likely to have read.

THREE CHARACTERISTICS OF WATER

Schwenk recognizes three characteristics of water. The first two are easy to observe and generally acknowledged. First, there is water's vital role in all metabolic processes in the earth, in the great aerial ocean, and in every living creature. Then it is clear that water is inseparable from the rhythmic processes that take place in space and time.

As Schwenk writes in *Sensitive Chaos,* "When water stops dancing and flowing, it stagnates, loses its life, as though paralyzed. The flowing and rhythmic patterns of water are central to Nature's essence. Thus we find the audible rhythms of brooks and of the ocean mimic the patterns of waves and meandering watercourses, and the fibrous structures of the brain mimic water flow . . . Every twig dangling in a river causes a train of vortices in the rhythmic sequence; about every surface of contact between two streams there is a rhythmic play of waves and vortices."[1]

The last characteristic is that water is the antenna that picks up influences far beyond Earth. This can be intuited only by very close observation of the inner boundary surfaces that permeate every body of moving water, and which arise from the interplay of constantly changing laminar structures. They act like membranes with the sensitivity of sense organs, which is what inspired the philosopher Novalis to designate water as "sensitive chaos."

WATER'S SENSITIVITY

The skin of any organism is its antenna, its sensitivity, its contact with the outside world. Division surfaces or boundary layers appear not only between water and air but also within the water mass.

The essential structure of water is laminar. Moving water consists of layers flowing past each other at different speeds, causing deflection and rolling-up, which create vortices (that mark the boundary between inner and outer space). A flowing movement increases the complexity of these laminar structures, or membranes, allowing them to expand, contract, or make rhythmical waves.

Each layer has a boundary surface that responds to outside influences, even those deep within the water body. It may be that different layers pick up different vibrational levels, like radio bands, so that bringing together all these vibrations forms a great cosmic orchestral symphony.

These surfaces become waved, curling over and forming a circling vortex. Where streams flow past each other at different speeds, there are surfaces of contact. As long as water is moving it absorbs information. When it stops moving it ceases to absorb information—like turning off a tape recorder.

Water's sensitivity is as great as that of the human ear. It is in its nature for water to be sensitive to the slightest stimuli. A gentle breeze immediately creases the surface of water into the smallest of capillary waves. A small obstruction creates a whole system of tension waves.

Tree sap, the water-based fluid of trees, changes according to the phase of the moon and its position in the zodiac. Thus, timber felled at new moon in winter is the most durable. In parts of South America still, trunks of valuable hardwoods are stamped indicating the phase of the moon when they were felled, increasing their commercial value.

Even within the earth, water rises and falls with the changes of the moon, which can affect the digging of a well. Steiner recommended planting seeds and plants at specific phases of the moon in order to maximize their potential for healthy growth.

Schwenk perceived the vortex as following Kepler's second law of planetary movement, the great starry universe in miniature: "The vortex is a moving part within a moving whole. It has its own rhythms, forms its own inner surfaces, and is connected to distant cosmic surroundings."[2]

He says that water is not itself alive. Life manifests itself in many ways, through growth, reproduction, digestion of food, excretion of wastes, and other metabolic functions. Water has none of these, yet without water there can be no life. These attributes of life depend on water. Water does not grow because it is life itself—the universal element.

There is a constant exchange between elements of air and water. Water is the regulator of climate and of meteorological processes and their rhythms.

The key to water's role in the human body is that water's specific heat of 98.4°F precisely matches normal blood temperature. The role of water in the human body is to bathe, cleanse, and nourish every cell. Our brain floats in water, which facilitates thinking. The composition of seawater and blood are almost identical, except that seawater contains magnesium and blood contains iron. Healthy drinking water is balanced between acidity and alkalinity.

Schwenk produced remarkable photographs of trains of vortices made by pulling a rod through a glycerin-topped body of water. The fractal model of reproduction can be seen through the repetition of smaller vortices in these trains. They are also found in Nature in the generation of smaller cyclones from parent systems.

WATER AS MEDIATOR BETWEEN COSMOS AND EARTH

Schwenk studied how cosmic rhythms are mirrored in moving water, in the trickling stream, the rolling river, the rhythmical ebb and flow of the waves, in the foam of the breakers, and concluded that "water becomes an image of the stream of time itself, permeated with the rhythms of the starry world. All the creatures of the Earth live in this stream of time; it flows within them and, as long as it flows, it sustains them in the stream of life."[3]

All living organisms show, in their form, that they have been through a watery phase of development. Some solidify only slightly. Others leave the world of water and become dependent on earth. Does the impressionable nature of water make it sensitive to living, formative forces and creative form and expression? Perhaps water is the vehicle that allows cosmic forces to penetrate the material world in order to create living organisms. (See figure 13.2.)

Theodor Schwenk tells the remarkable story of the smelt, which is distantly related to the salmon. Once a year at spawning time in May, smelt approach the coast of California. They wait patiently near the shore until the tide reaches its highest on the third day after full moon. Then, choosing the highest wave, they allow themselves to be carried up onto the beach. There the females lay their eggs, the males fertilize them, and with the next wave, they return again to the open sea.

The high tide does not reach this level for another fourteen days, when the spawn of the smelt hatches a few minutes before being washed out to sea, not to return until years later, for a moment on the third day after the May full moon.

Amazingly, then, moving water—the earth's antenna—absorbs the shifting vibrations of the sun, moon, and planets and passes along this information to the sea and land creatures.

Schwenk noted that the more we've learned about the physical nature of water, the more we've been able to control it with great dams and transport it in huge pipes to drive turbines. It seemed to make sense to drain wetlands and straighten rivers. The new technology gave us a sense of power, but at the cost of ceasing to understand the true nature of water. He observed that when we are concerned only with what is profitable, we perceive the individual, and not interconnection, as having primary importance. Connections are abundant in Nature, but we have stopped observing Nature. The artist still observes and comments, but contemporary society values the scientist more highly than the artist.

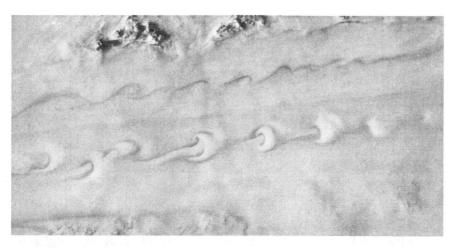

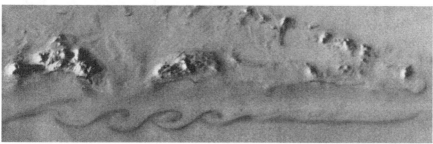

Figure 13.2. Beach vortices. Bell-shaped forms, which travel along with the current, arise in water flowing around a submerged stone. They are here made visible by the water stirring up the fine clay. Top: Bell shapes form after passing a submerged stone. Bottom: A train of vortices develops after an obstacle.

TEMPLATES FOR ORGANIC GROWTH AND EVOLUTION

Nature is a whole system comprised of two opposing qualities in balance. The sun charges the positive (yang) energy requirements of life, while Earth herself provides the balancing negative (yin) energies. Without this interplay there would be no water, plants, or chemical compounds. You may remember we described the metabolism of the tree as an example of this interchange (see chapter 8).

Pioneering research conducted by Lawrence Edwards, an anthroposophical mathematician, indicated that there are universal laws, as yet not fully understood, that guide an organism's growth into prede-termined patterns. He devoted his entire life to examining in minute detail the influence of celestial motion on the growth patterns of plants and on the form of embryos, the heart, and other organs. Edwards used detailed measurement and analysis to compare these with ideal geomet-ric forms and concluded that living forms are affected by patterns in time as well as space, with all of Nature passing through vast cycles of change.

He found that many tree buds, in their dormant winter stage, are far from asleep. They are influenced by the moon, usually in combina-tion with another planet, to open very slightly and then close again in roughly fortnightly rhythms (that is, the moon's full and new phases). The oak does this at 0° and 90° angular aspects of moon to Mars; the ash, moon to sun; beech, moon to Saturn; birch, moon to Venus; syca-more, moon to Jupiter; it's a kind of astrology of Nature.*

Almost all rhythms, from moon rhythms reflected in the hydro-sphere and planetary rhythms known to affect plant growth to the many physiological rhythms found in every living organism, are based on the pulsation of water.

PLANTING BY THE MOON

Planting seeds at the full moon has been practiced since time immemo-rial, but the science behind it has been tested only in modern times. The most famous innovator was Maria Thun of Darmstadt, Germany, whose research was supported by biodynamic farmers. In the 1950s, Thun planted seeds according to varying phases of the moon and found that potatoes planted at full moon always did best, whereas those planted at new moon invariably did poorly.

Her subsequent discovery was revolutionary. She found that pota-

---

*Lawrence Edwards's *The Vortex of Life* is the fascinating record of his rigorous research. He shows how the moon, particularly when amplified by certain aspects of Saturn and Mars, can create a cyclical effect in the growth of tree buds.

toes planted when the moon was in the constellations of Taurus, Virgo, or Capricorn (all earth signs) were more prolific than those planted in other constellations.

Dr. Frank Brown of Northwestern University conducted his own set of meticulous tests over a ten-year period. He found that plants absorbed the most water at full moon and least at new moon. Rudolf Steiner established that the elements of earth, air, fire, and water correspond to different parts of the plant; earth corresponds to root, water to leaf growth, fire to seed production, and air to flowers. He deduced that root crops should be planted when the moon is in an earth sign.

Another theory is that a waxing moon stimulates leaf growth, while a waning moon encourages root growth. Biodynamic methods are based on more complex astronomical positions of the moon, taking into account low and high points in the moon's orbit, ascending and descending, and eclipses.

With interest in biodynamic methods increasing, we can expect greater interest in planting by the moon.

A LIVING EARTH

Once again we ask, "What is living water?" We cannot understand the real significance of water until we understand the wider context of the living earth and the living cosmos.

I believe that many people have a race memory of being part of Nature, even though for many centuries this has been lost to modern culture. Much as we may appreciate the idea that Nature is evolving toward greater complexity and biodiversity, it is more difficult to comprehend how Earth herself might be going through her own evolution as part of a rising consciousness in the greater cosmos. Plutarch, Leonardo da Vinci, and Goethe all espoused this concept. In modern times, Kepler, Steiner, Schauberger, Lovelock, Bohm, and others have shown that this is more than mere theory and can be apprehended through human experience.

One very familiar Earth process is the weather, which involves a constant exchange of water between the vast surface of the oceans and the different layers of the atmospheric ocean. Meteorologists often find themselves describing such processes as if they were something alive. August Schmass writes of "biological concepts in meteorology" and of an "orchestral score" with "entrances" in the changing seasons.[4]

Paul Raethjen writes about cyclones that "behave like a living creature":

> Cyclones have a metabolic process without which they could not exist; they constantly draw new masses of air into their vortices and excrete other masses in their outward-spiralings . . . They have a typical life history with characteristic beginning, developing, and aging phases. They reproduce themselves, not a wave-like spreading out in space, but like a living creature, in the sense that a young "frontal cyclone" is born out of the womb of an adult "central cyclone."[5]

Information is knowing that water is H_2O; knowledge is being able to make it rain.

INCA SAYING

FOURTEEN

WATER AS A COMMUNICATION CHANNEL

Water plays the role of the untiring carrier of light, energy, and heat. First and foremost, it is the carrier of all the substances that create and sustain life.

VIKTOR SCHAUBERGER, *FERTILE EARTH*

DOWSING

Dowsing (water divining) has always had a connection with water, particularly spiraling water. Traditionally dowsers are skilled in finding and discovering the locality, quality, and reliability of underground water supplies or, sometimes, minerals. This skill is much depreciated today, as dowsing does not easily pass the conventional tests of repeatability under laboratory conditions. In the same way that homeopathy is dismissed by most scientists, dowsing is invalidated as pseudoscience, mainly, I suspect, because the scientific template does not cover subtle energies and the way they work.*

---

*An exception was Albert Einstein, who was known to have experimented with dowsing (Alanna Moore, *The Wisdom of Water*).

The august British Society of Dowsers (BSD), founded in 1933, seems to attract very practical people. Its list of past presidents includes doctors and high-ranking army engineers, but dowsing has broadened into many fields. The BSD includes a number of special interest groups, for instance, archaeology, water divining, earth energies, and health. Other themes are also explored, such as map dowsing, lost objects, missing persons, and kinesiology.

Dowsers use a variety of instruments. Most common, for fieldwork, are parallel rods, which might be as simple as a pair of coat hangers bent at a right angle, or something a bit more sophisticated. Some still use a forked hazel twig. For medical dowsing and most indoor work, a pendulum is most commonly used. The experienced water dowser is able to discern not only the presence of water but also its amount, depth, flow, salinity, pH, and other qualities, just by asking questions internally.

In 1995, Hans Dieter Benz, a physicist at the University of Munich, published research showing the efficacy of dowsing in arid regions of the world.[1] The German government supported his project to drill more than two thousand sites in several Asian and African countries. The results were impressive; for example, in Sri Lanka, there was a 96 percent success rate for locating drinkable water.

The occupational hazard of any form of dowsing is the possibility of a self-fulfilling outcome. One of the basic premises in any kind of research work is that the attitude or mind-set of the researcher can influence the result of the experiment, a truism that unfortunately is not widely recognized in conventional scientific protocols. An essential part of the training of any dowsing hopeful is learning how to reduce this risk.

It seems that many dowsers have a facility for one area over another. For example, I am drawn to map dowsing and site dating but am not much good at water divining. Maybe it's like memory. Someone says he has a bad memory in general (for example, for names), but it may turn out that he has a good memory for place and direction.

Dowsers often find what are called "blind springs," where a column of water rises vertically underground. It does not reach the surface, but pushes horizontally along rock fractures as an underground stream. Blind springs are often associated with places of power, and many European traditional sacred sites are blind spring locations.

Most experienced dowsers are certainly skilled, but for many of us, dowsing is based on intuition. It is not a science, and it should be scrutinized by its results, not its repeatability. For the expert, dowsing is very reliable, but for me, sometimes it works, sometimes not. It is not unlike my experience with homeopathy, which I know can have miraculous results—but sometimes it doesn't. Or when I drive into the main crowded street in central Bath, I try to visualize a parking space appearing for my car. It manifests often enough to vindicate the method; but when it doesn't, I'm not disheartened.

The universe, down to the smallest subatomic particles, is in a constant state of vibration, at speeds beyond the mind's comprehension. A living organism's different organs have different rates of vibration. Animals, trees, stone circles, and sacred sites all have characteristic vibrational levels. The subtle energy of their common denominator is water, which can be measured with a biometer, called a Bovis scale.

This looks like a semicircular protractor, with a scale going up to 20,000 gigaherz. Dynamic energy level is measured by swinging a pendulum over the center where the lines intersect, while asking the question "What is the energy level of this . . ." The pendulum should choose to swing up and down one particular line to indicate the appropriate energy level. If the water is in a small container, you can try enhancing the subtle energy level with the mind or, as Masaru Emoto does, with the emotive power of certain words (see chapter 15).

Kinesiology—muscle testing to discover the body's affinity with specific substances—is a form of dowsing that illustrates the principle of resonance. To discover whether, for example, a certain wine is good for a person or might produce a toxic reaction, the subject holds the bottle of wine against his abdomen with the left hand, and raises his right arm (if he is right-handed) until it is horizontal with the floor. A companion then attempts to push down the extended arm, which the subject is instructed to resist.

If the subject can't keep the arm horizontal, it is because the substance (in this case, the wine) has caused the musculature to lose its integrity. Muscles are 70 percent water, and biological water is in tune with the subject's sense of integrity, which is being challenged by the potential toxicity of what is being presented. This is an instantaneous reaction and is so reliable that many integrative doctors and practitioners use kinesiology for diagnostic testing. If you've never tried muscle testing, why don't you give it a go? It discounts placebo or wishful thinking.

Many experienced dowsers give up the tools and dowse with their whole bodies. Australian Aborigines dowse through the soles of their feet. This is presumably pure intuition at work. The body as a whole organism (like a bee colony) has insight.

We are mistaken to regard the brain as the source of wisdom. Its role is more like that of a computer designed to cope with the daily demands of survival, rational deduction, and other important individual functions. Consciousness exists on two levels: ordinary consciousness is a brain function, whereas elevated, or collective (that is, nonindividual), cosmic consciousness is a function of the whole body, mediated by water. Our biological water, which is connected to the vast watery network of the wisdom of the cosmos, is the key to our inner knowledge, of which our central nervous system is an integral part.

Subtle Energy Research on Water in Russia and the East

Russian and many eastern European and Far Eastern societies seem to be more detached from the Newtonian model of reality than are the American and British. They are not as skeptical of extrasensory and nonmaterial phenomena and often have an interest in relevant spiritual experience. They are generally accepting of dowsing as an important tool. They take a more holistic view and ask the questions "how" and "why" more readily.

A 2007 documentary film, "APA—Water, The Great Mystery," which features mostly distinguished Russian scientists, is well worth viewing to appreciate their research with subtle energies in water. It comprises interviews with eight Russian, three Far Eastern, four European, and three American scientists and physicians and six specialists from five religious traditions based in Russia and Israel.*

Some Findings of the Water Research Reported in the Romanian Film

- The molecular structure of water is more important for life than its chemistry. The molecules are organized into constantly changing structures that are continually forming and reforming, which allows a long-lasting memory to be retained.

  In the molecules there are memory cells working like a magnetic tape; in each of these cells are 440,000 information panels, each of which is responsible for recording a particular environmental energy level (Rustum Roy, Penn. State University).

- The structural memory of water allows it to record everything that happens around it, and every one of us is a link in the chain of information and also a source of information, for water connects everything.

- German scientific archives have an apocryphal story of water's memory: In the autumn of 1632, a poor farmer named Ganz, who had no memory of his origins, set out on a journey from Hessen to Italy to seek his fortune. Passing through the province of Konstanz the land felt familiar. His legs led him into a grove in which there was a spring; drinking from it, the memory of his parents and his childhood flooded back. Tradition has it that water at any place carries an individual imprint that, when absorbed by anyone at birth, is carried

---

*The Romanian film is a good summary of studies into the subtle energies of water. It can be viewed (in English) at the following link:
http://video.google.com/videoplay?docid=−2933349021550318008.

like an identity card for the rest of one's life, giving meaning to the concept of a physical connection to one's homeland.

- Structured water produces better results in agriculture—bringing earlier ripening and requiring less fertilizer. It has also been shown to restore the electrical charge in the blood, helping to deliver more oxygen and providing a more alkaline pH.

- When an extremely weak electromagnetic current was introduced into a fish tank, the fish all developed an identical stripe and behaved in a more collective way. Could this herald a new human population-control technique (Alexander Solodilov, Russian Acadamy of Science)?

- Water can be affected by both negative and positive energies even at great distances; this quality of water assists remote communication (Masaru Emoto).

- Information absorbed by water supplies in its distribution systems is more harmful than the energy of physical pollutants. The natural structure of water breaks down in water supply pipes, especially in bends, delivering virtually dead water to the consumer.

- Victor Inyushin, a biophysicist from Kazakhstan, researching the Soviet desert hydrogen bomb testing ground, found that the groundwater thousands of kilometers from the explosion site had lost its "life force" as a result of the explosion and believes that this caused disruption in the brain health of people in that vast area.

- Social studies of areas with high levels of violence show a correlation with degraded water.

- There are anecdotes of purifying undrinkable water through focusing of the mind. The power of prayer and directed visualization for healing and also for influencing events, such as weather behavior, are shown in a number of experiments conducted by the scientists. Tests were also conducted on water with healing qualities from different parts of the world.

CLEVE BACKSTER'S
BIOCOMMUNICATION RESEARCH

Cleve Backster, an expert on polygraph lie detectors, is the originator of the Backster Zone Comparison Test, the standard used by lie detection examiners worldwide. He developed the polygraph lie detector in 1966, while under contract with the New York City police department. When a criminal is afraid of being "unmasked" under questioning, the threat he feels to his well-being will make his skin become saturated with perspiration (water), which decreases the skin's electrical resistance.

Lie detectors work on the principle that when someone feels threatened, or his feeling of safety is compromised, he will respond physiologically in predictable ways. In this case, the galvanometer (part of the polygraph) registers a sudden drop in electrical resistance between electrodes applied to the skin's surface, known as the galvanic skin response, which is then inked on a disc recording chart.

Backster experimented with two plants, a rubber plant and a dracaena cane plant that was about three feet tall. He gave the latter a saturation watering, and to measure how long it would take for moisture to reach the top, he attached wired clips from the galvanic part of the polygraph—the part that measures skin resistance—to the end of a leaf to record the drop in resistance as moisture reached the leaves.

A spike on the recording chart resembled a human response of emotional disturbance on a lie detector test, so he began to experiment with threatening the well-being of the plant. First he put a leaf from the rubber plant into a warm cup of coffee. The graph showed a downward trend that resembled boredom. Then, at nearly fourteen minutes into the experiment, it occurred to him to burn the leaf, and although he didn't make a move to actually do it, the plant's response was instant and the pen went right off the chart.

When Backster removed the threat by taking the matches back to the secretary's desk, the plant's responses stabilized. For this he could find no possible mechanistic explanations, and he was alone in the building. When he questioned scientists from different disciplines to see if any could explain this phenomenon, he could find no satisfactory answer.

This couldn't be called extrasensory perception because plants don't have the human five senses. This plant's awareness seemed to take place on a much more basic level, thus he coined the term "primary perception." His conviction that the plant was responding to his intention changed his worldview and convinced him to make research into this strange phenomenon his first priority, which continued through thirty years of experiments.

Backster found that plants responded to a wide variety of microscopic life-forms. One time when he poured boiling water down the sink near a plant that was wired up, the plant responded so dramatically that Backster wondered whether the plant might have regarded the demise of the drain bacteria as a potential threat.

> This was confirmed several months later when I took samples out of the sink drain and inspected them under a microscope. There turned out to be a jungle of life-forms present, somewhat similar to the cantina scene from *Star Wars*—all kinds of bizarre life-forms.[2]

He developed a more complex experiment to measure whether the plant would respond to the sudden death of brine shrimp dropped automatically into boiling water at random intervals. While recording their responses at the other end of the lab, he found that they did indeed respond. It was difficult, however, to eliminate the energy connection between the experimenter and the plant being tested. If he tended the plants in any way, even for a short time, they became attuned to him. Plants are relational. They will be aware of connections between rooms but not to another unrelated area that may be physically closer.

When Backster automated the experiment, leaving the lab and setting a time-delay switch for random intervals unbeknownst to him, the plants remained attuned to his person. Backster and his partner would go to a bar a block away (in noisy, downtown Manhattan), and results indicated the plants were not responding to the death of the brine shrimp but to changing levels of the experimenters' excitement.

So the next control was to get someone else to store the plants in a part of the building that Backster and his friend didn't frequent. On the day of the experiment they fetched the plants and brought them to the strange environment of the lab. They were electroded in the usual way and wired to a complex mechanical programmer in a central location. Having been "abandoned" by the experimenter, the plants would have looked around for something to connect with in their environment. The living shrimp were put in dump cups, which were emptied into the boiling water in random timing. The plants responded to the shrimps' demise with significant regularity.

This classic experiment, written up in the December 1967 *Journal of Parapsychology,* met with predictable condemnations from icons of scientific respectability. At the 1975 American Association for the Advancement of Science meetings, an attempt to discredit him failed. However, in the following few years, feature articles appeared in large circulation popular magazines. Backster, who was keen to stimulate interest in his findings, gave thirty-four lectures to scientific and academic groups and appeared on TV interviews in several countries over the next few years.

After publication in *Electro-Technology* magazine (December 1969), he received five thousand requests from scientists for more information. Peter Tompkins and Christopher Bird wrote about the experiment in *The Secret Life of Plants* (1973), which became an international bestseller.

Quite a few scientists at the time tried to replicate the brine shrimp experiment, but they always seemed to fail; Backster thought it was because they misunderstood the need for mental detachment. The particular training scientists receive renders them incapable of grasping the idea that the consciousness of the experimenter can influence the outcome of the experiment. Therefore, when scientists tried to replicate his work with brine shrimp, they thought they were being rigorous by going into the next room and using closed-circuit TV to observe what happened. What they should have done was wait to bring the plants in immediately before the experimental run, so they would not become attuned to their experimenters. Because of their misunderstanding of Backster's protocols, they also did such irrelevant things as washing the leaves with distilled water.

The point is that they were not removing their consciousness from the experiment. It is actually very easy to fail with that experiment. Backster believed that they would probably be relieved to have failed, because to succeed would have gone against widely accepted scientific "laws." However, the insistence of repeatability as the criterion for scientific proof is actually anti-life, as life itself is not predicable. Repeatability is about control, which is the hallmark of Western science and culture. It is a feature of machines, not living systems.

Backster instructed his students, "Don't do anything. Go about your work. Keep notes, so later you can tell what you were doing at specific times, and then transfer them to your chart recording of tracing changes. But don't plan anything or the experiment won't work."[3]

Backster usually found a new line of research by accident. Working late at night, he was stirring the jam at the bottom of a strawberry yogurt carton when he noticed an unusual reaction on the plant's chart. He then electroded live yogurt cells, which turned out to be some of his most productive research—the bacteria in yogurt seem to be particularly attuned to human interaction in their immediate surroundings.

It was challenging to design appropriate equipment, because even observing an experiment allows your consciousness to interact with the experiment, which can affect the outcome. Once he designed an experimental technique that randomized the timing, he was able to withdraw from being actually part of the experiment.

In 1979, the Backster School of Lie Detection, now located in San Diego, held a reception on two floors of the building, each with a bar, for hundreds of people attending a polygraph conference. Before the crowd arrived, Backster electroded some plain yogurt, expecting chaotic readings because of all the commotion. Usually experiments were conducted in a controlled environment, but he wanted to demonstrate only the receptivity of the bacteria.

The bacteria were particularly sensitive to local human behavior and provided an example of selectivity. They were much more "interested" in other bacteria being killed by alcohol being consumed than by the human activity. This ability to prioritize was an example of a primary perception process similar to human psychology, but on a bacterial level.

Elisabet Sahtouris, an evolutionary biologist, noted, "Bacteria are responsible for forming the larger cells from which all other life kingdoms are constituted. Further, bacteria are the only creatures that could survive without all the others. Why should bacteria not think, if they could think, that the world is all theirs?"[4]

A cytologist, Dr. Howard Miller, in a review of Backster's research in *Medical World News,* predicted that Backster "may have discovered a kind of cellular consciousness." (See, for example, figure 14.1 on p. 206.)

Having successfully logged meaningful evidence that suggested the possibility of biocommunication in plants, shrimp, chickens, and a variety of bacteria, Backster wondered about cellular level response in humans. Studying in-body (in vivo) cells, he thought, might involve too many complexities with nervous system activity. So he decided to find a way of extracting living cells (in vitro) in order to see if, when electroded, they might communicate with their host organism. Research with blood would require medical supervision. However, a dental researcher he'd met had developed a method of obtaining white blood cells (leukocytes) by centrifuging cells obtained from the donor's mouth, which would not require medical supervision. (He describes these procedures in his book, *Primary Perception.*)

The most extraordinary test done with mouth swabs showed that when the parent organism (a doctor) was several hundred miles away, the cells were still "conscious" of stressful events in her life. As Backster observed, "Sentience does not seem to stop at the cellular level. It may go

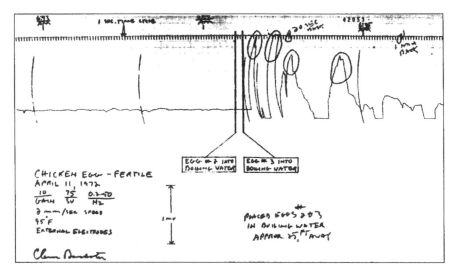

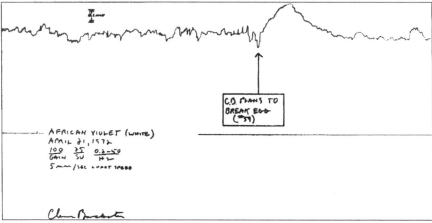

Figure 14.1. The violet and the chicken's egg. Cleve Backster wired an African violet to a polygraph galvanometer (lie detector). It recorded the moment when he planned to break an egg. (Cleve Backster)

down to the molecular and beyond. All sorts of things that have conventionally been considered to be inanimate may have to be reevaluated."[5]

It is one thing to say that repeatability is a feature of machines, not of living systems, which seem to be more spontaneous. Chaos theory gives a glimpse into a different world. Backster's experiments showed that you can't fool plants by pretending. A lot of insincere or hypocritical human behavior is accepted as normal. At the etheric level, this doesn't seem to work. If our human consciousness were at the etheric level, is it possible that we would be altogether more transparent?

There has been really no support for his research in the United States or in western Europe. However, in eastern Europe and Russia, where psychological, emotional, and spiritual factors are more accepted, Backster's research is celebrated as pioneering.

Backster has received only disinterest or scorn from U.S. scientists. The Western scientific model requires repeatability, predictability, and control to validate any experiment. This emphasis on repeatability is, however, anti-life in the sense that life's experiences are inherently non-repeatable. Science has not yet accepted that the attitude, emotional state, and bias of the researcher can affect the outcome of an experiment; that mind can influence results.

There can be no such thing as truly objective research unless self-consciousness gets out of the way. Backster arranged randomized triggers to stimulate responses in the plant or culture to ensure that the researcher was not influencing these responses.

Our current worldview insists that only humans experience consciousness and that it is a function of the brain. Backster's research disproves both of these assumptions. It would be difficult to overestimate the importance of this research, for it goes to the heart of the basis of life—that all of life is interconnected and interdependent and that all actions have wider consequences. It lifts a little the edge of the intricate web of life.

There seems to be a consciousness at the heart of Nature that may be the engine for a higher evolutionary meaning and purpose, and evidence shows that water is the vehicle of this consciousness. Water (including the water in blood and sap), the main constituent of all living things, is, as Viktor Schauberger pointed out, the carrier and fountain of life itself.

Backster's observations showed that a signal could travel instantaneously dozens, even hundreds of miles. To test whether it might be electromagnetic, he placed the plant in a Faraday cage or in a lead container, the normal screening devices, but they made no difference to the plant's receptivity. He was convinced that it did not fall within the electromagnetic spectrum.[6]* He did not consider water as a communication channel common to all life-forms, cellular and molecular, for such a weird possibility was then not on the radar. It now remains a strong possibility, but how does it work?

QUANTUM ENTANGLEMENT

When Backster wrote up his research, there were no explanatory models for how biocommunication could work. It clearly must have a quantum element, and the new theory of quantum entanglement, which we discussed earlier in the context of Mae-Wan Ho's experiments, could throw some light on it (see chapter 11).

Quantum entanglement is a mathematical description of what happens between a pair of particles. In a typical experiment, a light particle, called a photon, is made to split into two (daughters) to observe how they behave. They are not preprogrammed, but it is found that they respond spontaneously, independently, and in an interconnected manner.

It is the act of observation that makes them appear, and time and location seem to be completely irrelevant.[†] It seems that we could use pairs of entangled particles for an instant communication system, perhaps similar to what Ho describes happening in chains of collagen fibers in the human body, for what she calls "quantum coherence" in

---

*Backster's controversial research was first published in *The Secret Life of Plants* (1973), by Peter Tompkins and Christopher Bird. It took another thirty years for Backster to publish his own account of his fascinating research in his book *Primary Perception,* which was well received by his peers: Deepak Chopra says, "Cleve Backster's research has profound implications for humanity and its future evolution." Jean Houston concurs, saying, "The implications of this work are enormous for science, society, and ecology."

†This is one of the basic theories of quantum mechanics: an active observer is required for anything to become manifest.

the organism; this is the next stage up from quantum entanglement.

There are more complex conditions that govern the existence of particles. The first is that their properties do not exist apart from the act of observation; they are aspects of mathematical measurement. Second, spatial and temporal considerations do not enter into the calculations; the particles could be anywhere. Lastly, the quantum field ensures that everything is entangled, so very special conditions need to exist to produce particles that are not entangled.

This could be an explanation for telepathy or paranormal experiences; and why not for empathy? Quantum information theory is an exciting new branch of physics that looks into ways information within organisms can be transmitted, through a combination of entanglement and classical information transfer.

Mathematician Chris Clarke sees the world as a nested lattice of quantum organisms, with constant resonating between organisms and the greater whole. He calls this "living in coherence," and it may be a metaphor for the influence of a supreme intelligence. Clarke posits, "This suggests that the world, rather than being a collection of isolated particles pushing each other around, is more like an intricate web of subtle interconnections."[7]

If we can conceive of water as a vehicle of consciousness, it may not be such a stretch to consider that water may have memory.

FIFTEEN

THE MEMORY OF WATER

"The water will tell you," said the guide, when the travelers asked how deep was the water.

PLATO, *THEAETETUS*

INFORMATION TRANSFER

Ecological theory teaches us that all life is interconnected, interdependent. The idea of sustainability follows Nature's way of conserving energy—as circles within circles, nothing is ever wasted. At the end of its term, everything is recycled and contributes again to the whole with a new role, perhaps a more purposeful one. Nature employs closed systems with organisms to promote enhanced evolutionary change and growth. This allows energy to be conserved, raised, and reused.

A machine, on the other hand, is an open system. It obeys the second law of thermodynamics, which says that every system runs down and that entropy or energy loss results. An automobile, for example, no matter how well designed and constructed, is a machine that will wear out with constant use. If our bodies were machines, in accordance with Newtonian physics, they should wear out in a year or two. The fact that our bodies can last seventy years, or in optimal conditions even twice that, shows that they have properties of a closed system, one that conserves energy.

Mainstream science recognizes many of water's qualities, including the anomalous: it is a powerful solvent, versatile, has a need to move and pulsate, and balances temperature. However, mainstream science does not comprehend the energetic or quantum aspects of water: it stores and transmits information, self-organizes, self-purifies, and exhibits some of the properties of an organism.

All living cells, tissues, organs, and organisms have their own fields. The networks of living systems are regulated by the information clusters that the morphic fields create through their living memory bank, which is connected to the collective memory banks of similar objects or organisms. The enrichment of this memory, according to biochemist and plant biologist Rupert Sheldrake, is what drives evolution.

Sheldrake observed that nature tends to convey information as a repetitive signal. So the repeating geometric form of the fractal is what Nature uses to relate the macro world to the micro, through morphic resonance, which influences both form and behavior. Sheldrake's research shows that it is easier for humans and animals to learn a new skill that other humans/animals have already learned (the hundredth monkey theory).

FRACTALS

Fractal geometry was born out of chaos science, which demonstrates that the natural order is not random, because out of chaos there inevitably emerges an infinite order. Everything in Nature is organized into repeating geometrical forms. If we look at the irregular shape of a coastline, we find that its particular irregularity is constant at every scale. The world is regular in its irregularity.

Fractals describe the arrangement of beach sand, a river's tributaries, a lightning strike, lines in a palm, formation of clouds, and bronchia of the lung. Fractals are generated by the quantum field working with

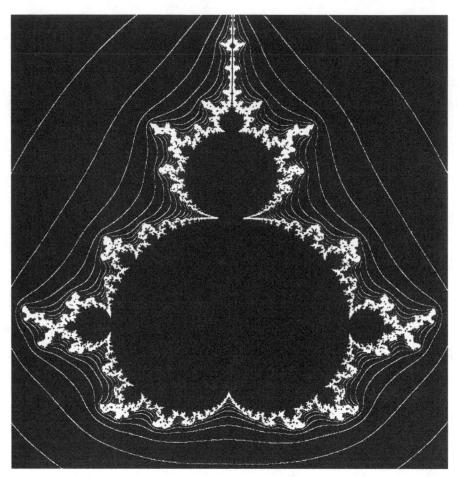

Figure 15.1. The Mandelbrot fractal. The Mandelbrot set is the best known of several mathematical fractal models that explain such seeming unpredictables as weather systems, natural turbulence, wave development, and the growth of plants. Sets are created on a computer by applying numbers to a plane according to a given formula, repetitively, at speed. The boundary area just beyond the black shape oscillates continuously, producing magical shapes and colors, the basic pattern of the set repeating itself with successive enlargements. (A. Bartholomew)

water in the transfer of information. As we saw in the study of vortices, turbulence or chaos in water provides the opportunity for the transfer of high-quality subtle energy or information.

Plate 1. A stream in Somerset, England. (A. Bartholomew)

Plate 2. Snowbound treetops. (Microsoft)

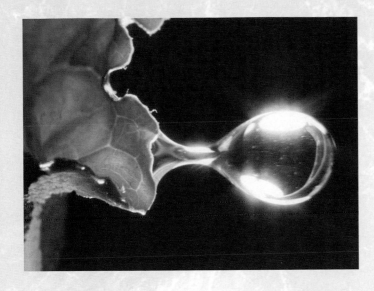

Plate 5. A spherical drop of water. Viktor Schauberger often said, "One drop of water contains the whole universe." (Nigel Catlin/ NLPA)

▲ Plate 3. A surfer going "down the tube." (Russell Ord)

Plate 4. Raindrops on an Alchemilla mollis leaf. (John Munro)

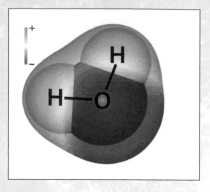

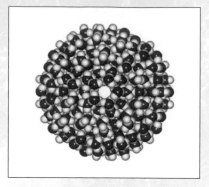

Plate 6. Model of the water molecule showing its charges. (Martin Chaplin)

Plate 7. A theoretical supercluster of 13 interpenetrating icosahedra, showing how they easily self-replicate like fractals. (Martin Chaplin)

Plate 8. The icosahedron Platonic solid. (Martin Chaplin)

Plate 9. The aurora borealis, with its dynamic motion, behaves as water does on Earth, often forming spirals and whirlpools. (From Falck-Ytter, Aurora)

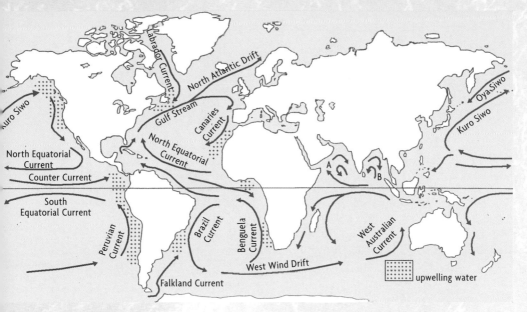

Plate 10. World ocean currents: The main ocean currents follow the prevailing wind systems—blue lines for cold currents, red for warm. The reversal of the monsoon wind system causes a reversal of ocean currents in the Arabian Sea (A) and the Bay of Bengal (B). Upwelling water brings up nutrients that support rich breeding areas for fish and cetaceans. (R. B. Bunnet)

Plate 11. A Dartmoor spring. (A. Bartholomew)

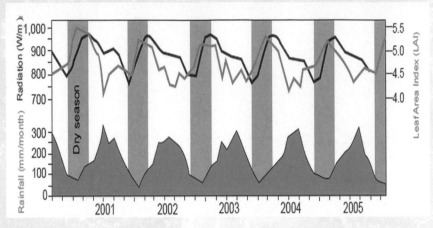

Plate 12. The intelligence of the rain forest: The Amazon rain forest plays a crucial role in moderating the world's climates. Just before the start of the dry season the forest increases new leaf growth so as to maintain this powerful heat engine's essential output of evapotranspiration. The amount of sunlight reaching forest canopy (red line) and the leaf density (green line) vary together: high in the dry season (pink bar) low in the wet season. Rainfall (blue graph) is the opposite: low in the dry season, high in the wet season when the rain clouds block sunlight. (Peter Bunyard)

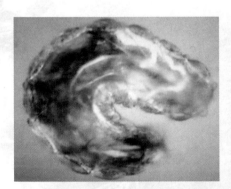

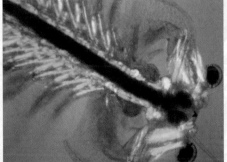

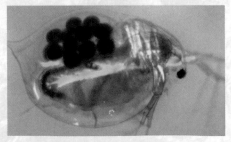

Plate 13. Stills from Mae-Wan Ho's Quantum Jazz *video of living organisms seen through a polarizing (x 40) microscope, their pulsating energy shown in vivid colors: twisting worm, artemia, and daphnia. (Institute of Science in Society)*

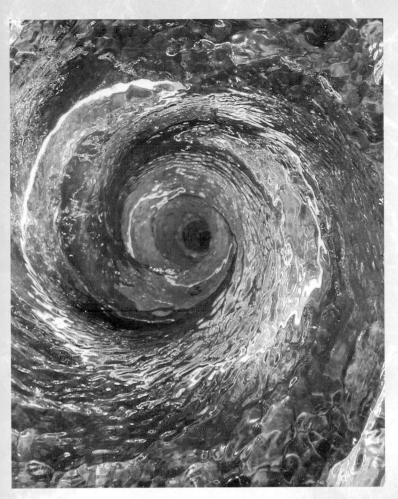

Plate 14. *A whirlpool vortex. (Pythagoras-Kepler School)*

Plate 15. *Double-egg vortexer (developed by Ralf Roessner to restructure and reenergize drinking water). This device demonstrates how the orientation of an egg affects the treatment of water: yang (expansion) in the top egg and yin (contraction) in the lower, allow the whole water body to be coherently transformed. (A Bartholomew)*

Plate 17. Varna flowform. (J. Wilkes)

Plate 18. Asymmetrical Olympia flowforms at the ING Bank, Amsterdam. (J. Wilkes)

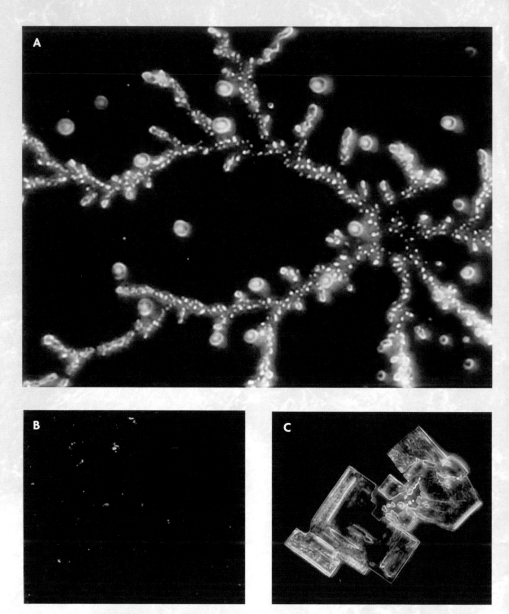

Plate 19. David Schweitzer's dark field microscope photos of water samples: These photos were taken through a polarizing filter at a magnification of 4,000x. Tap water was treated with a vortex energizer, and two areas of the sample showed different structures. The dendritic form, in A above, is thought to represent what Schauberger called the female or yin aspect of water and the crystalline formation, in C below, represents the male or yang. Image B shows tap water before treatment with the vortex energizer. (Centre for Implosion Research)

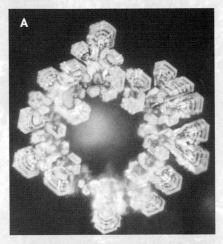

Plate 20. Masaru Emoto's ice crystals, frozen samples of water subjected to energy either at source or from words attached to a sample bottle. (Masaru Emoto)
A. Lourdes
B. Fujiwara Dam (before a healing prayer)
C. Fujiwara Dam (after a healing prayer)
D. Bach's Air on a G String
E. Heavy metal music

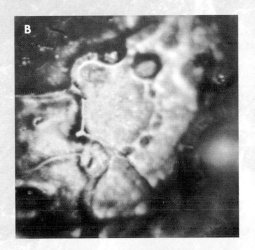

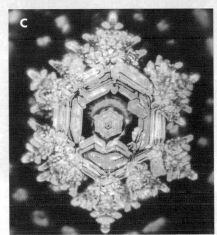

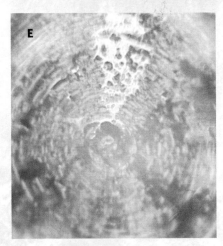

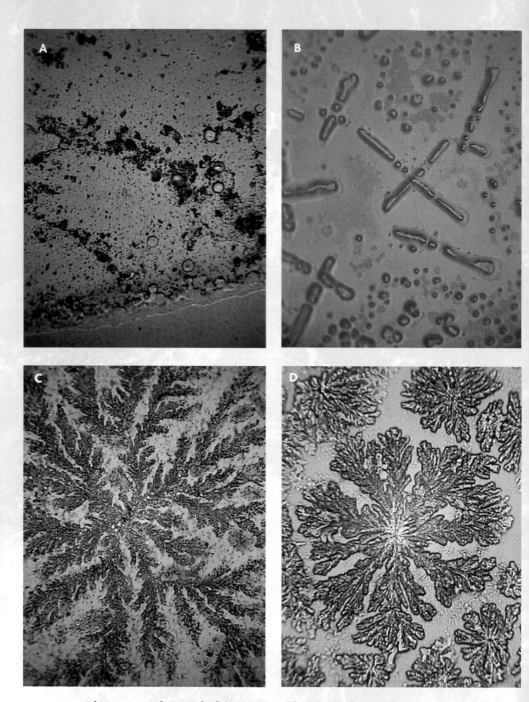

Plate 21. Andreas Schulz's water analysis crystals: Analysis based on the angular relationship between crystals formed from a combination of distilled and desiccated samples. A. Paris tap water; B. Stuttgart mains water (c. 300x); C. Spring water from New Zealand (c. 100x); D. Spring water from La Palma (c. 300x). (Andreas Schulz)

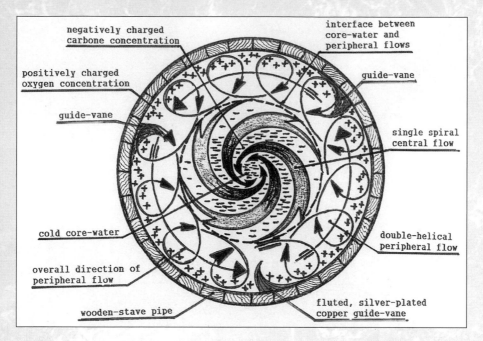

Plate 22. Cross-section of Schauberger's pipe. Action of the toroidal vortex where the concentration of positive oxygen destroys the pathogenic bacteria, acting as the river's immune system. Schauberger added the guide vanes to maximize the toroidal effect in the pipe. (Callum Coats)

Plate 23. Longitudinal section of Schauberger's wooden water pipe. Guide vanes create toroidal counter-vortices to transfer impurities to the pipe walls, where the oxygen concentration destroys the pathogenic bacteria. They also act like ball bearings to enhance forward movement. A natural stream or river has a longitudinal vortex running down its center. (Callum Coats)

Plate 24. Regions at most risk from water shortages, c.2090. Areas of drought (red) are predicted for southern Europe, the Mediterranean, the Middle East, northwest and southwest United States, the Caribbean (surprisingly), South Africa, and Brazil. Meanwhile, increased precipitation (blue) is predicted for China, equatorial areas, North Polar regions and below 60°S latitude. (IPCC scenario 2007, changes relative to 1980–1999) (A. Bartholomew)

Equator

Plate 25. Dry reservoir in Australia resulting from Australian climate change. (Claver Carroll/FLPA).

Plate 26. Flood victim in Jakarta. (Colin Marshall/FLPA)

Jacques Benveniste (see p. 216) was one of the first to discover that water could be biologically active in the absence of solutes, which contradicts a fundamental biological law: that biological activity in water requires a significant amount of the actual substance in solution.

About the time Benveniste was publishing accounts of his research with high dilutions of biologically active chemicals, Emilio Del Giudice and Giuliano Preparata, physicists at the University of Milan, were working on a model of molecular vibrations in water, which they called the theory of "electrodynamic coherence." They postulated a magnetic memory built by means of coherent molecular vibrations (water molecules pulsating in phase with their magnetic field). Through quantum mechanics they determined that packed molecules go from a chaotic to a coherent state, if that ordered state contains less dynamic energy. According to Preparata and Del Giudice, stability can be achieved only through the existence of long-range energy forces, which lead to collective behavior. This is called the theory of coherent domains, an example of holism (as opposed to discreteness).

Biological water is the vehicle for electromagnetic fields (through metals and minerals), biological fields (in organic substances), and by coherent domains and is influenced, either beneficially or harmfully, by all of these.

One of the anomalies of quantum water is its high dielectric value, which allows large electric fields within living cells. Martin Chaplin (see chapter 11), in his two states of water research, discovered a change in electromagnetic qualities from the less dense (noncoherent) phase, wherein the atoms of different polarity repelled each other, to the dense (coherent) phase, wherein they clustered closely, regardless of their conflicting polarities.

According to quantum theory, every particle is connected or "entangled" with every other particle at every scale from micro to macro. These connections within an organism or between organisms are based on the quantum coherence of water-based life.

Life is possible only because the quantum qualities of water allow it to transcend its own chemistry. The key seems to be that the hydrogen bonds between molecules are ten times weaker than hydrogen-oxygen bonding, which enables water's structures to resist compression, vibrating continuously—bonding and breaking in order to retain its energy and cohesion.

What happens with DNA is even more remarkable. It has the densest, most complex structure imaginable in order to synthesize proteins. When a protein approaches DNA, the water molecules surrounding it stop vibrating. The specific protein structure causes the interfacial water to break the DNA strand at an appropriate point in order to allow the transfer of information from the protein to the DNA—an extraordinarily sophisticated process.*

Quantum phenomena can be quite fickle. For example, light can behave either as a collection of particles or as a wave, depending on the observer's point of view. This makes reductionist scientists wary, just as they are with the placebo effect in medicine (even though it is an example of one of the most creative aspects of the human mind).

MEMORY OR RECORDING?

Does water have a memory? The suggestion is confusing, for memory is considered to be a brain-based activity, with many stored memories able to be accessed at a later time. This is rather like the discussion we had in the preceding chapter about the receptivity of plants. Biological cells have the capacity to record events.

I've heard of people claiming that memories can be inherited. A common example is of a daughter who insists she has the exact dreams her mother used to have. Is it possible that a family's biological water may play a part in this?

When it is moving, water is sensitive and records vibrations. At

---

*Monika Fuxreiter's research at the Institute of Embryology, Budapest (cited by Mae-Wan Ho), demonstrates that DNA is inseparable from water. It may be that water records the information to be conveyed to the DNA.

some future time we will learn how these may be observed, perhaps as a complex spectrum of resonances of the kind used in vibrational healing techniques. These therapies recognize that each organ of the body (some even say each molecule) has its own resonant frequency. They are like numbers on the atomic scale, but for energies.

Water records qualities and resonances, not memories as such. The great Antarctic ice sheet contains physical records, such as dust, pollen, and air bubbles, which can tell us things about ancient climates. Perhaps the ice also records resonant information.

This means that the medium of greater coherence—the etheric—is able under certain circumstances, such as in a river's immune system, to raise the water's dynamic energy level. Viktor Schauberger's technological applications were based on water's abilities to absorb, retain, and enhance energies. The problem for mainstream science is that these energy qualities are not easily quantifiable; they are difficult to measure.

PHOTONS AND WATER

Water's subtle energies are difficult to measure. One of the controversial areas of energy study is photon research. Photons were discovered only in the past couple of decades, with the development of dark field photomicroscopy, and are usually interpreted as a sign of life force. They appear as bright spots of light against a dark field. Some go as far as to say that energy equals light.

Unhealthy blood will show low photon presence, while a sample of blood from a healthy person will reveal an abundance of photon light spots. This analytical method should revolutionize medical symptom research, but unfortunately it is still met with much skepticism. One of the pioneers of this research is David Schweitzer, known particularly for his research into blood. He analyzed different samples of water in his dark field microscope, demonstrating that the quantity of photons indicated the vitality, and probably the quality, of the water sample (see plate 19).

Schweitzer found that blood cells have an esoteric geometric structure and harmonious colors. In 1996 he discovered a way to photograph the stored frequencies in homeopathic remedies and to record the influence of positive or negative thoughts on bodily fluids.

Since good-quality, living water is vital for our health, we need to be able to discriminate among the many who claim that their water treatment products are the best.

INFORMATION STORAGE

When water is flowing as its nature dictates, energetically in spirals and vortices, its molecules organize themselves into the structure necessary for it to carry constructive information. These microclusters of vibrating dynamic energy centers are constantly receiving and transmuting energy from every contact the water body makes.

The vortical movement creates polymer liquid crystalline chains and the laminar structure that generates dynamic energy from the interaction of their plane surfaces against each other. These structures can be observed with a suitable microscope. The more powerful the vortical action, the greater the storage capacity of information (like adding "memory" to a computer). Thus, water put through Viktor Schauberger's implosion (powerfully vorticized) process can enhance the energy of organisms that imbibe it.

The clusters have the ability to store vibrational impressions or imprints. If these are beneficial, they may be able to restore healthy resonance in the human body. On the other hand, if they are the imprints of toxins or pollutants in the drinking water, they may be carriers of disharmony and disease (see pp. 237–38).

JACQUES BENVENISTE AND HOMEOPATHY

Dr. Jacques Benveniste (1946–2005) had a particular interest in immunology. Working at the French National Institute for Health and

Medical Research (INSERM), he studied the effect of extremely weak solutions of antigens (compounds that elicit antibody responses) on basophils. Basophils are specific cells in the bloodstream that contain tiny granules of histamine, the substance released in classic allergic reactions, such as hay fever. The antidote is to take antihistamines.

When antigens bind to special receptors on the surface of basophils, they trigger a reaction that causes the basophils to degranulate and release histamine. According to classical Newtonian theory, progressively larger amounts of antigen should produce progressively stronger cellular reactions, and more dilute solutions of antigen should produce weaker cellular responses. Beyond a certain dilution there should be no reaction at all, simply because there would, statistically, be not even one molecule of antigen in the test sample.

Contrary to established scientific theories, and to his great surprise, Benveniste discovered that ultra-weak solutions of anti-immunoglobulin E (algE), containing no molecules of antigen, were still able to induce significant basophil reactions, causing cells to degranulate and release their histamine.

In homeopathy, common practice is to shake a remedy vigorously in water, then dilute with nine parts pure water. Ten such dilutions are called a "decimal." After twelve decimals there are no molecules left of the original substance. Nevertheless, the remedy still has biological activity, and increased dilution can make the remedy even more potent. How is this possible?

Benveniste knew that his research results were so controversial that his only chance of publication was to have other scientists duplicate his work. After his experiment was replicated in several laboratories around the world, Benveniste's conclusions were finally published by the influential magazine *Nature*. The article was accompanied by an editorial that questioned whether this research was to be believed, because it contradicted current scientific theory.

Because the article in *Nature* seemed to validate the principle of homeopathy, a healing practice considered bogus by most of its readership, it launched a worldwide storm of controversy between old-world Newtonian thinkers and new-world Einsteinian theorists and clinicians. Within four days *Nature*'s editor, John Maddox, descended on Benveniste's lab in Paris accompanied by both a physicist specializing in scientific fraud and a professional magician known for his work in "debunking psychics and paranormal phenomena." They stayed for five days and derided successful experiments that they witnessed as fraud. Maddox himself tried to repeat the experiment without the protocols. Shortly afterward, Maddox published a damning report in *Nature:* "High Dilution Experiments a Delusion."

What the debunking team failed to understand was that these experiments measured subtle energy effects. There was no consideration given to the possibility that the researchers' attitudes influenced the outcome of the experiments.

Indeed, later Benveniste so despaired of laboratories trying, but failing, to reproduce his results that he automated the experiments with what he called a "robot" to ensure that the method was standardized. Even so, there seemed to be researchers in a couple of laboratories who could not succeed. Eventually he discerned that the researchers were emitting a blocking signal; one of them was a frequency scrambler.

Benveniste described observations that cannot be explained by current theories. In his final years, he investigated the possibility of recording electromagnetic signals in biological water. Life depends on these signals between molecules. He digitally recorded the waveforms of some thirty substances (for instance, bacteria, antibodies, and so on) on a computer hard drive. These electromagnetic reproductions produced the same reactions as the original substances.

"The Benveniste Affair" is notable because it shows the extent to which the scientific establishment will go to discredit anyone who challenges cherished theories, even going against well-founded ideals of openmindedness. The fallback position is: "We can't explain it, so it can't be true."

Just before the visit of the *Nature* fraud squad, Dr. Atrias, a homeopathic doctor, had persuaded Benveniste to try out an electrical machine that he claimed transmitted chemical information. This machine transmitted information from a solution of algE potentized to thirty decimals into a glass tube containing a dummy dilution. Benveniste had long suspected that the electromagnetic properties of the cell played a part in storing information in the water before the molecule disappeared, making it able to be recalled at a later time.

While it certainly appeared that Benveniste's team was able to successfully demonstrate that a chemical signal could be transmitted without its original molecular support, it now looked as though an electromagnetic image of the original molecule could be held. He also confirmed that without the medium of water, signals cannot be transmitted in the body.

Homeopathy works on the coherence of the whole organism, so you would expect it to respond to quantum, rather than material, principles. One of the issues with testing homeopathic reactions is to discover methods appropriate to the individual person. Normal detection methods apply to examining individual molecules, rather than the collective global properties of an organism.[1]

The question remains: How can widely spaced molecules communicate with each other, and how does water store information?

MASARU EMOTO'S RESEARCH

In 1986, Dr. Masaru Emoto was searching for low-frequency therapy equipment for his Japanese health products agency, which supplied acupuncturists and moxibustion practitioners. He was concerned that although technology existed for measuring water's content, there was none to measure its quality.

When he asked Dr. Lee Lorenzen, who was later to develop microcluster water, if there was such technology in the United States, Lorenzen sent him three biocellular analyzers (magnetic resonance analyzers, or MRAs, used in homeopathy for measuring levels of vibrational energy), but Emoto didn't know how to work with them. Some time later, after losing his business, Masaru began experimenting with the three MRAs in his basement. Eventually, using one of these machines he was able to produce high-quality water, which he called Hado water, that seemed to produce healing effects in those who drank it.

Hado is a magnetic resonance pattern of wave motion measured as a vibrational rate, known in Chinese tradition as chi, a vital energy originating "from the circulation of electrons around the atomic nucleus."[2] Emoto believes that the hado changes according to the consciousness of the observer. (Since 2005 he has used the term to mean all the subtle energy that exists in the universe.)

Knowing that there are no two snowflakes that are alike, Emoto realized that taking pictures of the water before and after treatment with hado (MRA treated)—frozen as crystals—would show how information can be imprinted on water. Ice crystals produce a time-freeze of vibrational energy.

The method for producing good crystals from water samples proved to be tricky, but ultimately Emoto and a colleague found a technique. Drops of the water to be sampled are put into petri dishes and frozen for three hours at -25°C (-13°F). They are then warmed in the lab to a temperature near the freezing point. At about -15°C (-5°F) a crystal may form, but only for some twenty seconds, so it must be quickly photographed under the microscope (see plate 20).

Each water sample produces mixed results: if the water is of good quality, some crystals are well formed, others not, and some of the ice grains remain amorphous. Apparently, though, it is possible to find a common theme among the better formed crystals (none of which will be identical). Their interpretation must be more art than science.

This cannot be regarded as a scientific method, because the results are variable, unpredictable, and possibly subjective, but this does not worry Emoto. However, this aspect of his method means he is unlikely to get mainstream support for his research, and other researchers have difficulty replicating his experiments.

Emoto tested many sources of drinking water and found that most municipal supplies produced a poor crystalline structure—hardly surprising, since they contain chlorine. The few that did make crystals had significant proportions of groundwater. Sacred springs, such as Lourdes, or mountain springs produced the finest crystals.

Music and Resonance

One of Emoto's assistants suggested exposing water to music, which proved to be very successful. A bottle of distilled water was placed between two loudspeakers to produce samples. Works of the great composers—Bach, Mozart, and Beethoven—produced beautiful crystals, whereas crystals formed during exposure to heavy metal rock bands were ugly and ill formed. The great works are composed according to natural laws of harmony, which would show up as resonance in the crystal structures.

Resonance occurs between two systems when their vibrational rates are in harmony or at a critical point of disharmony. It can be associated with either creative or destructive phenomena. You've probably heard that a specific musical note can shatter a fragile wineglass.

It is possible that resonance operates through both the water medium and the etheric medium. A relationship between human beings or between a human and an animal can be seen as an emotional resonance through the medium of water. On the other hand, when you resonate with a particular gemstone or mineral, that would be through the medium of the etheric.

David Tame, author of *The Secret Power of Music,* believes that the degeneration of popular music has often preceded the fall of great civilizations.[3] Holistic medical doctor John Diamond describes the way certain types of heavy metal and rock music weaken the body's muscle tone and lead to decreased performance of children in school.[4] A more flowing natural rhythm corresponds more to the heart rhythm, supporting a natural balance in the body.

The human body's high water content means that we respond

deeply to different kinds of sacred music. It should be possible to calculate mathematically the geometrical structure of a Bach fugue, just as has been done with Rembrandt paintings.

Dr. John Ott asserts that the body has its own natural resonant frequency that can be supported, overstimulated, or suppressed by various light, sound, or electromagnetic frequencies and vibrations.[5] Long-term constant bombardment by electromagnetic emissions from high-tension electricity cables, TV, radar, microwave, and transmitters has a significant effect on our overall health and collective behavior.

Water as a medium is very sensitive to resonance. Its electromagnetic qualities make it the ideal path for the intercommunication of resonant frequencies. Ralf Roessner, who developed the double-egg water vortexer, noticed that a change also occurred in his own bodily fluids—the "instrument" of the whirling, observing person—when he held the egg vortexer against his body.

Language and Water

Masaru Emoto experimented with words taped to a bottle to see if they would carry dynamic energy into the water. He reports they did, in whatever language they were written. Phrases such as "I love you" and "I hate you" produced the anticipated results. He insists that words alone carry a subtle energy, which may puzzle some who prefer to believe that words carry the consciousness behind their creator. When a sensitive person declares that a book has good vibrations, he is surely perceiving the insight (subtle energy level) of its author, not just the words.

If the quality of water improves or deteriorates according to the information to which it is exposed, Emoto deduced, the human body is likely to be more healthy when receiving good information (energy) and to suffer when exposed to bad energy.

Masaru Emoto's Philosophy

Emoto's research has gone far beyond a laboratory. Perhaps the most dramatic research he has directed was to organize large groups of pilgrims to pray by lakes in order to help purify the quality of the water. Because his reach is so broad, it might be helpful to summarize key points of his message.

- Quantum mechanics acknowledges that substance is vibration, and vibration is at the core of Emoto's message. He describes how, at the microscopic level, the number and shape of the electrons orbiting the nucleus of each atom give a substance a particular set of vibrational frequencies. Whatever the object, nothing is solid; the appearance of solidity is the nucleus surrounded by a wave rotating endlessly at great speed.
- Each human individual vibrates at a unique frequency, depending on his or her energetic state of love, joy, or negative intention. Emoto believes the same principles apply to objects and locations. For example, there are places where accidents seem to happen, others where enterprises are successful, and objects that seem to bring tragedy to successive owners. Intense subtle energy can even produce natural disasters.
- When water freezes, the particles link together to form a crystal nucleus. If the nucleus grows coherently, a visible water crystal appears; but when information is present that is not in harmony with Nature, an incomplete crystal results.
- Everything in a state of vibration also emits sound. This is why crystal formations are affected by music, and why the subtle energy of specific words can affect the quality of crystal formation. Water can convert these vibrations into a pattern visible to the human eye.
- Emoto believes that in harmonious Nature only vibrations of love and gratitude are present—trees and plants show respect for each other, and animals take only as much food as they require. He believes that humans learned words and language from Nature, and that words like "gratitude" and "love" form the fundamental laws of Nature and the phenomena of life. However, phrases like

"you fool" do not exist in Nature. Such words and thoughts are created by humans.

- Natural water sources produce beautiful crystals, but much of Earth's water, whether in the atmosphere, on the surface, or even underground, is polluted. He says that pollution originates in human consciousness; it is the creation of our selfishness and our egos.

- Emoto claims that human beings vibrate 570 trillion times a second. A human being contains a universe within, filled with overlapping frequencies that produce a symphony of cosmic proportions.[6] When one being creates a frequency and another responds with the same sound, they resonate. People who generate similar frequencies attract each other. When their frequencies are incompatible, they cannot resonate and they do not accept each other.

- Our emotions affect the world moment by moment. If you send out harmonious thoughts, you will help create a beautiful world. The key to what is possible for you lies in your heart to know and your will to make happen. What we imagine becomes our world.*

- Our state of consciousness affects the world around us. If you bake a cake lovingly, some will note that it tastes better. I know others will scoff at these claims, but most readers will know what I mean, despite the difficulty of proving it scientifically.

- Emoto notes that a common thread of the great teachings of the world's religions is that intentional thought can change the quality of what we experience. This can be practiced through the meditative technique called visualization. We all have the power to visualize a protective shield for ourselves or others; a state of becoming more healthy, a homeopathic remedy. A champion tennis player cannot succeed without a powerful ability to visualize

---

*My mother believed in the inherent goodness in all people. That this was not just naïveté was shown by the fact that some people with a poor social reputation could respond to her with unaccustomed cooperation. However, in the past fifty years, basic standards of morality have given way to greater self-indulgence and lack of honesty.

his best shots. The power of the mind to effect outcomes is really extraordinary, but we need to exercise it with careful judgment and humility (see "Epigenetics," in chapter 9).

- Most objects in Nature emit stable frequencies. Each sparrow sounds basically similar, and the sounds made by dogs and cats do not vary much. But humans are able to use a full scale to make beautiful melodies.

- Emoto says that humans are the only creatures who can resonate with all other creatures and objects in Nature; we can give out energy and receive it in return. This is why it is vital that we change our way of thinking and live in harmony with Nature. If you fill your heart with love and gratitude, your life will give you what you seek. But if you emit signals of dissatisfaction and hate, your life will become this.

Water is neutral, but our terrible abuse of the earth has turned it into a carrier of disease. Emoto shows us how water can also be a medium of healing. If we were really to take on board the idea that we can heal Earth's groundwater, I believe that Nature would respond, for the groundwater is a key to the health of Gaia. It could happen quickly, given the will. We caused the pollution; we can clean it up by being the channels of its healing. In this way we can demonstrate our responsiility as Earth guardians.

ANDREAS SCHULZ'S WATER CRYSTAL RESEARCH

Andreas Schulz's water crystal analysis is a method of assessing the quality of a water sample without adding anything to it, which attracted a lot of interest when it was introduced in 1993 at an exhibition in Freiburg, Germany. It is easily understood by a lay person and is surprisingly simple, not requiring particularly complex equipment.

The water sample is first distilled at a relatively low temperature

(70–80°C).* A portion of the sample is dessicated into a powdery residue that is combined with some of the distilled liquid, placed on a glass slide, and allowed to crystallize at room temperature. The resulting crystals are photographed through an electron microscope (see plate 21).

In contrast to Masaru Emoto's analytical method, Schulz's process for testing the quality of a water sample has a standardized protocol. For example, crystals form particular angles. When more star-shaped crystals and 60° angles appear, the water quality is higher. A tendency toward 90° angles indicates low energy and polluted water. When the 90° structures predominate, the water is not suitable for drinking. Other criteria include the strength and spread of the crystal formations, fields of darkness, border structures, and so on.

In conventional crystal research, the microcrystalline structure of substances is dependent on the mineral composition of the sample; for example, rhombic, tetrahedral, or hexagonal forms. Such information can help assess the material characteristics, such as strength and load capacity. This method, however, will not help determine the quality of a food sample, its level of toxicity, or its ability to improve the quality of human life.

Schulz's method of crystal analysis depends on macrocrystalline (larger) structures, shapes that are independent of the chemical composition. So, while the conventional microcrystalline structure reveals cubic salt crystals in seawater, the macrocrystalline sample of high-energy sea water will tend to show rounded shapes with different angular structures. As this method is more specific and reliable than Emoto's and has a high level of precision, it has achieved broad scientific acceptance.

Chemically purified water may pass physical tests but still not be high quality. Consumers are often confused by the technical language of water analysis coming from municipal or commercial water companies that rely only on physical analysis. The value of the Schulz method

---

*Distillation is normally done at a temperature of 100°C or higher.

is that the energy level of the samples, which is paramount for quality, is easily seen.

Contributing to the overall picture given by the sample are the inner structure of water, arrangement of cluster structures, total information content, and the state of the water's vital energy, which will be affected by any form of energy pollution. This makes it a more reliable measure of water sample quality for drinking, as well as for evaluation of the quality of food, medicine, cosmetics, and a range of products.

PART THREE

CONFRONTING THE WATER CRISIS

SIXTEEN

HOW WE TREAT WATER

But there is not, as they say, any worse water than water
*   that sleeps.*
(Mais il n'est, comme on dit, pire eau que l'eau qui dort.)
                              MOLIÈRE, *TARTUFFE*

Other than in times of flood or drought, we mostly ignore water. In Europe and most industrialized countries, we seldom need to think about it. It's there when we turn on our taps, and then it drains away somewhere else. We can bathe when we choose and water lawns on a whim, and the fountains in our parks keep flowing.

Most thoughtful people accept that our culture is at war with the environment. The early Native Americans would have been horrified that we are extracting uranium from the earth in order to make energy to move vehicles, because they knew its important role in balancing the earth's energy.* But how many realize that our desecration of fresh water is even more damaging to our planet? Water is much more than just a resource; it is the handmaiden of the quantum field in guiding

---

*Is it accidental that the largest concentration of megalithic monuments of spiritual significance in Britain are found on the Orkney Islands, the only area in the British Isles where mineable uranium can be found?

life and evolution. As we are beginning to see, water is the essence of life itself (see chapter 19).

Our water supplies are in grave danger, because we don't know how to manage or care for fresh water. In California, for example, 78 percent of the water supply is used for agricultural irrigation (often poorly managed), leaving only 22 percent for industrial, domestic, and environmental use. It can take a thousand gallons of fresh water to produce enough grain for an eight-ounce steak. The United States uses three times as much fresh water per day as any European country, and enormously more water than any developing country.[1]

Climate change is bringing redistribution of (often torrential) rainfall and increasing drought. These unfamiliar conditions will force us to become much more careful with water. Undoubtedly, they will also bring conflict between nations.

OUR VIRTUAL WORLD

Global warming was blamed for the devastating floods in England in July 2007. While some local authorities had made preparations for a flood of this proportion (for example, by building collection basins) and fared better as a result, we need to look much deeper, to the heart of our problem with water. Climate change may indeed play a part in flood unpredictability, but there is another cause that we urgently need to recognize. We have forgotten what our forefathers understood—that natural land is like a giant sponge that can absorb almost any deluge.

Many of the major floods of recent decades—Mozambique, Colombia, Costa Rica, Bangladesh—were due to heedless destruction of the most important part of that protective sponge: the forests of the watershed. Denuded land sheds a downpour like water off a duck's back, for rain will soak into the ground only if the surface is cooler than the rain.

It is tragic how little understanding there is of the importance of tree cover to prevent soil erosion by increasingly violent storms. The terrible floods in Haiti in the wake of the 2009 hurricanes were due to deforestation brought on by population growth, dependence on charcoal for fuel, and building on the floodplain.

Our culture is completely ignorant of the importance of healthy river systems to keep the environment in healthy balance. Excessive deforestation clogs the rivers with silt, and loss of riparian vegetation causes overheating and energy loss from the rivers. The Ganges and Yellow Rivers are almost stagnant from siltation and upstream water extraction, and the Ganges from fecal coliform pollution.[2]

Our ancestors who lived on the land knew their land intimately and understood how important it was to keep the soil, woodland, bogs, and wetland in good condition. Their farming methods kept the soil healthy and encouraged countless species of bacteria, microbes, and worms. They also had the wisdom to keep off flood plains, the land that is most susceptible to periodic flooding.

Modern industrial farming practices are usually neither ecofriendly nor sustainable. The land is used as an anchor for plants that are chemically treated or genetically modified and often watered by wasteful irrigation. The chemicals kill many of the microbes and worms, damaging the soil structure and making it less able to retain moisture, and reducing its nutritional value. Their over-deep plowing techniques use steel blades that put an alien positive electric charge into the soil, which encourages pests that have to be dealt with by more chemicals.

This is virtual farming by virtual farmers, many of whom, ranging around their vast acreages in enormous air-conditioned, radio-equipped tractor cabs, have lost contact with Nature and even with their own land.

As we shall see, water is the driver of all natural processes in Nature. Our shortsighted obsession with profit has driven the destruction of the equatorial rain forests, the vital mechanism for moderating world climate. With no respect for Nature's laws, the modern technologist, fueled by cheap oil, greedily exploits Earth's resources, carving angry wounds in her skin to mine her minerals, felling the great trees for pro-

The Perils of Genetically Modified Agriculture

Agricultural biotechnology cannot alleviate the existing food crisis. On the contrary it is inherently unsustainable and extremely hazardous to biodiversity and to human and animal health.

- The increased use of toxic pesticides causes illness in farm workers and contamination of food and drinking water.
- The carrier genes can create new pathogenic bacteria and viruses that affect the gut and even the cell's genome, causing serious illness.
- The vector (carrier) can recombine to generate new virulent strains of viruses, especially in transgenic plants engineered for viral resistance with viral genes.
- The main danger is that increased use of toxic herbicides with herbicide-resistant transgenic plants leads to large-scale elimination of indigenous agricultural and natural species, destroying natural fertility and yield.[3]

digious Western beef appetites, and creating unsustainable biofuel deserts to power insatiable automobiles.

Equally disquieting, however, is how much of our experience today is increasingly virtual, controlled by electronic gadgets, computers, and televisions that create sensory deprivation of touch, smell, and even sound. For many of us, even our travel is virtual, with no real contact with the land or its inhabitants. How many of us listen to the music of a rushing stream, respond to the haunting owl's call, or are entranced by the wonder of a Perseid meteor shower undimmed by light pollution?

DWINDLING WATER SUPPLIES

Before they were seduced by the luxuries of modern living, people the world over followed sustainable practices of personal hygiene. In Asia in particular, daily collection of "night soil" ensured the fertility of the land. You can still see this in China and Tibet. In many parts of the world, the long-drop privy was the standard toilet. Now, from Aden to Singapore, houses are built with flush toilets and plumbed showers, causing crises in water supply. One traveler, anxious to impress his Aden family, brought back a shiny white porcelain toilet that stood unused in the corner of a room.[4]

In May 2008, oceangoing water tankers delivered fresh water to Barcelona, which was suffering drought from poor water management. Spain's rainfall has markedly fallen and temperatures have risen, but local authorities still persist in watering golf courses and filling swimming pools for tourists. It is salutary, though, to compare Barcelona's daily water consumption of 114 liters per person with Mexico City's average of 300 liters per person for its 20 million people.[5] The poorest districts in Mexico City depend on twice weekly tanker deliveries, while the prosperous suburbs are profligate in their water use. Infrastructure problems result in leaks consuming 38 percent of the supply, and there is little recycling or use of rainwater.

The subject of water is very topical, mainly because usable water is in short supply (see plate 24). Predictions are now common that wars will be fought over access to water, and it's easy to see why. Countries that control the headwaters of important rivers can restrict their flow downstream: Turkey to Iraq, Israel to Jordan, Syria to Israel, Sudan to Egypt, India to Bangladesh.

Twenty percent of the world's population does not have clean drinking water, and nearly half the world does not have modern sanitation. One hundred cities in northern China now ration water, and Beijing's future as China's capital has been under review because its growth has outstripped its water resources. Even those countries that have sufficient water treat it so badly that, when delivering it to homes, they kill it with chlorine, fluoride, and other chemicals, ostensibly to prevent disease. This actually depresses our immune systems and makes us more open to infection.

How has this come about? Water is in great abundance on this marvelous planet, but only about 0.5 percent is available as surface fresh water. The rest is salt water, inaccessible groundwater, precious aquifers, or frozen polar or mountain ice. While the world's population is increasing by 85 million a year, cities are expanding at double that rate. Cities and industries consume the most water (industrial water consumption is set to double by 2025).[6]

Twenty-four countries, mainly in Africa, will not have enough water to meet 2025 projected needs.[7] In addition, according to a recent UN report, world population could rise from 6.1 billion in 2000 to at least 8.2 billion by 2050.[8] Today, 1.2 billion drink unclean water, and 2.5 billion lack proper toilets or sewage systems.[9] What will be the situation in ten years?

Globally, about 70 percent of water diverted from rivers or drawn irresponsibly from aquifers is used for irrigation. This is hugely wasteful; leaking pipes and channels, along with evaporation from reservoirs and irrigation sprays, means that about 60 percent of the water does not reach plant roots. China's greatest river, the Yellow River, has run dry and in several years since 1985 has failed to reach the ocean.[10] The once-mighty Nile, Ganges, and Colorado Rivers barely reach the sea in dry seasons. The introduction of industrial agriculture has led to dangerous lowering of the water table in India and northern China.[11]

WATER FOR PROFIT

Perhaps the most telling judgment of our society's ethical standards is our relationship to water. Water has become one of the liveliest traded products on the commodities exchange. To regard water as a commodity is as despicable and immoral as claiming ownership and patenting seeds. These are God-given sources of life.

The construction of large dams, whether for hydroelectric power or for irrigation, does incalculable environmental damage and annihilates viable human communities. Dams destroy ecosystems and sever the balancing of dynamic energy from one part of the landscape to another. Since 1970, when Egypt's Aswan High Dam came into operation, the number of commercially harvested fish species in the Nile has dropped by two-thirds, and the Mediterranean sardine catch has fallen by 80 percent.[12]

Vast new networks of supply and disposal pipes must be built in cities if basic water needs are to be met. Governments, unwilling these days to invest in social infrastructure, are privatizing water utilities, but the results seldom benefit the consumer. A shortage in any essential commodity brings out the profiteers and extortionists. Pro-privatization propaganda reached a climax at the Water Forum meetings in The Hague in March 2000, but the abuses and inadequacies of commercial control have become apparent. Water barons collude to keep prices high, pay enormous bribes to obtain water contracts, and have a low record of efficiency.

One study showed that Swedish municipal water authorities delivered water at around a third of the cost, had operating costs of about half, and produced nearly three times higher return on capital than English private water companies of similar size.[13] After the economic downturn of 2001, several English private water companies experienced financial difficulties and were bought by foreign companies. It is complete nonsense that essential water supplies should be subject to the ups and downs of the financial markets.

In April 2000, protesting citizens of Cochabamba in Bolivia suffered more than 180 casualties at the hands of its own police before their government revoked the right of International Waters of London to impose a 35 percent price hike in water prices. The government has since reconsidered its policy of privatizing all public water supplies.

The great danger to our water comes from the globalization of supply. Multinational companies are unaccountable and have more interest in profit than in a sustainable environment. A group of water companies tried at the 2001 Hague Water Forum conference to foist a new water order on the world, in effect, to remove water supplies from public control. American companies are negotiating to build dams in India that would displace countless communities and destroy their environments. Three French companies already control more than 70 percent of the world's private market.[14] Increasing numbers of privatized water schemes are linked to ventures to extract more water through vast dams and reservoirs, with bulk water supply schemes that guarantee profits by requiring consumption regardless of need.

MODERN WATER TREATMENTS

Nearly all modern water treatments involve the use of toxic chemicals. Although urban water supplies pass routine tests for basic safety, this does not mean they are vital or even free of contaminants.[15]

Chlorination

Because public water is not treated with the care required to keep water pulsating and alive as Schauberger demonstrated it must be, it degenerates and attracts pathogenic organisms. As a result, authorities routinely treat it with chlorine to prevent the transmission of water-borne diseases. A powerful disinfectant removes all types of bacteria, beneficial and harmful alike, and in so doing, eventually destroys or seriously weakens many of the immune-enhancing microorganisms in the body.

It is a major contributor to lowered immune resistance in older people. Medical authorities say the amount of chlorine ingested is too small to have this impact, but they fail to take into account that chlorine accumulates in the fatty tissue of the body so that the dosage is cumulative, nor that there is a homeopathic action that amplifies the effect on the body. In addition to the drinking water, hot showers and washing machines can produce debilitating chloroform gas that is absorbed by upholstery and carpets. Viktor Schauberger had strong views about compulsory chlorination.

Those of us who live in cities and are forced year-in and year-out to drink sterilized water should seriously consider the fate of that "organism" whose naturally ordained ability to create life has been forcibly removed by chemical compounds. Sterilized and physically destroyed water not only brings about physical decay, but also gives rise to mental deterioration and hence to the systematic degeneration of humanity and other life-forms.

If we have any common sense remaining, we should refuse to continue to drink water prepared in this way. Otherwise we risk a future as cancer-prone, mentally and physically decrepit, physically and morally inferior individuals.[16]

It is, in fact, not difficult to remove chlorine from our domestic water supplies (see pp. 300–301).

Fluoridation

The issue of routinely adding fluorosilicates (fluoride) to drinking water is one of the worst outrages in public health policy. This is not the naturally occurring calcium fluoride that is naturally present in some drinking water, usually at low levels of about 0.1ppm (parts per million). It is a by-product of a number of industrial processes, initially the iron, copper, and aluminium, and now the phosphate fertilizer industries, and also contains a number of heavy metals. It is a potent toxic cocktail.[17]

Many dentists claim that fluoride protects teeth from decay. As the disposal of industrial wastes is very costly, the cynical proposal to add them to public water supplies was started in the United States, lobbied largely by the Mellon family, owners of ALCOA aluminum. Starting with Grand Rapids, Michigan, in 1945, it was introduced within two years to a hundred cities. It was basically a dirty-tricks campaign that labeled opposers as crackpots (and during the McCarthy era, as left-wing subversives) and has never completed convincing tests, nor produced adequate evidence of its efficacy or safety. It was political, not a scientific health issue, and in the same way as the more recent genetically modified food campaign, became a major U.S. export.[18]

Fluoridation of water supplies is current policy in much of the English-speaking world, and in a few other countries, such as Chile, it is permitted, usually at levels of about 1ppm (or 1mg fluoride per liter of water). In many other countries, however, it is often strongly opposed by citizens' groups and scientists who have decided that the risks are too high. The five countries that still fluoridate to a large extent are Ireland (75 percent of the population), Australia (66 percent), United States, Canada, and New Zealand (50 percent); Britain is lagging at 10 percent (mostly in the West Midlands and the Northeast), but the UK government has now strengthened legislation to enable fluoridation to become mandatory.

The World Health Organization and American Medical Association have been persuaded to back the policy. The FDA (Food and Drug Administration) has backed off slightly from its 100 percent endorsement of the practice, due to public exposure of the scam, but today 130 million Americans in 9,600 communities continue to drink fluoridated water.[19]

The addition of fluoride as a policy is justified by the claim that it reduces dental cavities, especially in children. Independent research challenges this claim, showing that the body accumulates levels of fluoride in the bones and certain organs, and there is evidence of increased risk of cancer, brain function impairment, kidney malfunction, and premature aging. At higher dosage levels, fluorosilicates are an effective rat poison.

Unfortunately fluoride is also added to many processed foods, fruit juice, milk, and toothpaste. Fluoride is released into food cooked in Teflon-coated cookware, so the actual intake may be significant, even if you don't live in a fluoridated water area. For reasons that are difficult to comprehend, but which are clearly political in nature, many dental and health authorities seem to support this mass medication of whole populations, and politicians seem happy to go along with it.[20]

Health researcher Barry Groves's study of U.S. fluoride policy concludes that:

Fluoridation is the longest, most expensive, and most spectacularly unsuccessful marketing campaign ever to come out of the United States . . . This is an example of a cynical alliance between industrial leaders, mainstream science, and the politicians we elect, which shows complete contempt for public health and welfare, and indeed, for the truth; it shows that we have to be extremely vigilant to preserve our freedoms, and indeed, our health.[21]*

RECYCLING WATER

It is urgent that we learn how to recycle water rather than flush it into drains and the sea. The first step is to capture rainwater in water butts (specially designed barrels that attach to downward drainpipes) to irrigate our gardens. The next is to filter and reuse gray water—that is, domestic waste water. Then comes the acid test of sustainability— recycling human water waste. Recycling of human urine (after treatment) and feces has been practiced for centuries in Himalayan communities, and untreated urine's high nitrogen content makes it an effective compost activator.

TRANSMUTING WATER'S MEMORY

Most communities make genuine efforts to remove physical pollutants from public water supplies, but there are so many toxins produced by industrial agriculture that it is wise to consider good filtration to reduce the dangers of pollutants and heavy metals. There are a number of effective, affordable under-counter and whole-house filters that remove most of the physical contaminants. However, what our water treatment policies must consider is that the physical removal of a pollutant is only part of making water safe.

---

*In Australia some of the fluoride laws are so draconian that people may be prosecuted for speaking out against water fluoridation ("Living in a Democratic Fluoridated Country," *Australian Fluoridation News*).

Typically, urban public water supplies are recycled as many as twenty times. Even if the physical contaminants have been removed, their vibrational imprint is still carried in the water in its memory bank, no matter how many times it is recycled. The purpose of some of the better vortex treatment systems is to recluster the water using superimposed natural energies to erase the memory of the water's previous abuse. A vortex, being the enabling gateway between different qualities or levels of energy, allows water to absorb the etheric energy that surrounds us all. The best domestic plan is a combination of an efficient plumbed-in filter with a vortex-type reenergizing system (see appendix 1, Water and Health).

WATER MAINS MATERIAL

Archaeological research has shown that in ancient times, from the Babylonians to the Greeks, water mains were constructed of high-quality wood or natural stone. Later, the Romans experimented with different metals and often used lead, which brought its own problems of lead poisoning.

Before the expansion of cities during the Industrial Revolution, many water mains in Europe, and even in New York, were constructed of wood, which allowed the water to breathe and interact with its environment. However, Vienna's water mains were extended to new suburbs between 1920 and 1931 using steel or iron pipes internally coated with tar, and according to Viktor Schauberger, the incidence of cancer more than doubled.[22]

The laminar structure of water quickly disintegrates owing to its chaotic flow through a cylindrical pipe. Friction with the pipe walls heats up the water, decomposing dissolved trace elements. The oxygen in the water is reduced when it interacts with the iron to form rust, which, in turn, encourages disease-promoting bacteria. The accumulating rust decreases the pipe's diameter and constricts the water flow, and what is ultimately delivered is dead water that has to be disinfected with chlorine.

The Wooden Water Main

Schauberger knew that water can maintain its vitality and dynamic energy only if it is allowed to tumble about in a spiraling vortical manner, so in 1930 he designed a pipe that actually encouraged this movement (see plates 22 and 23). It was constructed of wooden staves, like a barrel, which allowed the moisture to seep through, transferring a cooling effect (as in sweating) to the water in the pipe. The spiraling movement was created by a series of guide vanes, which acted like rifling in a gun barrel. These were made of silver plated copper to enhance the subtle energies and fluted so as to direct movement toward the center, thus reducing the heating effects of friction.*

Plates 22 and 23 illustrate how this configuration sets up a double-spiral longitudinal vortex, creating a water flow that is faster than that of a conventional cylindrical pipe. The centripetal flow of the main water body helps to cool and accelerate it, as the heavier water draws the specifically lighter outer water along in its wake. The centripetal spiraling of the toroidal "doughnuts" created by the guide vanes makes oxygen from the main water body available, transferring any pathogenic bacteria to the pipe walls, where they are eliminated by the aggressive oxygen. The higher quality microorganisms survive, because they require higher levels of oxygen.

This brilliant design imitates the pulsating flow of water in a natural vessel and delivers water that purifies and cools itself through its motion, eliminating the need for any processing or additives. Ideally, these wooden water mains should be embedded in sand, which allows them to breathe and protects them from light and heat. In such conditions they should outlast a steel pipe.

---

*Essentially growth-promoting dynagens created by the bimetal composition: silver (male) and copper (female). The silver also has bactericidal properties. Dynagens are also produced by the centripetal movement of the main water body, raising the overall vitality, life energy, and wholesomeness of the water.

WATER STORAGE

Water's enemies are excessive heat and light. Water contains oxygen, which is essential for both growth and decay. At temperatures lower than 9°C (48°F), its oxygen is used for growth; higher than that, it promotes decomposition. As the temperature rises above 10°C (50°F), the oxygen becomes increasingly more aggressive, promoting pathogenic bacteria that can transmit disease.

A tank that is above ground needs to be well insulated and painted white to reflect the sun's heat. If it is mostly below the surface of the earth, the walls will not require insulation, but the top must be painted white. However, Viktor Schauberger urged us to observe the shapes that Nature uses to propagate and maintain life. Nature abhors squares (cubes), rectangles (water tanks), and circles (cylinders). He said that we should not be surprised that our dependence on these unnatural shapes for storage results in the deterioration of our water. Although it is impractical for larger containers, we should attempt to use a more natural shape for smaller containers.

Because it behaves like a living organism, water needs to be in constant movement to maintain its health. The one container that allows this is the egg shape. The material of containment is very important because water needs to keep cool; the best materials are natural stone, wood, or terra-cotta. The ancient Greeks understood this and kept their water (and wine) in *amphorae,* egg-shaped vessels that allowed the liquid to breathe. In amphorae discovered in archaeological digs, grains have been found to be preserved so well after two thousand years that they germinated when planted, proving the effectiveness of the egg shape for preservation.

EARTH HEALING

There are many traditions that recognize a spirit of water. The Saami people of Arctic Scandinavia call her Mere-Ama, whose blessing is often sought for good health and fertility. The water mother spirit may be identified as a deva who can be sought for advice on personal matters of health and welfare. In many old cultures, working with the water mother was a women's ritual.

Australia has been suffering terrible drought for a century. Alanna Moore, the Australian geomancer, tells of a Buddhist group that conducted a rain-making ritual near Bendigo, Victoria, in 2006. "Monks from the Atisha Center (site of the largest *stupa* in the Western world) gathered in bushland beside a dry watercourse for their rain ceremony," explained Moore. "It had been one of the driest years on record, yet a few days later a local deluge of some 60 millimeters (more than two inches) of rain fell," according to a friend of hers who attended.[23]

HOLY WATER

Many spiritual traditions celebrate water as a sacred medium. In the desert environment of the Middle East, which cradled the great monotheistic religions, water was clearly the precious source of all life. Jesus often referred to the spiritual qualities of water. His miracle of turning water into wine is very symbolic of the key role that water has in any healing activity.

Masaru Emoto's experiments showed that praying over a specific sample of water improved its quality. Many of the world's religious practices, going back millennia, are based on this eternal truth. The practice of prayer before a meal is based on this belief, though many who do it have lost touch with its relevance.

We live by the grace of water.
NATIONAL GEOGRAPHIC SPECIAL EDITION,
NOVEMBER 1993

SEVENTEEN

WATER AND CLIMATE CHANGE

Where least expected, water breaks forth.
(Dove non si crede, l'acqua rompe.)

ITALIAN PROVERB

CLIMATE CHANGE IS SYMPTOM, NOT CAUSE

Human society is in crisis not from the catastrophic effects of climate change but because we don't yet acknowledge how we got into this situation. Climate change is not the issue; it is a symptom of our disconnection from the environment. Nature will always have the last word, and unless we are willing to learn from her, future prospects for Man are poor. Humility is a rare quality and there is, as yet, almost no sign of a change of heart; we still think we can reduce the effects of global warming through our clever technology. I believe, however, that water can show us how to reconnect with our source (see chapter 19).

ECONOMIC AND POLITICAL INSTABILITY

In 1820 the world population hit one billion. The growth of population since then to 6.8 billion (2009) has been possible only with the exploitation of fossil fuels. Oil, the most versatile fuel ever discovered, has brought about an unprecedented revolution in methods of transport and has spawned a raft of technologies, from industrial farming to the chemical industry, to computers, medicine and health, myriad consumer goods, world trade, and tourism. Our livelihoods are dependent on it.

The creation of enormous wealth has always destabilized human societies. The prodigious wealth conferred by fossil fuels, particularly oil, in the past 190 years has been absorbed by the economically developed nations, with disproportionate excess going into the hands of a few, including multinational corporations that are beyond national laws or regulation. Political institutions collude with these centers of power, and the losers are the organic health and well-being of human society and the environment.

As increased demand for oil begins to overtake decreasing supply, oil production will start to run down—by 2035, it is predicted to be about 60 percent of the present peak level—and will no longer be a reliable source of energy; countries that still have oil reserves will want to hold on to them or use them for strategic bargaining. Undoubtedly, wars to control oil supplies will become more numerous, and the countries that have depended on fast economic growth will be most vulnerable to economic decline. The web of world trade is now so interdependent that the failure of its transport system could be catastrophic.

THE POPULATION BOMB

This is often referred to as the elephant in the room, because many people don't want to talk about it. Earth's resources would have difficulty supporting a global population predicted to rise to 9.5 billion well before the end of this century, particularly since food production is likely to be seriously disrupted by the effects of climate change. This will affect all countries and may dampen the rate of population growth in developing countries.

As we have seen, Nature's main priority is balance, and if any species becomes too dominant or grows too fast, Nature will find a way to adjust it. Why should Man be exempt from this? The adjustment could take the form of anything from serious climate change and economic collapse to decimating wars and global pandemics. The main threat to global stability will come from the billion or more people migrating from countries most affected by climate change to wealthier countries that feel less impact. The potential for violence will be great. It is likely that by the end of this century, Earth may not have the capacity to support our entire anticipated population, but perhaps only half our current numbers of 6.8 billion.

WATER UNDER STRESS

It would be difficult to overstate the seriousness of the prospects for fresh water all over our planet during the rest of this century. News reports are being phrased in increasingly apocalyptic terms.

> *Climate change:* Freshwater supplies will be endangered by change in the distribution and intensity of rainfall. Global warming will greatly increase the amount of water that the air can hold. This will result in more frequent downpours, similar to the monsoons of the tropics, in temperate latitudes, such as the British Isles and northern U.S. regions. Some areas that used to have rain may experience drought; increased desertification will spread, especially in Africa, southern Europe, and the American Southwest.

> *Effects of Global Warming:* The atmosphere and the oceans together behave as a single organic whole, changes in one part of which can affect the opposite side of the globe. So a hotter tropical climate can result in increased desertification in the center of continents (e.g., central Asia), as well as bringing more extreme precipitation nearer the coasts. And the destruction and dieback of the tropical rain forests will result in more extreme

atmospheric conditions, with more violent hurricanes, typhoons, deluges, and floods, and less rain in continental interiors.

Oceans: The effects of ocean warming are presently poorly understood. One of the more alarming concerns is the effect this has on phytoplankton that are not only the base of the food chain but also one of the principal absorbers of CO_2, which is stored in their bodies on the ocean floor. They are very sensitive to ocean temperature, preferring a cooler range. The collapse of their populations would affect not only a wide range of ocean creatures (and fish supply) but also the viability of the oceans as a carbon sink.

Deforestation: Forests, especially tropical, create and recycle rain. The failure of the Amazon rain forest will reduce rainfall north and south of Amazonia, and the Atlantic shores are likely to lose the moderating influence of the Gulf Stream.

Melting glaciers: The river systems of India, Pakistan, and Southeast Asia depend on Himalayan meltwater, and there will be acute summer water shortages when the glaciers disappear. Europe's largest rivers are presently fed by Alpine melt and may well start to run dry in hot summers. Rivers beyond 50° latitude are likely to be less affected.

Exhaustion of aquifers: Agriculture in the continental interior of North America has, for the past century, been dependent on immense stores of ancient water in deep aquifers below the plains. These have been drained far beyond the point at which natural replenishment can take place. The Australian basin's aquifer is also dangerously low (see "Regional Problems" on p. 252).

Increasing population: Population increase and rise in living standards has put a great strain on water supplies. This is particularly evident in northern China, parts of India, Indonesia, Mexico, and California. Economic immigrants can also strain local resources, and dwindling dependable water supplies could spell famine in many parts of the world, especially in Africa.

Competition for water resources is likely to bring even more conflict between nations than that caused by the exhaustion of oil reserves, because there are no alternatives to water.

Some nations are in a position to control their neighbors' sources of water (for example, China could regulate water in Thailand, Laos, and Cambodia through its control of the Tibetan plateau). This will happen on a local scale throughout the world.*

WATER SCARCITY

The map of water scarcity in currently populated regions shows five areas under severe stress (in rising order): the American Southwest and Mexico, the North African coast (especially Algeria), Palestine and the Nile Delta, Pakistan and South India, and northern China (see plate 24). The causes vary from population pressure and economic growth to inappropriate irrigation technologies and change in rainfall patterns.

The American Southwest has experienced substantial immigration from Mexico into both Southern California and Texas, putting a strain on the infrastructure and on the demand for fresh water. Northern California has one-third of the state's population, but 75 percent of the state's water resources. Aqueducts and canals, begun in the 1930s, bring surplus water from the north to the farming regions of the Central Valley and to the Los Angeles conurbation, which also receives water from the Colorado River.

Agriculture consumes 80 percent of captured freshwater, leaving domestic, industrial, and environmental needs to compete for the remainder. Much of the irrigation effort is wasteful. There have been efforts to recycle "brown" wastewater for irrigation, but there is resistance to its use for domestic purposes. The main problem here, as in every area of

---

*The Uru Chipaya, the ancient "water people" of Bolivia, blame their upstream neighbors for diverting precious supplies (*Guardian Weekly,* 1 May 2009). Competition over the water of the River Jordan is a flashpoint in the Near East.

water stress in the world, is the excessive pumping of groundwater; this is nonsustainable, because these resources are irreplaceable.

Mexico City is one of the largest and fastest-growing cities in the world, yet it has exhausted its underground aquifer and there is no infrastructure to bring in adequate supplies of fresh water from the mountains.

Coastal North Africa has seen much higher temperatures in recent years, as well as a decrease in rainfall. Urbanization has compounded the water problem.

The highly populated Nile Delta, which is threatened by sea level rise, is the main source of Egypt's food. Cairo's population has greatly increased, and along with the rest of the Mediterranean region, it suffers from the effect of warming.

Israel is a pioneer in soil irrigation that goes directly to plants' roots, but the water table has dropped seriously throughout the region.

LAND UNDER STRESS

As a result of climate change, the prognosis for the latter part of the century is that land suitable for growing crops will be limited to higher latitudes. Parts of western Russia might still be able to grow crops, but areas such as Siberia, Canada, parts of northern Europe, and southern South America will become the breadbaskets of a much-reduced world population. Presumably the taiga pine forests of Siberia would be sacrificed for agriculture. The equatorial rain forests will die out if global warming accelerates.

Apart from drought, the main problem of food security will be our dependence on the monoculture of grain types. Because they are not protected by diversity of species, monoculture crops are vulnerable to the types of global disease that caused the Irish potato famine and problems with wheat rust. There is an urgent need for crop breeders to develop a wide range of alternative species, using the wild plant bank.[1] Industrial agriculture chooses to be blind to this predictable situation.

SALINE AGRONOMY

It is most likely that climate change will render fresh water supplies in many parts of the world insufficient to grow the food we'll need for future populations. Currently, less than 1 percent of the world's available water is fresh, and most of this is locked in the polar icecaps, which are melting without benefit to humanity. Another 1 percent is brackish (less salty than the oceans), and then there are the unlimited oceans. Many plants can be grown in saline water, for food, for minerals, and for energy.[2]

WATER IN THE LANDSCAPE

Water creates vibrant life appropriate to each climatic landscape. Whether this is driven by the intelligence of Nature, cosmic design, or even some inherent intelligence of water may be beside the point. Man has irreparably damaged water's natural role of optimizing the fertility and biodiversity of the landscape.

When we leave water to its own devices, as Peter Andrews did in Australia (see chapter 18), apparent miracles can happen. But when we interfere, as when the mangrove swamps defending the tropical coasts of Africa and Southeast Asia were removed to make way for monocultured shrimp farms, disaster often ensues; those coastal communities were devastated by the tsunami of 2004.

The most prolific natural environment is the equatorial tropical forest. Temperate climates cannot sustain such complex biological wealth, but temperate latitudes are more sought after for human settlement and agriculture.

People have always chosen rivers as their main focus for settlement, as they provide fresh water and easier connection to the rest of the world. But when population density increases, water features are sometimes crowded out of the landscape. Apart from increasing biodiversity and ecological richness, water features absorb high levels of precipitation. Rising temperatures increase evaporation from the oceans, resulting in higher atmospheric humidity, which produces more torrential and unpredictable rainfall. Where will this go if we remove the sponges that allow slow release of water? Woodland and forest, especially on watersheds and in tropical environments, have a primary importance in preventing flooding and develop absorbent biological richness.

Permaculture, an organic form of cultivation with minimal input, optimizes biodiversity via a variety of perennial plants and the recycling of water. This system makes a good sponge and often uses water features.

Swamps, marshes, ponds, bogs, and wetlands all encourage the richest diversity of fauna and flora, starting with the tiniest forms of life at the base of the food chain—bacteria, bugs, insects, and microscopic invertebrates. They are essential in a system of water purification and recycling but have been disappearing from Europe as demand for commercial use of the land increases. With their return, septic tanks and human effluent can be treated by horizontal or vertical flow reed beds, wherein plants take oxygen down to the roots to aerate the water. Toxic farm effluent can be treated by serpentine channels of ditches planted with willow. A staircase of flowforms can oxygenate and energize the cleaned water.*

We have all heard that Earth is warming at an alarming rate, unprecedented for many thousands of years. The increase in CO_2 emissions is the main contributor, but this is exacerbated by secondary negative feedback mechanisms that act like a row of dominoes pushing each other over. For example, warming in the Arctic tundra melts the permafrost, which releases vast stores of methane (the most powerful greenhouse gas) that have been safely locked up for millennia, which accelerates global warming, and so on in a relentless cycle.

REGIONAL PROBLEMS

The need for fresh water is as universal as the obstacles to a sufficient supply, the difference being that Man creates most of the obstacles.

---

*The Water Association (1992) is a pioneering European group of like-minded scientifically trained innovators of sustainable systems for purifying and reenergizing waste water with reed beds, ditches, flowforms, and other water resources.

Australia

The early colonists destroyed the land's water balance and soil fertility by draining wetlands to create pasture and cropland, then exacerbated the problem with artificial fertilizers. Victoria's rivers were systematically cleared of debris, which affected the biological balance of the region, encouraging invasive species. Without logs and other materials that create turbulence and deep holes, which are important for fish to thrive, the Murray/Darling river system has been overwhelmed by invasive carp, destroying the biodiversity of the water species.[3]

The Australian subcontinent has been experiencing a warming trend for thirty to forty years, the past eleven of which have brought severe drought conditions to the south and parts of the eastern coast (see plate 25). Significantly, the per capita consumption of water is the highest in the world, yet Australia is also the driest continent.

A campaign for stringent water conservation and rainwater harvesting for use in cooking, washing, and cleaning has been implemented in the cities. When properly filtered, this water is also used for drinking. The national norm is a three-minute maximum for showering, and no car washing. Many people have installed septic tank systems with aerobic digesters and filters that recycle toilet water many times over.

Some authorities are experimenting with solar power desalination plants to convert seawater into drinking water. Australian climatologists believe that drought conditions will persist and worsen. When Ross Young, executive director of the Water Services Association, was asked what can be learned from the Australian experience, he wrote in *The Australian:* "When climate change begins to have an impact on water supplies, it does so in a far more rapid and dramatic manner than any of the experts ever predicted. That's why everyone must be proactive."

The El Niño phenomenon, when the temperature of the Pacific tropical ocean current becomes much warmer (see box), is usually identified as the cause of Australia's drought in the north and east in the past forty years. The Murray-Darling basin, which accounts for 41 percent of the nation's food production, has been particularly badly affected. The basin covers an area of more than one million square kilometers, with a catchment from Queensland's tropical north to the Darling River and from the Murray's source in the Snowy Mountains in the east down to South Australia near Adelaide.

El Niño

The phenomenon of El Niño is caused by an oscillation in air pressure and ocean temperature between the eastern and western sides of the tropical Pacific Ocean. Normally pressure and ocean temperature are low off the coast of South America and high in the western Pacific.

The tropical trade winds drive the ocean currents westward across the Pacific Ocean, bringing rainfall to Indonesia and eastern Australia and helping to create the monsoon in the Bay of Bengal.

With El Niño the trade winds weaken or switch to westerly, and the ocean temperature in the eastern part of the tropical Pacific can be 6°C (10°F) higher. This changes rainfall patterns so that in general, western-facing coasts receive more rain and eastern-facing coasts can experience drought. Previously El Niño occurred every five or so years. Now it can occur several years running, with increasing severity.

Deforestation weakens the evapotranspiration cycle of the tropical rain forest that pulls in the trade winds from the Atlantic. As a result of rising ocean temperatures and deforestation, El Niño more frequently brings drought to eastern Australia and Brazil, warmer winters in the Pacific northwest and northern midwestern states of the United States, winter downpours in central and southern California, and disruption of the vital Indian monsoon. Climate scientists warn that the increasing frequency of El Niño in the 2010s will exacerbate global warming.

La Niña is the opposite oscillation in air pressure and ocean temperature to El Niño. During La Niña the eastern Pacific Ocean temperatures may be 6°C (10°F) lower than average. Its effects on rainfall across the world are the opposite to those of El Niño.

In 1949 the federal government created the Snowy hydro scheme to generate hydroelectric power and capture water from the spring snowmelt in two large lakes in order to regulate the flow of the Murray River so that farmers downstream could draw water for irrigation in their dry summers. For a time this worked well, but the allocations were not scaled down as the drought began to set in, and a combination of overextraction and decreasing winter rainfall has reduced the Murray to a trickle that often does not reach the ocean.

Australia's experience of such a prolonged dry spell may be a fore-taste of what is to come. Tim Flannery, the Australian climate change guru, believes that crippling drought could now happen in other parts of the world, including northern India, northern China or western America, precipitating widespread water crises.

Asia

Pakistan's Indus Valley has been dry for centuries, and with increasing industrialization, underground water sources are becoming seriously overexploited. In both Pakistan and southern India, the introduction of industrialized agriculture and water-hungry industries (such as Coca-Cola) have increased water stress in a region where rainfall is becoming more unpredictable.

Climate change is particularly worrying in northern India. Across the country, from Gujarat to Hyderabad, and in Andhra Pradesh, "the rice bowl of India," the monsoon season figures fell 43 percent.[4] There are reports of communities at war, and of some who were drawing water being "hacked to death by angry neighbors accusing them of stealing water."[5] In Bhopal, where 100,000 people depend on water tankers, fights break out regularly.

Northern China suffers from the most serious water stress situation, especially around Beijing, which has seen enormous population growth and industrialization. The water table in the region has been shrinking alarmingly, about a foot a year for the past ten years.

An ambitious plan to bring water from the moist Yangtze basin in the south to the dry lands above the Yellow River was envisioned by Mao Zedong in 1962. Plans included building three channels, each more than six-hundred-miles long. These would be twice the cost of the Three Gorges dam, and three times the length of the railway to Tibet. Ecological, political, and financial pressures have delayed the project. One reason is that the pollution of the Yellow River is very serious, and regional political authorities feel their needs are greater than those of the northern cities.[6] China's great push toward record economic growth could become stalled for want of sufficient water for its people and its industry.

India has a particular problem, as its traditional sustainable farming has been the target for the water-hungry "green revolution" chemical technologies in the West (see box). Add to this genetically engineered monoculture planting, and there is a serious water shortage.

The Case for Biodiversity

The chemical monocultures of the Green Revolution use ten times more water than biodiverse ecological farming systems. World Bank funding to mine groundwater resources has exacerbated the water famine. Indian governments are continually in collusion with multinational companies that would like to industrialize Indian food production. There remains congenital skepticism in international agricultural agencies regarding maximizing biodiversity and organic matter in the soil (destroyed by chemicals), which simultaneously increases climate resilience and both food and water security. The effect of the 2009 monsoon pointed up the dangers of this intransigence.[7]

Europe

The Mediterranean countries will become hotter and even drier. Spain in particular has been feeling the change already. In 2007 the country suffered its worst drought in sixty years. Catalonia, of which Barcelona is the capital, has been worst hit, with its reservoirs almost empty. In May 2005 this city chartered six huge tankers to bring fresh water to alleviate the shortage. Spaniards must become better water misers.[8]

In Greece, Athens experienced frightening fires in 2009. There is danger that the damaged land could degrade into desert unless it is quickly reforested. Tree planting is always the best protection against climate change in warm climates.

Britain is predicted to have wetter winters and hotter summers. It will certainly be subjected to more violent weather, with floods, storm surges, coastal erosion, and flooding. If the Gulf Stream slows down much more than it already has, the British Isles may lose some of the warmth it has taken for granted for several millennia. The position of these islands at the boundaries of several climate systems makes the changes they face more unpredictable.

North America

Most climatologists agree that the interior of the United States will receive less rain, creating serious problems for food production. Southern California and the Southwest, and states west of the Rockies, are already experiencing droughts. There is likely to be an increase in the number and severity of typhoons and hurricanes.

In 2009 the first hearing of the world's top scientists to the U.S. Congress warned of severe droughts throughout the west, searing heat in the cities, dropping water levels on the Great Lakes, and increasing heat-related health problems. Big battles are foreseen between the Democratic leadership alerted by concerned scientists and climate-change-denying politicians.[9]*

One consequence of these droughts, exacerbated by population increase and poor land management, is an increase in dust storms.

---

*In 2009 Christopher Field of the Carnegie Institute of Science testified: "With severe drought from California to Oklahoma, a broad swath of the southwest is basically robbed of having a sustainable lifestyle. We are close to a threshold in a very large number of American cities where uncomfortable heat waves make cities uninhabitable. Sacramento could face heatwaves for up to one hundred days a year."

When dust settles on mountain snowpack that normally reflects the sun's heat back into space, premature melting of the snow takes place, which changes the blossoming and growing times of vegetation.[10]

Many coastal cities, such as New York, Los Angeles, Seattle, and Portland, will be at risk from rising sea levels. Much of Florida is low lying and will gradually be flooded by a rising sea level. In addition, the coast between New York and South Carolina is falling at about fifteen centimeters (about six inches) a century, due to isostatic adjustment after the last ice age, which means greater loss of coastlands here.[11]

Reduction in the Polar Ice Caps

How could the optimum climate be designed to encourage maximum biodiversity (the evolutionary imperative) and favor the emergence of *Homo sapiens*? And while we're at it, one that is self-correcting in the event of variation in the sun's radiation? By creating polar ice caps!

The polar ice sheets have existed for the past ten million years and have coincided with the development of unprecedented biodiversity. Tropical and temperate forests have flourished, with great fertility and soil depth in the temperate latitudes. The balance between hot, humid tropical latitudes and polar ice has allowed temperate climates to develop in the middle latitudes. This period has also seen the emergence of higher mammals and hominids. Will they have a future if the ice caps disappear?

The climate of the past few thousand years has been very kind to humanity, allowing us to spread to almost every corner of the globe. With the availability of fossil fuels, we have enjoyed optimum conditions. This will all soon change. A shift in global temperatures reduces the range of environments that can sustain human life. During the past ice age when the average world temperature was 4°C (39°F), humans were restricted to the warmer lower latitudes. Global warming will have the opposite effect, driving people to cooler higher latitudes.

The initial cause of climate change is generally acknowledged to be an increase in greenhouse emissions. When the average increase in global temperature exceeds 3°C (5°F), the remains of the equatorial rain forests are likely to die off, completing the process we have initiated through mindless deforestation. The forests' destruction may turn out to be a more potent cause of world climate change than CO_2 emissions and will make the equatorial climate more extreme and all climates less predictable.

The warming effect of climate change has been most marked in the Arctic, where it has been three times the rate of Earth as a whole.* The sea ice has been shrinking in the summer months at an unprecedented rate.[12] The Northwest Passage linking the North Atlantic to the Bering Strait, and onward by the Northeast Passage to Europe, is predicted to be navigable within a few years.†

The sea ice shelf reflects most of the sun's radiation (once again, the albedo effect). Its melting allows the Arctic Ocean to absorb the sun's heat, a positive feedback effect that cumulatively, year by year, accelerates the rate of warming in the Arctic and releases methane from the sea bottom (see box on p. 60). Greenland's glaciers and ice cap are melting at an ever-increasing rate, causing enormous pools of fresh water that could close down the Gulf Stream if they escaped from the Arctic basin, south of the Spitzbergen ridge. The melting of all of Greenland's ice would raise world sea levels by more than seven meters (twenty-three feet), inundating most coastal cities and fertile agricultural land. The Antarctic ice cap is melting at the edges, its rate currently predicted to be much slower than that of Greenland's ice.

---

*It is more marked than in the Antarctic because most of the world's CO_2 emissions originate in the Northern Hemisphere.

†A German plan to build the most advanced polar research vessel in the world is being funded by the European Commission, to be commissioned in 2012. The research icebreaker *Aurora Borealis* will have a multifunctional role of deep-sea drilling and supporting climate/environmental research in both Arctic and Antarctic regions. See http://eri-aurora-borealis.eu.

The Methane Threat

Crystalline methane hydrides are also deposited on the continental shelves, especially off the eastern coasts of North and South America. They are stable within a limited temperature range, but it is believed they could be suddenly released if the sea temperature rose to a critical level. No one knows just what that tipping point might be, but when it comes, the release of methane would be fast and catastrophic to global warming levels, as methane is a twenty times more powerful greenhouse gas than CO_2.

The IPCC (International Panel on Climate Change), which revises its predictions regularly, now looks toward an earlier dramatic rise in sea level. Their reports look optimistic because they are usually already out of date when published. Warming of the ocean also increases its volume. The IPCC estimates that, by midcentury, significant flooding of centers of population will have started. Minute changes in ocean temperatures have a dramatic effect (see plate 26).

PORTENT OF THE SIXTH MASS EXTINCTION?*

We understand very little about the oceans, which contain 90 percent of Earth's biomass. Barely 1 percent of their life-forms have been identified and studied. Only recently we have learned that they absorb more CO_2 than land vegetation, especially in colder waters. The oceans' ability to absorb CO_2 will be compromised by temperature rise. New research indicates that the Arctic Ocean is becoming more acidic as the CO_2 discharged from the water is turning into carbonic acid, posing a threat to the important base of the oceanic food chain, the phytoplankton, which thrive in cold water (see the following box).

*See the geological time chart, figure 2.1, which shows the timing of the five previous mass extinctions.

The Growing Acid Problem in the Arctic Ocean

Professor Jean-Pierre Gattuso of the Centre National de la Récherche Scientifique at a European Commission "Oceans of Tomorrow" international conference in Barcelona, October 6, 2009, reported research from Svalbard (Spitzbergen) projecting that the Arctic Ocean will be 10 percent corrosively acidic by 2018, 50 percent by 2050, and 100 percent by 2100. This has the most serious implications for ocean biodiversity, because the bottom of the food chain, from small mollusks to the vast numbers of zoo-plankton, will be particularly vulnerable and would not survive such changes. Acid dissolves the bony structure of these tiny animals. Bioengineering technology to solve this crisis was discussed at the conference but quickly dismissed as impractical. Probably the only way to slow this collapse is the immediate abandonment of fossil fuels and/or the precipitate reduction of the human population to a third of its present level. The Northern Hemisphere receives the most human-produced CO_2, but we should expect this phenomenon to spread later to the Southern Hemisphere.[13]

This could lead, later this century, to a collapse of the rich biodiversity of the oceans, which would affect biodiversity on the land (as part of the same biosphere), already suffering under unprecedented species loss. The implications of species loss are apocalyptic.

The Great Barrier Reef, one of the Seven Wonders of the Natural World, has one of the greatest densities of biodiversity, including many endangered species. It has already suffered bleaching from increased sea temperatures, and a number of scientists have predicted its demise as a living habitat as soon as 2020.

MAN'S IMPACT ON THE EARTH

Some geologists are now calling the past 12,000 years the "Anthropocene period" (human-influenced), because in these years humankind has completely changed the face of Earth and altered its climates, and has precipitated a species collapse. This began with the wholesale deforestation that accompanied the development of agriculture, which caused a release of CO_2 from plants and soil into the atmosphere. Geologist and television host Iain Stewart believes that this gradual increase in greenhouse gases has maintained the momentum of the present interglacial period, which otherwise would probably have ended by now.

Agriculture brings with it significant loss of topsoil and reduction in fertility, as well as, in modern times, widespread pollution of the water table. It is insatiable in its demand for water. We have disrupted the great natural water cycles, and the only major rivers that maintain their energy levels and flow naturally are in the remote tundra areas of northern Canada and Siberia.

The past 12,000 years, with the tectonic uplift of the Himalayas and other more recent Asian mountain systems (augmented by the still orogenically active older Rockies and Andes), have also seen a great increase in the amount of weathered minerals deposited on the land and in the oceans. Stewart suggested in his BBC television series, *How Earth Made Us,* that these deposits, by enhancing carbon sequestration, must have been helping to keep the planet cool and fit for life.

WATER AS A SOURCE OF ENERGY

Wind power has claimed the greater part of investment in renewable energy. Its main disadvantage is the intermittency of effective wind. On the other hand, water provides a much more reliable source. Small-scale hydroelectric plants were common on private estates a century ago, and larger systems came in the 1930s. The mammoth projects have had a damaging effect on the environment, from the Hoover Dam built on the Colorado River in the 1930s, to the Three Gorges hydroelectric project on the Yellow River in China.

The development of wave and tidal power projects have been slower because of necessary research in the siting of projects, and higher development cost of the machines. But there is no reason why costs will not come down for sites such as the Pentland Firth off the Orkney Isles, the Severn Estuary in the West of England, or the Bay of Fundy off Nova Scotia, all of which have tremendous potential for energy generation. We'll need all the renewable potential we can find to replace fossil fuel sources.

Viktor Schauberger developed implosion machines that produced power multiples in excess of conventional generators. They were not very stable, and nobody has yet been able to replicate them. Both Viktor and his son Walter said the problems people encountered stemmed from trying to build these appliances without the humility to first study and learn from Nature.*

Some have developed simple adaptations of automobile engines to run on hybrid fuels—water and gasoline, or even water alone (through hydrogen generation or "Brown's gas"). There is even intriguing research indicating that salt water can be ignited when exposed to a radio frequency beam. I believe that when the time is right and we are ready, Nature will release some of her secrets for power generation.[14]

---

*Both Viktor and Walter Schauberger criticized people who tried to produce "free" energy with no understanding of what was involved. They claimed that the energies of the fifth and six dimensions require a state of humility and commitment in order to be cooperative.

EIGHTEEN

THE FUTURE OF FOOD PRODUCTION

Organic soil has a greater capacity to retain water and nutrients, such as nitrogen. It contains significantly more nutrients—vitamin C, iron, magnesium, and phosphorus—and is significantly lower in nitrates than conventionally tilled soil. Organic soil is also more efficient as a carbon sink, and organic management saves on fossil fuels.

MAE-WAN HO, *FOOD FOR THE FUTURE*

The availability of water for growing food will be one of our greatest challenges going forward. We have seen the way water works in the natural environment and in organisms. Above all, we have seen the importance of the water cycles. Nature is the great conservator, the recycler, never wasting energy. One might even suggest that man invented the second law of thermodynamics in order to justify his prodigal, unthinking ways.

We shall end this last part of the book by meeting head on the real issue of what we do with our water, for at least two-thirds of our precious fresh water goes to food production. The way we use water for agriculture clearly illustrates how our present way of thinking and dependence on unsustainable practices is our own undoing.

WORLD FOOD TRADE DISTORTS WATER RESOURCES

It takes massive amounts of water to produce food. This is called virtual water. North America is the biggest exporter of virtual water, followed by South America and Africa. Asia and Europe, as a whole, are not importers. A net exporter, like Spain, which is suffering from increasing water shortage, actually exports water it needs for itself via its food exports. The water resources of a country like Britain, which is a net importer of food, will suffer more water shortage when it is forced to grow more of its own food as rising oil costs make long-distance shipping too costly.

THE PRACTICE OF IRRIGATION

Earth has accessible water storage systems in its lakes and groundwater. Most of its subterranean water is too deep to exploit, but for millennia, Man has been boring into the earth to obtain water. In earlier times, when food growing methods were less demanding, it was a sustainable practice; we borrowed in lean times, and it was topped up in times of plenty. However, the great continental aquifers (which are mostly at least a million years old) are now being dangerously depleted, especially in North America, China, and Australia.

From 60 to 70 percent of the total fresh water we use goes to agriculture, and in many parts of the world demand outstrips sustainable supply. Irrigation from rivers is the main source, which is often wasteful—much of the water is lost to evaporation and fails to reach plant roots.

Our freshwater use is increasing at twice the rate of population increase in many parts of the world. Climate change will redistribute rainfall and overconsumption threatens the world's natural storage systems. It is difficult to see how the required revolution in our awareness can take place while the population time bomb is ticking away.

The likelihood of water wars has become a frequent topic of debate. Until humanity learns that negotiation is more effective than aggression, neighboring countries will compete to control the waters of a shared river, and the increasing scarcity of water will trigger conflicts greater than the ones already happening over oil.

The next generation will see the biggest revolution in agriculture and food production that the world has experienced for a century. The rise of industrial farming techniques of the past one hundred years has been totally dependent on cheap and easily available oil. World production of oil has now peaked, and demand is starting to overtake supply. Future supplies will be of poorer quality, at escalating cost, and subject to tricky geopolitical bartering with those nations that have oil reserves they prefer to retain for their own long-term needs.

Modern farming is highly mechanized and uses complex machinery that demands large amounts of fossil fuels to manufacture. Even more desperately, modern agriculture depends on oil-based chemicals—fertilizers, pesticides, insecticides, and herbicides.

An additional danger is the rush to produce genetically modified crops and transgenic foods using inadequately researched technologies, backed by opportunistic politicians and reductionist scientists who refuse to heed the Pandora's box of dangers involved.*

The damage that industrial farming has done to the world environment is incalculable. It's caused massive soil erosion and loss of biodiversity, fertility, and rainfall; desertification; pollution of the water table; species' loss; mudslides and flooding; and loss of woodland and forest. There is so much power vested in the industry that a voluntary change to sustainable practice is unlikely.

If you can't see the consequences of your actions, if all your life you've held a myopic worldview, a change to the long view would be like St. Paul's conversion on the road to Damascus—and probably unlikely to happen. Our exploitation of fossil fuels is reaping its own rewards and most economic activity will have to localize, including food production, and revert to more labor-intensive patterns.

---

*Mae-Wan Ho, in her book *Genetic Engineering: Dream or Nightmare?*, describes the large-scale release of transgenic organisms as "much worse than nuclear weapons as a means of mass destruction—as genes can replicate indefinitely, spread, and recombine."

READING THE LANDSCAPE

If only we could see that water is the essential lifeblood of the planet and cannot be separated from the natural environment, we could then start to work with Nature, whose husbandry of water is so efficient.

To be effective, water management has to take into account the whole ecosystem. Above all, there must be an awareness of the natural landscape, which over the ages develops a balance among woodland, wetlands, naturally flowing streams, lakes, and natural drainage. What modern farming at all scales tends to do is heedlessly impose a totally foreign and highly manipulative imprint on the landscape, the health of which is consequently bound to deteriorate.

On this planet of water, it comes as no surprise that the land skin is water-dependent. Its absence causes desertification. It's not always clear when important water cycles are disrupted by human activities, but the overall health and fertility of an ecosystem is usually dependent on the relationship between the river and the landscape through which it flows.

Australia has one of the worst records of land exploitation in modern history.[1] The first European explorers, before 1850, described the southern part of the country as verdant forest and sweet rivers. Deforestation and extractive agricultural practices and overstocking have transformed much of the subcontinent into an arid, infertile land. It is probable that the twelve-year drought that the wheat-producing region of the Murray-Darling basin has been suffering would not have been so bad without that history.

The early European settlers in Australia didn't like standing water. They drained the upland ponds and marshes, created irrigation canals, and hastened stream flow in this once-fertile area, not realizing that these manipulative practices would destroy the fertility and biodiversity, reduce balanced rainfall, cause eroded gullies and excessive salinity, and isolate the rivers from the landscape.

Thoroughbred-horse breeder Peter Andrews was brought up near Broken Hill and learned from Aboriginal elders how to read a landscape to learn where water wanted to flow. Thirty-five years ago, when he acquired 20,000 acres of grazing property in the Upper Hunter Valley, New South Wales, he knew what he had to do to revive the seriously degraded landscape. It took him several years to determine where the water had flowed when the land was healthy. He led the water back to those places and reconnected the streams to the flood plain, so that they could bring minerals and energy to nourish plant life.

This was not an expensive operation; it was sustainable and required no chemicals or costly engineering. The secret was to restore the natural pathways of water in the valley; to slow them down and allow them to re-create ponds, marshes, and riparian vegetation—all the elements that produce a healthy and biodiverse sponge that would restore fertility to the floodplain and slowly release water in times of drought, keeping the underground salts at bay.

The result is that in today's severe drought in the Murray-Darling basin, Andrews's land is a green oasis surrounded by aridity. Political bureaucracies and agricultural establishments have difficulty understanding the idea of wholeness of the land. Having fought official skepticism for a generation, his patience is being rewarded with acclaim from many quarters that recognize his natural-sequence farming methods as the answer to the challenge of climate change.[2]

It is nothing short of miraculous that water seems to have an innate knowledge of what functions to perform in each environment that it molds. But water is also the servant of Nature. This becomes apparent when we allow Nature to reclaim land that has been manipulated by Man. In the extreme case of chemically fertilized industrial farming it becomes a desert devoid of singing birds and fluttering butterflies.[3] When the rainfall becomes adequate, the reclaimed land soon becomes vibrant with life.

Water is sick (see Attenborough quotation on page 146) because we prevent it from doing what it must to promote and nourish life. What is desperately needed is a new profession of water wizardry for committed people who will develop the skills of the Aborigine shaman, the insights and understanding of quantum biology, and the vision and passion of Viktor Schauberger.

Nature has always ensured that the water planet has sufficient fresh water to nourish all life. Much of this needs to be stored in wetlands, marshes, lakes, and glaciers to be available during dry periods.

BIOLOGICAL AGRICULTURE

Healthy topsoil is the most important ingredient in sustainable agriculture. Topsoil is created by decayed vegetable matter and can vary in depth from a few centimeters to several meters. Forests created the deep soils of the world over millennia, but many of these have shrunk by as much as 80 percent in the past two hundred years.

Under natural conditions, friable soil is populated with a multitude of microbial and invertebrate fauna and is usually capped with a layer of humus, formed from decomposing leaves and other vegetable matter that retains water and is a valuable protection against drought. This rich mixture of life-forms comprises a processing factory essential to soil health and fertility, and everything should be done to help it flourish. We can never put enough organic material on the soil. Turning over or digging into the topsoil disturbs this rich biological treasure chest. The use of powerful modern tractors has turned the ancient art of plowing into land abuse. In the more purist forms of biological agriculture, a no-dig practice is being rediscovered.

Intensive farming practices have led to the exhaustion of the soil's minerals and dependence on artificial fertilizers. These destroy the rich biodiversity upon which the soil's fertility and the vibrancy of its energy depend. The land becomes a diversity desert, without earthworms, bees, birds, insects, or wildflowers.

Industrialized farming (at least 90 percent of total agriculture in most countries—more than 97 percent in the United Kingdom) is dependent on the chemical fertilizers nitrogen, phosphorus, and potassium (NPK) that have escalated in cost with the rise in the price of oil, and which are becoming uneconomical to use. It is also highly dependent on oil as a fuel for machinery and transport, and has a high consumption of electricity. The rise in costs through peak oil (when demand overtakes supply) is already beginning to hit conventional farming. Since it is doubtful we can develop sufficient alternative supplies to replace the vanishing oil and natural gas, we urgently need to develop new farming methods.

Governments, advised as they are by large corporations and their compliant scientists, seem blind to our approaching crisis of energy and food supplies. The food supply is 80 percent controlled by supermarkets that operate on a "just-in-time" basis and long supply lines that require heavy fuel consumption.

Are we prepared with an alternative? Growers with any foresight should be converting to organic, low-input methods. Organic methods of cultivation favor small-scale units that can supply local demand and are more energy- and water-efficient, and generally more productive.[4]

SOIL REMINERALIZATION

Agriculture was developed in the Middle East's Fertile Crescent, which benefited from annual floods that carried minerals down from the mountains. The early colonizers of the New World had the advantage of mineral-rich soils that had never been cultivated. In Europe, however, where cultivation had proceeded for centuries, the soil was becoming depleted of minerals. This was aggravated by the intensive farming practices introduced in the mid-twentieth century.

In 1894 an agricultural chemist, Julius Hensel, published *Bread from Stone,* a book that described the beneficial effects of fertilizing with rock dust, a by-product of highway building. His book was bought up and destroyed by the new chemical fertilizer companies that feared a threat to their profitable businesses.

Rock dust is composed of finely ground, mainly igneous rocks, such as granite and basalt, that ideally are ground in a cold process that retains the rocks' inherent energies. Because of their broad range of minerals, trace elements, and salts, when spread on the ground the dust encourages a wealth of different microorganisms.

Remineralization with rock dust was practiced in Switzerland 160 years ago. Its reintroduction was encouraged by *The Survival of Civilization,* a book written by John Hamaker and Don Weaver in 1975. They describe the importance of mineral and trace elements to plant growth and quality. Hamaker describes how he was able to use rock dust to increase the depth of the topsoil at his Michigan home, from about 10 centimeters (4 inches) to about 1.2 meters (4 feet) over a period of ten years. My wife has found that sprinkling rock dust on her garden beds has substantially increased the quality and size of her vegetables. Rock dust is normally available as a by-product of road metal quarries.

Rock dust has paramagnetic qualities—a weak attraction to a magnet, which increases the soil's ability to attract and hold energy. Water has a diamagnetic charge, a weak magnetic charge that repulses a magnet. The dynamic interplay between paramagnetic and diamagnetic (yang and yin) energies introduces productive oscillating energy effects in the soil.*

ORGANIC FARMING

Organic farming uses manure, farmyard slurry, and composted vegetable matter to increase the soil's fertility.† The introduction of chemical fertilizers in the nineteenth century quickly supplanted traditional

---

*The ancient round towers found in Ireland are thought to have been built to enhance the fertility of the soil by creating paramagnetic (yang) energy, which originates in the sun, whereas plants produce diamagnetic (yin) energy, stimulated by water (see Alanna Moore, *Stone Age Farming*).

†The use of human night soil is still widespread. According the *National Geographic* (June 12, 2010) nearly 200 million farmers in Tibet, Nepal, China, India, Vietnam, sub-Saharan Africa and Latin America feritilize their food crops with untreated human waste.

organic methods because it was much less labor intensive and appeared to give higher crop yields. A few farmers retained the traditional methods, and as evidence has accumulated about chemical pollution of the water table and rivers, there has been a renaissance of organic farming in the past fifty years.

The sustainability of organic farming derives from the recycling of organic material to maintain its fertility, just as it occurs in a natural forest. Modern organic composting tends to use green vegetable matter rather than dried, interleaved with layers of earth. Significant heat is generated in the pile with this method. Viktor Schauberger believed that since heat discourages earthworms, the resulting compost will not be of the best quality. His preference was for a cold process that produces a higher content of protein and immaterial, or "fructigenic," energies. He also believed it important to protect the compost from element-hungry juvenile rainwater that tends to leach nutrients.

Organic farming is more labor intensive than conventional. It requires greater strength than driving a tractor. A shift to organic would demand substantial numbers of younger people to become growers (in Britain the average age of farmers is more than sixty years). Organic agriculture and localized food systems mitigate 30 percent of the world's greenhouse gas emissions and save one-sixth of present energy consumption.[5]

It is such a threat to the trillion-dollar agricultural industry and to the trillions invested in genetic modification that they are disseminating misinformation and lies about organic farming and its ability to feed the world safely and sustainably, further delaying the change we so urgently need.

PERMACULTURE

In Australia in the mid 1970s, Bill Mollison and David Holmgren were the first to formalize a system of "permanent agriculture," which had earlier been described by American agricultural scientist Franklin

Hiram King in the early 1900s. They coined the term *permaculture* and based their system on the notion that if people were to feed themselves sustainably, they would need to reduce reliance on industrialized agriculture. Where industrial farms use technology powered by fossil fuels and each farm specializes in producing high yields of a single annual crop, permaculture stresses the value of low inputs and a rich mixture of perennial crops. The method is particularly suited to small holdings.

A permaculture garden is often created for a specific family or community. Ideally it is designed in the form of a forest garden in which trees are spaced to allow vegetables or fruit bushes to grow in between. As nearly as possible, the design is predicated on what Nature prefers, above all stressing biodiversity. Worms turn the soil, Nature provides fertilizers, and the biological diversity attracts a rich bird and insect life, all of which contrive to produce abundant crops.

A permaculture garden may look messy and disorganized, but it is planned with great forethought; the better the plan, the less upkeep is required. Typically hand tools are used. Every plant is important in some way: some provide essential nutrients like potassium, nitrogen, or phosphorus; others control pests, attract beneficial insects, or retain moisture. Plants may be grown in tiers to increase the density of food production.

The productive garden has great biodiversity and teems with life and health. An acre of garden designed for maximum production can feed ten people—double the output of a conventional farm. Grains may be less easy to grow, but a four-acre nut wood can produce two tons an acre, as much as four acres can produce of organic wheat.[6]

The Transition Network model for meeting the crisis of oil depletion encourages an abundance of small-scale home and market gardens for food production, which maximizes localized production and challenges the hidden costs of transporting food over large distances to their place of consumption.

Recently, permaculture has become a significant subject in university curriculum. It goes beyond food production to cover all the issues of community and a sustainable society and was the impetus for the Transition Towns movement (see box).

Transition Towns

The Transition Network was formed in 2003 in Totnes, Devon, UK, to meet the twin challenges of peak oil and climate change, emphasizing the values of community strength and self-sufficiency. It has grown quickly and is now helping to transform hundreds of enthusiastic communities in many countries around the world. See www.transitiontowns.org.

NEW MODELS

Mae-Wan Ho has proposed the idea that all sustainable systems act like organisms. They are sustainable precisely because the energy they produce moves in a cycle and is kept within the system, the surplus of one part being used by another, so there is very little waste.

Her Dream Farm 2 is an envisioned model of integrated food and energy systems that operate in an organic circular economy. The central component is a biogas digester that processes livestock manure and wastewater. Biogas is 60 percent methane that is used for cooking, heating, generating electricity, and driving cars. The solid residue is a rich fertilizer for crops and mushrooms.

Wastewater from the digester passes through an oxidizing cleanser with algae that produce oxygen through photosynthesis to oxidize the remaining pollutants. The cleansed water goes into fishponds that supply water to irrigate crops whose wastes go to raise earthworms or compost or are fed back into the digester. Algae from the pond can be harvested to feed hens, geese, and ducks. The remains of the mushroom harvest are fed to livestock, with the crops, and their manure goes back to the biogas digester to complete the cycle.

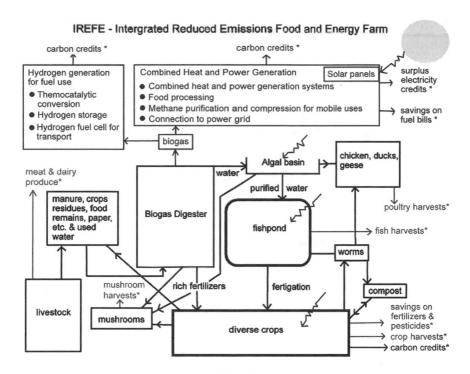

Figure 18.1. Mae-Wan Ho's Dream Farm 2.

Methane production can be augmented with other renewable sources, such as solar panels, windmills, and micro-hydroelectric generators. Such a farm could feed a thousand people and be totally energy self-sufficient. If Dream Farm 2 were universally adopted around the world, it would have the potential to mitigate 56.6 percent of greenhouse emissions and 50.5 percent of energy use.[7]

BIODIVERSITY

Biodiversity is Nature's essential principle, but it can also be appreciated on an energy level. The greater the biodiversity and complexity of interconnections among classes of organisms, the more efficiently is energy exchanged within a system and the higher the quantum effect. The concept of biodiversity is often as poorly understood as that of sustainability, because they are part of a holistic worldview that is difficult for students of our disjointed educational system to understand.

Forests are a powerful energy exchange system because of the extraordinarily rich biodiversity of their fauna and flora. When we degrade our precious forests, the whole environmental system suffers and water supplies are put at risk.

If Nature did not operate on closed energy systems—no waste, everything is recycled—Earth would heat up through entropy (waste energy). In a closed system, one organism's waste is put to use by another, so the energy generated is kept within the family, so to speak.

The problem we face today is of enormous waste of energy from farming systems, transport, building, manufacturing, and power generation, all of which cause entropy and contribute to global warming, apart from the greenhouse gas excesses. Can you wonder why our environment is overheating when the internal combustion engine wastes 70 percent of its energy, and the typical power station delivers only 40 percent of what it generates?

BIODYNAMIC CULTIVATION

It was Rudolf Steiner (see chapter 13), the Austrian teacher and philosopher who founded the spiritual philosophy of anthroposophy, who first introduced biodynamic farming. Its whole-organism approach to cultivation is similar to Schauberger's and designates energy as the primary cause and growth as the secondary effect. While it has been suggested that Steiner and Schauberger exchanged ideas, it is not clear if either influenced the other.

Among biodynamic farming's unique methods is an ancient practice of burying cow horns filled with cow dung (or, alternatively, powdered quartz) deep underground in the autumn. At this season the spiral shape of the horn draws in the active earth energies, transforming its contents into powerful fructigenic energies by the cold process of fermentation, encouraged by lower temperatures. The cow horns are disinterred in early spring, their contents having been converted into a fragrant, highly active substance (see figure 18.2).

This empowered material is the basis of the natural fertilizer known as "500 mix." Since 1947, it has been increasing widely used, and more than 1.25 million acres are fertilized in Australia using this system. The land where it has been spread, when seen from the air, stands out clearly from neighboring farms, due to the much greener pasture. Some cows on farms bordering rancher Alex de Podolinsky's did not eat for two or three days after having broken into the biodynamic farm, so high was the quality of the grass they had consumed.[8]

The 500 mix fertilizer is derived from an ancient Alpine tradition that Schauberger himself once observed being practiced by an

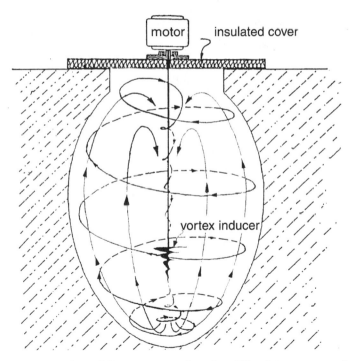

Figure 18.2. An egg-shaped fermentation chamber. This fermentation chamber is buried in the ground. The impeller induces a clockwise rotating vortex into the liquid, which allows the fermentation to draw in geospheric energy from the surrounding ground. (Callum Coats)

old mountain farmer who achieved amazing results from his fertilizer. The principle is similar to that of homeopathy. When a homeopathic medicine is made, the original remedy is stirred and shaken between the dilutions to increase its potency. To make the fertilizer, a small quantity of the converted cow dung is added to water and stirred first in one direction and then in the other, so as to create alternating vortices rotating about the vertical axis of the mixing vessel.

A left-hand vortex builds positive energy, and the right-hand vortex creates a negative energy that draws in the inseminating O_2. The alternating energy charge builds up the inherent energies of the 500 mix. This recalls the alternating left- and right-hand bends in a river building up its energy in a longitudinal vortex (see pp. 94 and 98).

As the vortices are alternately formed and destroyed in the stirring, the level of energy rises and the degree of chaos decreases until, after about an hour, the product is ready for use. This is sprayed on the fields toward evening within two to three hours of preparation and before the accumulated energies have dispersed.

In order to learn to live sustainably, we have first to understand how Nature works and accept her laws. Schauberger's life was devoted to this challenge.

> *The best guarantee that your food will be produced according to environmental and social principles is to meet the people who grow it.*
>
> MAE-WAN HO, *FOOD FOR THE FUTURE*

NINETEEN

THE BIG PICTURE

*A free people can grow only from a free Earth. Any people
that violate Mother Earth have no right to a homeland,
because high-quality races cannot survive in soils destroyed
by speculation, because they are divorced of all connection
with the Earth. Human societies without roots perish. They
have to experience the path of decay until, like unsuitable
fertilizers, they give up their stubborn wills; only then will
they be allowed to start again and re-enter the mighty
course of evolution.*

VIKTOR SCHAUBERGER, IN *IMPLOSION* MAGAZINE

THE HOLISTIC VIEW

If your contact with the environment is limited to what you can see
from your window, your understanding of the world will be minimal.
With the instant global communication we have today compared to a
century ago, you would expect our understanding of the world to be
immensely greater. So how is it that we still find it so difficult to see
the big picture?

Psychologists tell us that within the family is the best place to
appreciate life's lessons and learn to get along with people of different
temperaments, because there is a genetic requirement of mutual support

and protection. The family is an organic unit that encourages holistic interdependence. Frequently, however, dysfunctional family life in our self-absorbed, instant gratification society makes it hard to understand a holistic worldview. A genuine community is more holistic. Most religions and cultures teach holistic behavior, but to follow a way of life in which you value and appreciate every person with whom you come into contact may be idealistic to the point of sainthood.

If we see life systems only in mechanical terms, our worldview becomes blinkered and we are unaware of other levels of connection.[1*] It is the interconnectedness and interdependence of all of life that bring meaning to, and an understanding of, life and evolution. The prevailing worldview of Earth as a mechanism spills over into our need to rationalize every part of a process, a position that is uncomfortable with chicken/egg predicaments. The holistic worldview is more accepting of mysteries, believing that they will release their truth at the appropriate time.

We've talked a lot about holism in this book, but holism is an intellectual concept. Life is about experience, and it is quite difficult to *experience* the "knowing" that everything is interconnected; contemporary values and our education are firmly prejudiced against any such reality. This is the stuff of mysticism. The transpersonal psychologist Abraham Maslow coined the term "peak experience" for those extraordinary moments of insight when we see everything is actually one single reality.

My water epiphany came when I experienced for the first time that I am *embedded* in water. I saw water as the infinite continuum of life in which all living creatures are contained. This was much more powerful than the intellectual idea of being interconnected. "We are all one" because of water (see box).

---

*James Lovelock, on a visit to the Hadley Center, the UK's primary climate research center, while impressed by each scientist's expertise in his own area, noted that there was little overall recognition of Earth as a dynamic system in critical imbalance.

The Water Link

I find being close to horses a bit frightening. The field where I walk regularly has three mares with their growing foals just now. I like to take them apples for a treat, but when all six surround me, they can feel a bit threatening. When I tried to visualize these lovely, powerful animals as part of my family through the water link, they seemed to become more like family and more friendly. This is what you might call a "holistic connection." Try it yourself; it can even work with people.

Other peak experiences may not seem to have a water connection, but I believe they often do, because it is water that enables personal experience and emotions, perhaps prompted by its etheric partner, the divine plan. It might manifest as a sense of wonder at the infinite beauty of the night sky, a glorious sunset, the view from the mountaintop, the singing of a nightingale, or perhaps an insight gained during deep meditation. Any one of these may trigger a very deep sense of longing in our soul, precipitating a change in our priorities and in our life's direction. We may find that we want to help other people or serve the planet.

The challenge lies in knowing how to integrate such experiences into your life. They are a real gift, and to pass up the opportunity for change can be a source of major regret in later years. The highs experienced from taking drugs are less authentic, because they are a "dislocation" and incoherent with the whole organism (the "soul"), seldom bringing such changes to the person involved.

I find the whole story of water to be very exciting, for clearly water is the common denominator of all life, implying that the universe is a single organism, all its constituents being closely interdependent. I'm reminded of a phrase from Douglas Adams, author of *The Hitchhiker's Guide to the Galaxy:* "the fundamental interconnectedness of all things."

THE SEARCH FOR MEANING

For more than 99 percent of humanity's time on this planet we have been closely connected with Nature, which, until modern times, was always considered sacred. The various gods that people worshipped were mostly thought to be part of the natural environment, while the shamanic view was often of the raw power of Gaia. Some religions (for instance, Celtic Christianity) were a blend of pagan belief and more modern monotheism.

The scientific revolution of the Enlightenment brought a rise of secularism and the polarization of religion and science. The Catholic Church, which had had a stabilizing influence on society, lost the support of many people who now considered its doctrines to be controlling and simplistic.

We have created God in our own image, a childlike conception that dilutes our own responsibility and leads to division and wars. We have lost our sense of awe and the belief in a universal power that controls life, which has doubtless contributed to the breakdown in values and morality that we see today.

Humanity seems to be genetically wired to seek meaning in life. Traditionally this has been exercised at the tribal level; mass worship is still the norm in religious groups. Increasingly, however, a more mystical and spiritual form of seeking has emerged, one that transcends the Big Daddy version of the supreme intelligence/creator, yet allows a personal connection with a higher level of consciousness, with more emphasis on contemplation and meditation rather than worship.

One of the by-products of the Enlightenment was the utopian belief that increasing use of technologies could bring about transformation of society. This has encouraged the quick-fix attitude that dominates our policies toward everything from financial problems to global warming. It is the mark of a reductionist worldview.

In contrast, holistic science, especially at the quantum level, can demonstrate a level of meaning in all of life's processes. I can foresee a new spiritual consciousness arising as a result of people rediscovering the sacred in Nature and welcoming the idea of a universal intelligence behind creation, uninfluenced by male anthropomorphic constructions. Indeed, an appreciation of water's part in life is, I believe, the key to a new spiritual worldview.

HOLISM IN SOCIETY

We are mistaken to separate ourselves from the natural environment. As part of the planetary community we are subject to Nature's laws. As the crunch point has arrived for Nature, so it has for our human institutions. If they are not sustainable, they will fail. There is a strong link between sustainability and holism, for both are connected to water's qualities.

Water is the common denominator of all of life, the medium of communication within and between organisms. It is through water that the complex network of life is organized, creating interdependence among all life-forms.

Water is also the model of holism. Through studying water's qualities we can learn how to create sustainable enterprises and communities, where energy produced by one part can be recycled by another (little circles within the whole).

It was Mae-Wan Ho who proposed the model of energy sustainability for organisms that operate efficiently with minimum waste and entropy.[2] Entropy is merely dissipated energy that is useless for doing work and serves only to heat the environment.

As we saw in chapter 18, she applies the same model of zero waste and zero entropy to Dream Farm 2, where all parts of the system feed each other, keeping the energy "in the family."

An example for the sustainable community that fits poet Ben Okri's wish list is that of the transition movement, which was inspired in 2006 by environmentalist Rob Hopkins in response to the twin challenges of diminishing oil supplies (peak oil) and climate change.[3]

Most of us avoid thinking about what will happen when dwindling oil supplies make it too costly to depend on fossil fuels, but the transition movement shows how the profound and inevitable changes ahead can have a positive outcome if we are prepared (see chapter 18). In a Transition Town, people of all ages join to create a cohesive, resilient, self-reliant community that will grow its own food, generate its own energy, use local skills and creative talents, care for its people, and give everyone a sense of engagement and purpose. It is a recipe for increasing optimism in a future for humanity.

As of June 2010, there are 167 Transition Towns in the British Isles, 127 in the United States, and the movement is spreading in Australia, New Zealand, Canada, and Europe. It is a holistic movement in which controlling personalities are discouraged and everyone is encouraged to play a part.[4]

The word *sustainability* is fashionable but often misunderstood. If taking the long view is unfamiliar to you, you probably don't understand the concept. It is more often a rationalization than a heartfelt instinct. The best definition is Mae-Wan Ho's: to think of sustainable systems as organisms, in which all energy is kept within the whole, resulting in zero waste and zero entropy. Surplus energy from one part of the organism is used by another part.

Nature will not tolerate gross inequalities: water's role is to equalize, to level, to stimulate well-being of the whole, not individuals in isolation. Many now believe that inequality contributes more to our social ills and personal disaffections than any other factor.[5]*

The quantum view vindicates traditional values and what are sometimes called "natural laws." Ho made the extraordinary suggestion that

---

*Environmental economist Herman Daly asks: "What is the proper range of inequality (the highest income as a multiple of the lowest)—one that rewards real differences and contributions rather than just multiplying privilege? Plato thought it was a factor of 4. Universities, civil servants, and the military seem to manage with a factor of 10–20. In the U.S. corporate sector, it is 500–1000" ("Toward a Steady-State Economy," *Resurgence*). Endless economic growth, irresponsible banking, and unscrupulous advertising are basically unsustainable. A move away from these toward an awareness of fulfilling the needs of society as a whole would reduce inequalities.

the way coherent organisms become entangled with one another is a model for an idealized human society in which high ethical standards and universal love are accepted as the norm.

Water's fundamental property of holism (the interdependence of all life), was the model for human society until the human ego took over. This model is the ideal integrated community with true sustainability.[6]

SACRED CHAOS

The turmoil of 2008–2010 in the capitalist system—banking, credit, local and international markets, globalization of commerce—showed that our financial systems are unsustainable. The prevailing economic model of unlimited growth confuses money (exchange) with real wealth (goods and services).[7] It produces waste and entropy, compared to a natural system where energy is recycled within the system. True wealth involves the well-being and happiness of society and of the whole planet. Until there is a change in our worldview of the purpose of human society, don't expect our social and economic problems to go away.

CREATIVE PARTNERSHIP

It is clear that organisms, even across genera boundaries, are aware of each other. This awareness very likely comes through a shared grounding in the water element. On the micro level these are mostly electromagnetic relationships, governed by polarities. These polarities are the dynamos of life, creating the great dialectic principles that also carry complementary attributes—positive/negative, light/darkness, good/evil, heat/cold—that must be balanced for an understanding of the whole.[8]

Because the etheric field is universal and water is common in the universe, associated with life or potential life, it seems natural to view them as complementary, working together. In esoteric terms the etheric field (sometimes termed "the God field") may be seen as the masculine, initiating polarity; while water has the receptive, feminine role.

Many religions teach that God cannot act directly on the world stage, but only through incarnate life, which may be the reason for periodic visitations by great teachers to help correct imbalances that inevitably arise where free will is involved.

What Water Can Teach Us

- On a physical level, we are composed of at least 70 percent water. Therefore, just for health reasons, we should be aware of the way that water quality affects our bodies.

- Water is associated with the emotions and with creativity. Becoming more aware of water's dynamic energy will enrich our emotional and creative life.

- Water is the common denominator of all of life, so to understand life, we need to understand water and the sustainability it requires of life. All of life is linked by water—it is what gives humans a sense of connection with Nature and with other animals.

- Water molds the landscape, controls the weather and climate, growth and fertility, health and sickness, harmony and beauty, communication among organisms, pulsation and rhythm. Understanding how this works will help us to be better guardians of the earth.

- The most important lesson is that Nature will not tolerate gross inequalities: water's role is to bring down to size, to level, to stimulate fertility and productivity of the whole, not individuals in isolation.

- Humanity's growth has reached the point of smothering the rest of creation, and with its gross inequalities, human society has failed the test of a sustainable organism.

- Through water, quantum coherent organisms invariably become entangled with one another. A quantum world is a world of universal mutual entanglement, the prerequisite for universal love and ethics. Because we are all entangled, and each being is implicit in every other, the best way to benefit oneself is to benefit the other.

- Thinking like water, our personalities are able to soften, so that we can empathize better with others. Understanding why water flows the way it does will teach us that it is better to "go with the flow."

- An important role of water is to carry an electric charge, which it can do only when impure and unstable. Water teaches us that impurity and instability can stimulate creativity and growth.

- Water adapts itself to the shape of its container. If we are able to adapt to a situation that is presented to us, we will be better able to change negative situations.

- Its balance of flexibility and stability is a metaphor of physical reality and, ideally, of our relationships with ourselves and others.

- In the way it generates equilibrium and harmony, water is a brilliant ecological model. Its movement and rhythm cultivate the beauty of an aesthetic model.

- Water's fundamental property is that of holism (the interdependence of all life), which was the model for human society until individualism became rampant, the ego inflated, and when the lust for (seduction by) wealth and power became dominant. This earlier model is that of the ideal integrated community and of true sustainability.

- Solubility is the capacity to assimilate anything and everything into a context where all can coexist. This essential property of water provides us with a model of the ideal integrated community.

- Humanity's present identification with a mechanistic worldview and the falsity of our social and economic structures make a holistic worldview impossible; water can reveal our denial of the obvious.

- It is the restlessness of water that gives living systems the ability to become ever more complex and to strive toward the perfection they can never reach. As the driver of evolution, water is a model for our own striving, allowing us to evolve through our own mistakes. This is the self-empowerment process of holistic biology.

- Water raises its dynamic energy through turbulence and chaos, which, in the bigger picture, mirrors the turbulence of change in human society.

- The dynamic way that water creates energy shows up our technology's way of generating energy as wasteful, dangerous, and harmful to the environment.
- Perhaps an appreciation of what water contributes to the collective consciousness may help us better understand our own heritage, our past experiences, and our life purpose.

WATER AND CONSCIOUSNESS

The quantum field, the enormous web of interconnected subtle energy that seems to continue infinitely through space, is a kind of communication system, making all of creation aware of itself and its oneness. Viktor Schauberger called it "the eternally creative intelligence," or "the-all-that-is." It is the foundation of consciousness, also known as the "God field."

Some scientists call it the "zero point energy field" (or simply, "the field"), because changes in the field are still detectable at absolute zero when all matter has been removed and no motion is possible. It is now recognized that our concepts of space and time are relevant only at the material and not at the dynamic energy level.

We are clearly at the end of one epoch and embarking, albeit hesitatingly, on a new, uncertain one. The new quantum physics has started to rekindle ideas of a universal consciousness and spirituality. Science is proving the existence of a consciousness-like "God" or eternally creative intelligence, and that the universe does actually have meaning and probably even a purpose. But there is a lot about the traditional knowledge of the hierarchy of energies and dimensions, familiar to esotericists, that the new generation of quantum physicists still has not addressed.

An annual conference in London, called "Living the Field: the Marriage of Science and the Spirit," brings together scientists like David Bohm, Deepak Chopra, Brian Goodwin, Karl Pribram,

Rupert Sheldrake, and Russell Targ to announce these startling discoveries.[9]

To me, the zero point energy field has a certain barrenness about it; it is a cold, mental concept. I feel that it can be brought to life and closer to home with the concept of water as the medium of universal consciousness. After all, we live on such a beautiful planet full of color and diversity, made vibrant by living water.

COSMIC CORRESPONDENCES

Viktor Schauberger demonstrated that Nature's dynamic is the law of polarity. He said that unity of the whole is composed of two opposing qualities in balance. The dance of creation is the harmonious interplay through attraction and repulsion of polarized atoms, without which there would be no water, no plants, nor chemical compounds. The mutual attraction of 2x H and 1x O gives birth to the marvel of water. He showed how the sun, as inseminator of life, carries a positive (masculine) charge, while Earth's energy is receptive and feminine.

Turning around the principle of "as above, so below," it is reasonable to expect that the ultimate cosmic dynamic of life might be such a polarity. Substitute for the sun the etheric field, and for the earth the domain of water, and a whole list of correspondences appears that demonstrates how, even at the cosmic scale, reality and wholeness come with the resolution of the polarity of qualities. The etheric field is the initiator, the water domain the implementer.* Neither can work without the other. That is why I call water the "handmaiden of the etheric."

---

*Callum Coats describes the correspondences as dialectic pairs, which together make a whole (*Living Energies*, 63). John baptized Jesus with water and the spirit, a metaphor for the water domain and the etheric field, which together are unity.

COMPLEMENTARY ATTRIBUTES

The Quantum/Etheric Field	The Water Domain
Sun	Moon
The god field	Earth/Nature
The divine plan	Evolution
Positive/male/yang energy	Negative/feminine/yin energy
Will	Consciousness
Order	Chaos
Laws	Procedures
Initiating	Following through
Impulse	Implement/fulfill
Creating	Sustaining/nurturing
Formative	Relatedness
Detached	Intimate
Intellectual	Emotional
Theory	Practice
Idealism	Beauty
Determination	Appreciation
Goal orientation	Acceptance
Planning	Going with the flow
Implicate	Explicit

WATER AS SPIRITUAL MEDIATOR

This takes us back to what I said at the very beginning, about our collective amnesia and not living up to our potential.

From their inherited traditions, we know that our ancestors, who were self-aware and imaginative, believed in the divine nature of water and had a sense of how it connected all of life—that it is, in fact, a medium of universal consciousness. Even the surviving fragments of dysfunctional indigenous societies of more recent times acknowledge this.

Schauberger and Steiner both said that Earth's water acts as a mediator or transducer between the solar and cosmic energies on the one hand, and the energy of Earth and Nature on the other, to produce productive, balanced energy for the emergence and evolution of conscious life, for all life-forms and life processes.

My personal vision is that living water is the key to evolution, healing, and consciousness. Jesus was baptized with living water. We should venerate it as our forebears did. Having examined the extraordinary roles of water in the initiation, maintenance, and evolution of life, it is not hubris to say that water is the creator of life, for I believe it is the active part of the universal creative intelligence.

We need to have more faith in our instincts. Many of us may have a dim memory of when we were part of Nature. This is in our blood—or should I say, in our water memory! We must tell our children that the universe is a single unity, that all of Nature is one. We have been living under an illusion of separation.

In times like these, when many people are worried about their security, their jobs, and their savings, it is helpful to have a broader view of what life is really about. To contemplate the astronauts' view of the shining blue pearl of Earth, or to gaze up at the resplendent night sky, has a way of putting things in their true perspective. Our individual concerns diminish in the face of the unity of life. This is true holism.

We are beginning to witness a paradigm change in our attitude to all of life and to our worldview, to which an understanding of water as a medium of consciousness contributes substantially. Consciousness shifts at a personal level. Eventually the change in worldview will trickle down to mainstream science, but let's start with you and me.

WATER AND HEALTH

Water plays an essential part in health and healing. It is the source of either good health or of sickness. Our bodies literally run on water, so we ought to be drinking the best-quality water for our health. In developed countries, public water supplies are often unhealthy. They come mostly from underground sources, often laced with agricultural chemicals, heavy metals, and other toxins.

Many of the physical pollutants are filtered out by water authorities, but at the price of adding chlorine, fluoride, or other chemicals that can damage our bodies in the long term. In addition, the subtle energy of these pollutants are not removed by physical filtering and have to be dealt with by a quantum technique (for instance, Nature's method—the vortex).

Tragically, 35 percent of the world's population does not have access to drinkable water, never mind good-quality water.

QUALITIES OF DIFFERENT WATERS

Although good water is tasteless, without color or smell, it quenches our thirst like nothing else. In order to be healthy, we need to drink, according to most authorities, from five to nine pints (one or two liters) of good-quality water a day. Some types of water are more suitable for drinking than others. High-quality water should contain elements of both earth origin (female) and atmospheric (male).

Distilled Water

This is considered physically and chemically to be the purest form of water. Its nature is to extract or attract to itself all the substances it needs to become mature and therefore absorb everything within reach. Such water should not be drunk every day. The Kneipp cure uses distilled water for its short-term therapeutic effect, where it acts to purge the body of excessive deposits of particular substances. There is controversy about its safety. Some medical authorities justify the drinking of distilled water by asserting that only the unusable minerals are leached out of the body. I advise caution.

Rainwater

As long as it has not been affected by industrial pollution (acid rain), rainwater is the purest naturally available water. Though slightly richer through the absorption of atmospheric gases, like distilled water it is still unsuitable for drinking over the long term. When drunk as melted snow, it can also give rise to certain deficiencies; and if no other water is available it can on occasion result in goiter, the enlargement of the thyroid gland.

Juvenile Water

The symbol H_2O represents pure or distilled water. Schauberger called this water juvenile, because it has no developed character or qualities. When it is immature, water absorbs minerals with a voracious appetite, then gives back much-needed nourishment to its environment when it matures as a mountain spring. Juvenile water is immature water from deep underground sources, such as geysers. It has not mellowed sufficiently during its passage through the ground. It has not developed a mature structure and contains some minerals (geospheric elements) but few gases (atmospheric elements), so as drinking water, it is not very high grade (as compared to most spa waters, which arise from mineral rich depths). It becomes mature when it is suitably enriched with raw material, what we call "impurities," on which other organisms depend for their energy and life.

Surface Water

Water from dams and reservoirs contains some minerals and salts absorbed through contact with the soil and the atmosphere. Its quality deteriorates through exposure to the sun, to excessive warming, and to chemicals and other pollutants. Although most urban communities now depend on this source, generally speaking it is not good quality water.

Groundwater

Groundwater has a higher quality due to a larger amount of dissolved carbones and other trace salts.* This is water emanating from lower levels, seeping out at the surface after passage along an impervious rock surface. Often this is now polluted by the chemicals of industrial agriculture.

Spring Water

True spring water has a large amount of dissolved carbones and minerals. Its high quality is often revealed by its shimmering, vibrant bluish color. The product of infiltrating rainwater (with a full complement of atmospheric gases) and geospheric water (full complement of minerals, salts, and trace elements), this is the best water for drinking, and it often retains this quality in the upper reaches of a mountain stream. Commercially bottled spring water is unfortunately not always of the best quality, even if it is bottled in glass rather than the plastic that impairs its quality; and much does not emanate from true springs.

Other Groundwater

Aquifer water is obtained from boreholes and is of unpredictable quality. It may be saline, brackish, or fresh. Water from wells can vary from good to poor, depending on how deep the well is and what stratum of water is tapped. Wells can be polluted by nitrates and herbicides, but they can be purified with a vortex filtration system.

---

*Viktor Schauberger gave the term "carbone" to all the building blocks of matter with the exception of oxygen and hydrogen.

WATER TRANSPORT

It was not until the nineteenth century in Europe that priority was given to building sewers to remove waste. Before then, public hygiene was not a high priority. There was little understanding of the connection between water and health.

The Romans made wooden water pipes to let water "breathe" but drank wine from lead tankards. Pipes made of lead caused much illness for centuries. More recently, iron or steel pipes were lined with aluminum to prevent rust. It is no wonder that we still have a metal toxicity problem with our water supply. Make sure whatever filter you use removes heavy metals (see below).

Bottled Water

The United States spends $16 billion per year on bottled water, and we drink an average of 28.3 gallons per person (2007). With an average price of $1.29 for a 16-ounce bottle, it is far more expensive than gasoline. People seem to believe that bottled water is healthier than what comes from the tap, but this is not necessarily true. There are much stricter regulations regarding tap water purity than there are for bottled water (see box on p. 296). There is little evidence that bottled water is healthier, but this must depend on the tap water being compared. However, it is easy to filter and reenergize tap water to make it healthy and drinkable, and this need not be costly.

Health scares involving some of the better known brands—for example, benzene in Perrier in 1989, bromate in Dasani in 2004, and naphthalene in Volvic in 2005—and the occasional appearance of nitrates don't seem to have deterred people. The temptation to extend shelf life and make the water taste more interesting has led to the addition of preservatives and flavorings (not always listed on the label) that usually come from petrochemicals and often include neurotoxins, carcinogens, benzoates, and artificial sweeteners. Many of the brands have a high mineral content, which, over time, can put a strain on the kidneys.[1] Much commercial bottled water in the

> ### Bottled Water versus Tap Water
>
> The rule that city tap water must not contain E.coli or fecal coliform bacteria does not apply to bottled water, nor is bottled watered required to be filtered or disinfected, as is city water. City tap water is required to meet standards for certain toxic or cancer-causing chemicals, like phthalate (a chemical that can leach from plastic bottles); the industry persuaded the FDA to exempt bottled water from these requirements. Similar rules apply in Britain.
>
> Municipal water supply companies must tell consumers what is in their water. The bottling industry successfully killed this "right to know" requirement for bottled water.

United States is actually tap water that has been refiltered.

Perhaps more obvious, but seldom considered, is the fact that chemicals can leach out of the plastic into the water, particularly in strong light or warmer temperatures, or especially with reuse. Plastic bottles do not easily break down or recycle, so they are a major environmental problem, whether in landfill sites, on beaches, or in the ocean (for instance, the North Pacific gyre) and produce significant pollution when burned.*

If you're going to drink bottled water, choose a glass bottle and don't assume it's always good quality. You can fill a stainless steel screw-top thermos at home to take with you during the day, but glass is really the best type of container to use.

A good water filter, preferably plumbed-in, will remove physical pollutants (check to see what it does and does not remove) and reenergize and restructure the water to deal with the energies of those pol-

---

*Twice the size of Texas, the North Pacific gyre (one of the five major oceanic gyres) is an enormous garbage dump composed mostly of small fragments of plastic. It is formed and maintained by clockwise circulating ocean currents, and is a great hazard to fish and seabirds (nesting seabirds feed these bright bits to their chicks, and the chicks die of starvation).

lutants that the filter can't remove. The cost is a fraction of bottled water.

WATER PURIFICATION

We are all concerned about the quality of our drinking water. We hear that municipal water is recycled in the bigger cities, and in London and New York as many as twenty times. But it is filtered, isn't it? So it must be safe. Yes, it is filtered, but that doesn't remove all the germs, so chlorine is added. Viktor Schauberger did a lot of research on the effects of chlorine. We looked at chlorination and fluoridation in chapter 7.

Alkalinity
A water ionizer separates alkaline from acidic water by electrolysis. The minerals with negative ions (for instance, magnesium and calcium) are attracted by the positive electric anode, making that part of the water alkaline; while the negative cathode attracts the acid part of the water.

Alkaline water has a high oxygen reduction potential (ORP) that can neutralize free oxygen radicals, the source of much disease and premature aging. Many chronic diseases are encouraged by excess acidity in the body, which often stems from poor diet and lifestyle.

Conventional medical opinion is skeptical of the benefits of drinking alkaline water. It would be unwise to make generalizations about its possible benefit, because the reaction must be individual. Too much alkaline water is undoubtedly harmful to some; it must be a question of moderation and balance. Taking it between meals when the stomach acids are less active is preferable. (Alkaline water made from bicarbonate does not have the all-important ORP.)

Distillation
Distillation is an ancient process of vaporizing water so that the pure water molecules are separated as steam from the contaminants, which have a higher boiling point. The steam is allowed to condense through

tubes into another container. The distillation process removes minerals, viruses, bacteria, and any chemicals that have a higher boiling point than water.

It has been used for centuries in the making of whisky and other spirits, and in the 1970s was a popular method of home water purification. Distillation is often used as the preferred water purification method in developing nations or areas where the risk of waterborne disease is high, due to its unique capability to remove bacteria and viruses from drinking water.

However, there are reasons why distillation should not be used to treat water for drinking. It does not remove chemicals that have a lower boiling point than water, such as chlorine or its by-products; or volatile organic chemicals (VOCs), such as herbicides and insecticides, which have a lower boiling point than water. Municipal treatment of water removes bacteria and some heavy metals, but does not remove VOCs; nor does distillation, which many who still use it mistakenly believe.

The mineral-free water produced by distillation is acidic, and can be quite dangerous to the body. Acidic drinking water can dissolve the essential mineral constituents from bones and teeth. In addition, distillation is incredibly wasteful. Eighty percent of the water is removed and discarded with the contaminants, leaving only one gallon of purified water for every five gallons treated. This may be fine with sea water, but not justified with precious fresh water.

Distilled water has an important use in scientific experiments and in some industries that require mineral-free water. It removes heavy metal materials such as lead, arsenic, and mercury; and hardening agents, such as calcium and phosphorous.

Viktor Schauberger was adamant that drinking distilled water was undesirable. He called it "immature" water that is aggressive and "hungry," and can be destructive. When its energy is raised through vorticizing, this unpredictable quality can be magnified (like a young child's). This is why we advise against trying to restructure it through vorticizing. (Distilled water can't be ionized.)

Reverse Osmosis

Reverse osmosis is a modern system for purifying water. It was developed about forty years ago as a treatment for desalinating seawater. It seemed to be the answer for water purification at home, and was popular in the 1970s as a cheaper alternative to distillation.

In natural osmosis, water tends to migrate through a semipermeable membrane from a weaker to a stronger saline solution, balancing the saline composition of each solution. The reverse osmosis process also employs a semipermeable membrane, but water is forced through it under pressure.

The membrane blocks the passage of salt particles, which are physically larger than water molecules. It is widely thought to be the answer to water purification, because it also removes larger particles of other contaminants: lead, manganese, iron, calcium, and the dangerous fluoride that is sometimes added by municipal authorities.

However, there is a downside to this method. Reverse osmosis does not remove smaller particle contaminants, such as VOCs, which include chlorine. Like distillation, reverse osmosis removes alkaline mineral constituents of water and produces the acidic water that can dissolve calcium and other essential mineral constituents from bones and teeth. The removal of trace elements of minerals leaves drinking water tasteless and unhealthy. Taking supplements is not a convincing solution, for they are not delivered in the balanced form the body requires.

Reverse osmosis, although less wasteful than distillation, is still a most inefficient process. On average, it wastes three gallons of water for every one gallon of purified water it produces. Reverse osmosis was not used in Schauberger's day, but his criticisms of distillation would apply to osmotic filters.

WATER FILTERS

There is a wide variety of drinking water filters available, and the ones that cost $340 or more are no better than others selling for less than

$170. You'll need to know the quality and content of your water to choose the appropriate filter. (See Links and Resources.)

A good filter removes bacteria and suspended solids, heavy metals, chlorine and chemicals, and dissolved organic matter. The better brands offer alternative cartridges for specialized problems like fluoride, excessive agrochemicals, and calcium.

The Basic Filter Jug

This type of unit uses granulated carbon. It removes chlorine, some chemicals, mercury, large parasites, and particles. *Advantage:* cheap initial cost. *Disadvantages:* short cartridge life; won't remove bacteria, some heavy metals, asbestos, or radioactive material.

Plumbed-in Filters

Under-sink units come with a separate sink faucet and cartridges (most are easy to install yourself).

- Carbon block and activated carbon filters remove what the basic jug does, and also dissolved organic matter, such as pesticides and other chemicals, oil residues, and some radioactive substances. *Advantages:* usually relatively good value, long-lasting cartridge. *Disadvantages:* some of these do not remove heavy metals, fluoride, or viruses. However, some water filters offer a combination of cartridges that may include removal of: fluoride, nitrates, excess calcium or iron, and heavy metals.
- Ion exchange cartridge removes most heavy metals. It is often incorporated in a general purpose cartridge.
- Ceramic (often silver coated for antibiotic results) removes finer particles than the carbon does. A ceramic filter is usually more expensive.
- Negative ionization makes water more alkaline. It is widely believed that acidity produced by processed foods, drugs, stress, and pollution is a major cause of illness. We take the view, how-

ever, that eating more alkaline food (and less acidic) is a more successful way of balancing the body's pH than through expensive water ionization.

- Magnetizing water breaks up the normally tight structure of water molecules. This allows the body to absorb a greater amount of oxygen and hydrogen. Magnets also reduce the tendency of hard water to deposit chalky sediment. Magnets are also used to increase the efficiency of fuel oils as they also loosen the molecular structure of oils.

- Distillation and reverse osmosis are not recommended, for the reasons given above. The exception would be a specific medical need for immature, pure water. We favor retaining the minerals, salts, and trace elements as far as possible to maintain the water's maturity, while removing the dangerous metals and chemicals. It is really not practical to replace minerals artificially in distilled or osmotic water.

- Shower filter: Most showers use less water than a bath, but we still absorb chlorine and other chemicals through our skin. Chlorine also evaporates as chloroform, which can make us drowsy. A shower filter will greatly reduce these effects. It need not be expensive or reduce the pressure, and should improve alkalinity. If you don't want to plumb-in a whole-house filter, this might be a good idea.

- Point-of-entry whole-house filters provide filtered water to all baths, showers, and washing machines. When you filter all of the water entering your home, you improve not only the healthfulness of the water, but the indoor air quality as well, as it stops chemicals vaporizing (for instance, from your clothes in the washing machine). This reduces the risk of respiratory problems (see box on p. 302). A whole house filter need not be a big investment. Do shop around, because the expensive ones may not be any better than those more reasonably priced. (See Links and Resources.)

- Imploded water energy harmonizerss, produced by the Center for

Implosion Research (CIR), are by-products of Viktor Schauberger's technology. They create highly energized water spiraling in copper tubes that have been formed into beautiful organic sculptures. CIR has energy harmonizers for both personal and environmental protection from electromagnetic pollution. One type will clear algae growth or reduce calcification of water pipes.[2]

Chloroform Gas in the Home

According to the U.S. Environmental Protection Agency (EPA): "Every home in America has an elevated level of chloroform gas present due to the vaporization of chlorine . . . from tap and shower water." Chlorine vapors are an irritant that can cause respiratory problems, such as asthma, bronchitis, and allergies. Point-of-entry, whole-house filtration effectively reduces chlorine, VOCs (volatile organic compounds), and other chemicals that vaporize (for instance, from clothes in the washing machine) and contaminate the indoor air.

Water Restructuring

Nature does not destroy; it recycles. Nature purifies water by means of the vortex (see chapter 12), which raises the dynamic energy level of the water to that approaching, or higher than, our own intercellular water. This is the best form of water to drink. It means that the body will have to work less hard to produce quantum water, and will maintain a higher level of subtle energy in the body.

Some products claim that water spun counterclockwise (left spin) is harmful ("negative"). This is incorrect. Nature's way of raising energy is to induce an oscillating movement alternating between negative (yin) and positive (yang) electromagnetic qualities. (See introduction.) Each change of direction of spin raises the energy slightly, with cumulative effect. With energies, the term "negative" refers to polarity, not to quality (see chapter 19).

There are some filters available that include a vortexing function, but they are expensive and may not do what you want. In our house, we pour water from our plumbed-in filter into either a vortex jug or a double-egg vortexer.

HEALTH ASPECTS OF LIVING WATER

The essential requirements for living water are that it should be:

- *Clean:* free of biological or chemical contamination and harmful energies, (which increase oxidization and free radicals)
- *Mineralized:* especially magnesium, calcium, and trace minerals, which will produce greater alkalinity
- *Composed of smaller or looser molecular clusters:* (micro water or magnetized water) gives low surface tension—and easier absorption
- *Abundant with negative hydrogen:* produces a higher antioxidant potential
- *Energized:* with positive, beneficial etheric energies, best achieved through vorticizing

Polluting Energy
The energies of hospital wastes and hormones, such as estrogen, are not removed by filters, but can be neutralized through vorticizing.

Humidifiers (and Negative Ionizers)
Many people overheat their homes with central heating, which can render indoor air dry and unhealthy. An electric humidifier can be combined with the use of bactericidal essential oils to stop the spread of infection from people with colds or bronchitis. (A negative ionizer will also improve the indoor environment, especially in hot weather.)

Minerals

Water normally supplies a substantial part of the minerals we need. Many of our soils now suffer from mineral depletion, so that we receive less nutrition from our food. We would be wise to take as supplements those minerals in which we are deficient. (Hair analysis is usually a reliable way to determine deficiencies.)

Hydrotherapy

The tradition of water immersion goes back millennia, sometimes as a ritual for spiritual purification, but also very much for health. For Romans, the spa culture was an essential element in their social lives. Warmer water is particularly beneficial for sore bodies, arthritis, and physical recuperation.

Thalassotherapy is a specialized variation practiced with sea water, popular on the west coast of France, and on the Dead and Red Seas. It is considered beneficial for skin and circulatory disorders, as well as joint stiffness and arthritis.

The Turkish bath involves a steam room and a sweat room, followed by a cold plunge and a massage. The Scandinavian sauna is a steam bath often followed by a cold plunge. And in Japan, the wood-fired *ofuro* is a time-honored tradition.

Inhalation

This is an effective way of helping sinus or head cold symptoms. Place a few drops of an appropriate essential oil on the surface of a bowl of just boiled water, and put a towel over your head. Alternatively, an electric face steamer is a worthwhile purchase. Similarly, a neti pot is very effective for nasal irrigation.

Colonic Irrigation

This detoxifying therapy, dating as far back as Hippocrates, uses a (pressurized) water enema to cleanse the colon.

USING WATER AT HOME

You may live in a part of the country with plenty of rainfall, so why worry about water use?

Rainfall patterns are becoming less predictable, our population is growing, and our lifestyles are changing—we use 70 percent more water than we did forty years ago. In Southern California, investment is now being committed to distilling fresh water from the ocean. In southeast England (Kent), water supplies are so critically short that using nuclear power to distill seawater is being considered.

Water meters are becoming more common, with the incentive to reduce needless use.

Calculating Water Usage

The big users are:

A bath = 21 gallons
Five-minute power shower = 24 gallons
Five-minute ordinary shower = 9 gallons
Washing machine = 16 gallons
Dishwasher = 11 gallons
Hose or sprinkler = 143 gallons/hour

Tips on Water Economy

- Never leave a tap running. A dripping tap can waste more than 1,450 gallons a year.
- Store cold water in the refrigerator rather than waiting for the tap to run cold. Cold water has greater dynamic energy.
- When you make a cup of tea, fill the kettle only as much as you need.
- By installing dual-flush or slimline toilets, buying water-efficient appliances, and using low-flow taps, you can easily reduce your water consumption by 25 percent.
- Consider installing a whole house dechlorinating filter, which will make your home environment much healthier.

- Save even more by doing your dishes in a bowl in the sink; the same with a few clothes. Half-load washing machine programs are uneconomical in terms of water, energy, and cost.
- In temperate climates, the average roof collects enough of rain per year to fill 450 water butts with free water. (One water butt equals 126 gallons.)Use this for watering your garden, rather than wasting treated drinking water. It's a good plan to have a second butt to catch overflow from the first.
- Use a watering can for your plants. A sprinkler uses a lot of water.
- Water your plants early in the morning or late in the evening to reduce evaporation. Direct water to the roots of plants and give then a good, deep soak; twice weekly is enough, even in warm weather.
- Use gray water (from sinks, dishwasher, bath, washing machine) on flowers, but preferably not on vegetables.
- Group your vegetables according to their water need: leafy ones require the most, zucchini and cucumbers when their fruit begins to swell; root vegetables require the least.
- Build up the organic content of your soil by using lots of compost made from garden waste, vegetable and fruit peel and trimmings, paper, and cardboard.
- Mulch on the surface of the soil keeps the soil moist. Strips of cardboard or carpet will also keep down the weeds. The less you dig, hoe, and disturb the soil, the more efficiently will the organically rich humus thrive and retain the fertility and moisture of the soil. Permaculture is the most water-efficient method of gardening.

WATER ANOMALIES

(Summarized, with permission, from Martin Chaplin:
www.lsbu.ac.uk/water/anmlies.html)

Water is an apparently simple molecule (H_2O) with a highly complex character. As a gas it is one of the lightest known; as a liquid it is much denser than expected (in the chemical group of hydrogen compounds); and as a solid it is much lighter than expected. Much of the behavior of liquid water is quite different from what is found with other liquids, giving rise to the term "the anomalous properties of water" (see box on p. 308).

As liquid water is so commonplace in our everyday lives, it is often regarded as a "typical" liquid. In reality water is most atypical, behaving quite differently at low and high temperatures. It has often been stated that life depends on these anomalous properties of water. In particular, the large heat capacity, high thermal conductivity, and high water content in organisms contribute to thermal regulation and prevent local temperature fluctuations, thus allowing us to control our body temperature more easily. The high latent heat of evaporation gives resistance to dehydration and considerable evaporative cooling.

Water is an excellent solvent due to its polarity, high dielectric constant, and small molecular size, particularly for polar and ionic compounds and salts. It has unique hydration properties for biological macromolecules (particularly proteins and nucleic acids) that determine

The Opposite Properties of Hot and Cold Water

Notable amongst the anomalies of water are the opposite properties of hot and cold water, with the anomalous behavior more accentuated at low temperatures, where the properties of supercooled water often diverge from those of hexagonal ice. As a cold liquid, water shrinks when heated. It becomes less easy to compress, its refractive index increases, the speed of sound within it increases, gases become less soluble, and it is easier to heat and conducts heat more efficiently.

In contrast, as hot liquid water is heated it expands, becomes easier to compress, its refractive index is reduced, the speed of sound within it decreases, gases become more soluble, and it is more difficult to heat and becomes a poorer conductor of heat. With increasing pressure, cold water molecules move more quickly but hot water molecules move more slowly. Hot water freezes more quickly than cold water, and ice melts when compressed, except at high pressures when liquid water freezes when compressed. No other material is commonly found as solid, liquid, and gas within such a narrow temperature range as life on Earth requires.

their three-dimensional structures, and hence their functions, in solution. This hydration forms gels that can reversibly undergo the gel-sol phase transitions that underlie many cellular mechanisms. Water ionizes and allows easy proton exchange between molecules, thus contributing to the richness of ionic interactions.

At 39°F water expands on heating *or* cooling. This density maximum, together with low ice density, results in:

- The necessity that most of a body of fresh water (not just its surface) is close to 39°F before any freezing can occur.
- The freezing of rivers, lakes, and oceans is from the top down,

thus permitting survival of the bottom ecology, insulating the water from further freezing, reflecting back sunlight into space, and allowing rapid thawing.

- Density-driven thermal convection causing seasonal mixing in deeper temperate waters carries life-providing oxygen into the depths.

The large heat capacity of the oceans and seas allows them to act as heat reservoirs so that ocean temperatures vary only a third as much as land temperatures and so moderate our climate (for example, the Gulf Stream carries tropical warmth to northwestern Europe). The compressibility of water reduces the sea level by about forty meters, giving us 5 percent more land. Water's high surface tension plus its expansion on freezing encourages the erosion of rocks to give soil for forests and our agriculture.

THE MORAL BANKRUPTCY OF OUR CIVILIZATION

Ben Okri, Nigerian poet and novelist

(Reprinted from the *Times,* 30 October 2008, and
the *Network Review* 98.)

The crisis affecting our economy is a crisis of our civilization. The values that we hold dear are the very same ones that got us to this point. The meltdown in the economy is a harsh metaphor for the meltdown of some of our value systems. For decades, poets and artists have been crying in the wilderness about the wasteland, the debacle, the apocalypse. But apparent economic triumph has deafened us to these warnings. Now it is necessary to look at this crisis as a symptom of things gone wrong in our culture.

Individualism has been raised almost to a religion, appearance made more important than substance. Success justifies greed, and greed justifies indifference to fellow human beings. We thought that our actions affected only our own sphere, but the way that appalling decisions made in America have set off a domino effect makes it necessary to bring new ideas to the forefront of our civilization. The most important is that we are more connected than we suspected. A visible and invisible mesh links economies and cultures around the globe to the great military and economic centers. The only hope lies in a fundamental reexamination of the values that we have lived by over the past thirty years. It is not just banking that needs an overhaul, but our entire way of life.

There ought to be great cries in the land, great anger. But there is a strange silence. Why? Because we are all implicated. We have drifted to this dark, unacceptable place together. We took the success of our economy as proof of the rightness of its underlying philosophy. We are now at a crossroads. Our future depends not on whether we get through this, but on how deeply and truthfully we examine its causes . . . What we need now more than ever is a vision beyond the event—a vision of renewal.

In looking over the landscape of contemporary events, one thing becomes very striking. The people to whom we have delegated decision-making in economic matters cannot be unaware of the consequences. Those whose decisions led to the economic collapse revealed to us how profoundly lacking in vision they were. This is not surprising. These were never people of vision. They are capable of making decisions in the economic sphere, but how these decisions relate to the wider world was never part of their mental composition. This is a great flaw of our world.

To whom do we turn for guidance in our modern world? Teachers have had their scope limited by the prevailing fashions of education. Artists have become more appreciated for scandal than for important revelations about our lives. Writers are entertainers, provocateurs, or—if truly serious—more or less ignored. The Catholic Church speaks with a broken voice. Politicians are guided more by polls and donors than by vision. We have disemboweled our oracles. Anybody who claims to have something to say is immediately suspect.

So now that we have taken a blowtorch to the idea of sages, guides, bards, holy fools, and seers, what is left in our cultural landscape? Scientific rationality has proved inadequate to the unpredictabilities of the times . . . This is where we step out into a new space. What is most missing in the landscape of our times is the sustaining power of myths.

If we need a new vision for our times, what might it be? A vision that arises from necessity or one that orientates us toward a new future? I favor the latter (see "Holism in Society" in chapter 19,). It is too late to react only from necessity. One of our much neglected qualities is our creative ability to reshape our world. Our planet is under threat. We need a new one-planet thinking.

We must bring back into society a deeper sense of the purpose of living. The unhappiness in so many lives ought to tell us that success alone is not enough. Material success has brought us to a strange spiritual and moral bankruptcy.

If we look at alcoholism rates, suicide rates, and our sensation addiction, we must conclude that this banishment of higher things from the garden has not been a success. The more the society has succeeded, the more its heart has failed.

Everywhere parents are puzzled as to what to do with their children. Everywhere the children are puzzled as to what to do with themselves. The question everywhere is: You get your success, and then what?

Every society has a legend about a treasure that is lost. The message of the Fisher King is as true now as ever. Find the grail that was lost. Find the values that were so crucial to the birth of our civilization, but were lost in the intoxication of its triumphs.

We can enter a new future only by reconnecting with what is best in us, and adapting it to our times. We need a new social consciousness. The poor and the hungry need to be the focus of our economic and social responsibility. Education ought to be more global; we need to restore the preeminence of character over show, and wisdom over cleverness. We need to be more a people of the world.

All great cultures renew themselves by accepting the challenges of their times, and like the biblical David, forge their vision and courage in the secret laboratory of the wild, wrestling with their demons and perfecting their character. We must transform ourselves or perish.

LINKS AND RESOURCES

For more information about Viktor Schauberger or about any of the topics in this book, visit the websites below.

Viktor Schauberger website: www.Schauberger.co.uk
Author's website: www.AlickBartholomew.co.uk

OCEANIC AND CLIMATIC CHANGE RESEARCH

Although the oceans control the world's weather and climate and contain 90 percent of Earth's biomass, our knowledge about them is pitifully small. They hold the key to understanding climate change. Some good sources of information are:

Woods Hole Oceanographic Institute, Woods Hole, Massachusetts. The best known ocean research center in North America, which first drew attention about six years ago to the slowing of the Gulf Stream.

The Damocles Project (www.damocles-eu.org). European countries have cooperated to fund important research, such as this project, on climate change in the Arctic.

National Oceanographic Centre, University of Southampton. This

is the United Kingdom's center for oceanography research (www
.noc.soton.ac.uk).

Hadley Centre, Exeter, part of the government's Meteorological
Office, is the United Kingdom's influential center for climate
change research (www.metoffice.gov.uk/climatechange).

WATER TREATMENT

For more information on water quality, practical suggestions, water filters, and quantum water products, see www.Sulis-health.co.uk.

WATER'S CHEMISTRY

Good surveys can be found at:

Jill Granger's pages at http://witcombe.sbc.edu/water/
chemistrystructure.html
www.filtersfast.com/Water-Chemistry.asp
Martin Chaplin's excellent pages on water structure and science:
www.Isbu.ac.uk/water

THE INSTITUTE OF SCIENCE
IN SOCIETY (I-SIS)

If you want to be well informed on the big issues of the day—renewable
energy sources, climate change, food and energy issues, genetic engineering, the new biology, quantum physics, and so on, the Institute of
Science in Society (I-SiS) is a reliable source of independent information. Funded by private donation, to my mind they deserve our support
more than many of the environmental charities (any money you donate
to them will go much further).

The Institute of Science in Society (I-SiS) was founded in 1998 by
Dr. Mae-Wan Ho and her husband, Peter Saunders, professor of applied
mathematics at King's College, University of London. A small team

of dedicated pioneers supervises their pivotal research, lectures widely internationally, organizes and participates in conferences, and publishes books and their bimonthly illustrated magazine, *Science in Society*. It is the only truly independent institute of its kind in the world. Their excellent website is at www.i-sis.org.uk.

NOTES

Note: See Bibliography for full reference documentation.

I-SiS = Institute of Science in Society. Their magazine is *Science in Society* (*SiS*).

SMN = Scientific and Medical Network. Their magazine is *The Network Review*.

INTRODUCTION

1. Chris Clarke, "The Implications of Modern Science for a New World View."
2. Mae-Wan Ho, "Medicine in a New Key."
3. Fritjof Capra, "The Yin Yang Balance."

CHAPTER 1. THE IMPORTANCE OF WATER

1. Viktor Schauberger, "The Ox and the Chamois."
2. See *The Water Wizard* by Viktor Schauberger.

CHAPTER 2. THE COSMOS AND THE SOLAR SYSTEM

1. John McCreary in *The American Dowser,* November 1981.
2. Rob Gourlay, Australian groundwater specialist, www.eric.co.au.
3. Julian Caldecott, *Water: The Causes, Costs, and Future of a Global Crisis.*
4. D. S. Allan and J. B. Delair, *When the Earth Nearly Died.*

5. Ibid.

6. "Oceans and Global Warming," *SiS* (July 21, 2006).

CHAPTER 3. CHARACTERISTICS OF WATER

1. Paolo Consigli, *Water Pure and Simple.*
2. Quote provided by the Centre for Implosion Research: www.implosionresearch.com.
3. *SiS* 15 (September 2002).
4. See Mae-Wan Ho, *The Rainbow and the Worm.*
5. Listed on Martin Chaplin's website: www.isbu.ac.uk/water.

CHAPTER 4. THE BLOOD OF THE EARTH

1. Iain Stewart and John Lynch, *Earth.*
2. Vandana Shiva, "Climate Justice."
3. *Hutchinson Encyclopedia.*
4. Veronique Mistiaen, "Guarding Russia's Sacred Sea."

CHAPTER 5. THE GREAT WATER CYCLES

1. *Nexus,* April 2009.
2. IOC Tsunami Glossary by the Intergovernmental Oceanographic Commission (IOC) at the International Tsunami Information Centre (ITIC) of UNESCO. Accessed at ioc3.unesco.org/itic.

CHAPTER 6. SPRINGS AND RIVERS

1. Julian Caldecott, *Water: The Causes, Costs, and Future of a Global Crisis.*
2. Callum Coats in *Living Energies,* 176–77, describes one he studied.

CHAPTER 7. WATER AND THE HUMAN BODY

1. Paul Spinrad, *The RE/Search Guide to Bodily Fluids.*
2. Karol Sikora, *The Observer,* 18 May 2008.
3. BBC Radio 4, *Today,* 23 June 2008.
4. Coen Van der Kroon, *The Golden Fountain.*

CHAPTER 8. WATER CIRCULATION IN PLANTS

1. Viktor Schauberger, "The Dying Forest," 30.
2. BBC Radio 4, *Today,* 13 October 2008.
3. James Lovelock, *Observer,* 22 March 2009.
4. BBC Radio 4, *Today,* interview with Jim Naughtie, 15 May 2008.
5. See www.orangutan.org.uk.
6. David Attenborough's TV documentary on the Pacific salmon in *Nature's Great Events*: BBC, 18 February 2009.
7. Peter Bunyard, *The Breakdown of Climate.*

CHAPTER 9. THE EVOLUTION CONTROVERSY

1. Carl Safina, "For Evolution to Live, Darwin Must Die."
2. Charles Darwin, *The Origin of Species.*
3. Mae-Wan Ho, " Death of the Central Dogma."
4. See Darwin's 1886 letter to M. Wagner, in *Charles Darwin: Life and Letters,* ed. F. Darwin.
5. Bruce Lipton, *The Biology of Belief.*
6. See: www.emofree.com.
7. Mae-Wan Ho, "Epigenetic Inheritance: What Genes Remember."
8. Marcus Pembrey, "Sins of the Fathers, and Their Fathers."
9. Paul LaViolette, *Genesis of the Universe: The Ancient Science of Continuous Creation.*
10. Mae-Wan Ho, *Quantum Jazz: the Tao of Biology.*
11. See also: Fritjof Capra, *The Tao of Physics.*

CHAPTER 11. THE ORGANISM AND QUANTUM WATER

1. Rupert Sheldrake, *Dogs That Know when Their Owners are Coming Home.*
2. David Bohm, *Wholeness and the Implicate Order,* 145–47.
3. See Sheldrake, *Dogs That Know when Their Owners are Coming Home,* chapter 3, and Mae-Wan Ho, "Two States Water Explains All."
4. Mae-Wan Ho, *The Rainbow and the Worm.*
5. Mae-Wan Ho, "Quantum Coherent Liquid Crystalline Organism."
6. Ibid.
7. Mae-Wan Ho, "Quantum Jazz, the Tao of Biology."

8. J.-M. Zheng and G. H. Pollack, "Long-range forces extending from polymer-gel surfaces." See also Mae-Wan Ho, "Water Forms Massive Exclusion Zones."

9. I-SiS, March 31, 2008.

10. One of the "kitchen table" experiments of Gerald Pollack, professor of bioengineering, University of Washington, Seattle.

11. Mae-Wan Ho, "Quantum Coherence and Conscious Experience."

12. Mae-Wan Ho, "Collagen Structure Revealed."

13. G. D. Fullerton and M. R. Amurao, "Evidence that Collagen and Tendon Have Monolayer Water Coverage in the Native State."

14. Mae-Wan Ho, "Coherent Energy, Liquid Crystallinity, and Acupuncture."

CHAPTER 12. SPIRALS, THE VORTEX, AND THE ETHERIC

1. Callum Coats, *Living Energies,* 63.

2. Ibid., 65–72.

3. See: www.Sulis-health.co.uk/sulis/water.html#eggvortex.

CHAPTER 13. WATER'S COSMIC ROLE

1. Schwenk, *Sensitive Chaos,* 83.

2. Ibid., 44.

3. Ibid, 68.

4. August Schmauss, "Biologische Gedanken in der Meteorologie," 19.

5. Paul Raethjen, "Dynamics of Cyclones."

CHAPTER 14. WATER AS A COMMUNICATION CHANNEL

1. *The Journal of Scientific Exploration,* Stanford University, 1995.

2. Cleve Backster, *Primary Perception,* 34.

3. Ibid.

4. Elisabeth Sahtouris, *Earth Dance: Living Systems in Evolution.*

5. Backster, *Primary Perception,* 105.

6. Ibid., 41.

7. Chris Clarke, "Entanglement: The Explanation for Everything?"

CHAPTER 15. THE MEMORY OF WATER

1. Mae-Wan Ho, "The Strangeness of Water and Homeopathic 'Memory."
2. Mae-Wan Ho, "Crystal Clear: Messages from Water."
3. David Tame, *The Secret Power of Music.*
4. John Diamond, *Your Body Doesn't Lie.*
5. John Ott, *Health and Light.*
6. Compare with "Quantum Jazz" (the video), discussed on page 162.

CHAPTER 16. HOW WE TREAT WATER

1. *National Geographic* special edition on water, November 1993.
2. Jeffrey Sachs, U.N. Millennium Project, New Delhi, January 2007.
3. Mae-Wan Ho, Sam Burcher, and L. C. Lim, "Food Futures Now, Organic, Sustainable, Fossil Fuel Free."
4. *The Guardian,* 12 May 2008.
5. *Guardian Weekly,* 13 February 2009.
6. *The Ecologist,* May 1999.
7. International Management Institute.
8. *Guardian Weekly,* March 2001.
9. *National Geographic,* "Earth's Fresh Water under Pressure," September 2002.
10. Ibid.
11. *The Ecologist,* May 1999.
12. Ibid.
13. Caspar Henderson, *The Ecologist,* 2002.
14. Ibid.
15. See also appendix 1, Water and Health.
16. Viktor Schauberger, *Nature as Teacher.*
17. Waldblott, McKinney, and Burgstahler: *Fluoridation: The Great Dilemma,* 288.
18. Barry Groves, *Fluoride: Drinking Ourselves to Death?* Groves is a well-informed source on this topic.
19. *Journal of Dental Research* 69 (1990): 723–27.
20. Groves, *Fluoride,* 227.
21. Ibid.
22. Viktor Schauberger, *Our Senseless Toil,* Part II, 14.
23. Alanna Moore, *The Wisdom of Water.*

CHAPTER 17. WATER AND
CLIMATE CHANGE

1. BBC Radio 4: "Home Planet," 24 March 2009.
2. D. Bushnell, "Seawater/Saline Agriculture for Energy, Warming, Water, Rainfall, Land, Food, and Minerals." See also E. P. Glenn, J. J. Brown, and J. W. O'Leary, "Irrigating Crops with Seawater."
3. Alanna Moore, *The Wisdom of Water.*
4. *Guardian Weekly,* 17 July 2009.
5. *Guardian Weekly,* September 2009.
6. *The Guardian,* 19 May 2009.
7. Vandana Shiva, "Water Wisdom."
8. *Guardian Weekly,* 23 May 2005.
9. *Guardian Weekly,* 6 March 2009.
10. *Guardian Weekly,* 26 June 2009.
11. *Guardian Weekly,* 17 July 2009.
12. See University of Hamburg: animated video of ice cover changes on Arctic Ocean over nine years: www.youtube.com/watch?v=e2rt1QWC-9Q.
13. *The Observer,* 11 October 2009.
14. "Can Water Burn?' I-SiS, June 10, 2009.

CHAPTER 18. THE FUTURE OF
FOOD PRODUCTION

1. Alanna Moore, "Water in Australian Landscapes," *The Wisdom of Water.*
2. See: www.naturalsequenceassociation.org.au.
3. Rachel Carson, *Silent Spring.*
4. Mae-Wan Ho, Sam Burcher, and L. C. Lim, "Food Futures Now, Organic, Sustainable, Fossil Fuel Free."
5. "Science of the Organism and Sustainable Systems: Implications for Agricultural Policies," *SiS* (March 2009).
6. Rebecca Hosking, "A Farm for the Future."
7. Ho, Burcher, and Lim, "Food Futures Now, Organic, Sustainable, Fossil Fuel Free."
8. Peter Tomkins and Christopher Bird, *Secrets of the Soil.*

CHAPTER 19. THE BIG PICTURE

1. James Lovelock, Royal Society lecture, 18 October 2007.
2. Mae-Wan Ho, *The Rainbow and Worm.*
3. See Ben Okri, "The Moral Bankruptcy of our Civilization" (appendix 3).
4. See: www.transitionnetwork.org.
5. See Richard Wilkinson and Kate Pickett, *The Spirit Level: Why More Equal Societies Almost Always Do Better.*
6. There is an old saying that the flutter of a butterfly's wings on the far side of the world can affect the destiny of nations.

   In the new information age in which we live, the reaction of Far Eastern financial markets to a political decision in one European country instantaneously affects world economic health. Individual countries are now, to some extent, powerless to determine their own futures. National boundaries are meaningless.

   The Internet has done more to link together the world community than any other influence. It is less easily controlled than television for political and commercial purposes, and can therefore be a powerful medium for creative change.
7. David Korten, *The Great Turning: From Empire to Earth Community.*
8. See Coats, *Living Energies,* 63.
9. See Lynne McTaggart, *The Field.*

APPENDIX 1. WATER AND HEALTH

1. See *The Ecologist,* September 2007.
2. Available at www.Sulis-Health.co.uk.

BIBLIOGRAPHY

Note: I-SiS = Institute of Science in Society; *SiS* = Science in Society magazine; SMN = Scientific and Medical Network

Allan, D. S., and J. B. Delair. *When the Earth Nearly Died: Compelling Evidence of a World Cataclysm 11,500 Years Ago.* Bath: Gateway Books, 1994.
———. *Catastrophe.* Rochester, Vt.: Bear & Company, 1999. (U.S. edition of the above.)
Alexandersson, Olof. *Living Water: Viktor Schauberger and the Secrets of Natural Energy.* London: Turnstone, 1982.
Altman, Nathaniel. *Sacred Water: The Spiritual Source of Life.* Mahwah, N.J.: HiddenSpring, 2002.
Ash, David, and Peter Hewitt. *The Vortex: Key to Future Science.* Bath: Gateway, 1983.
Backster, Cleve. *Primary Perception: Biocommunication with Plants, Living Foods and Human Cells.* Anza, Calif.: White Rose Millennium Press, 2003. (A classic.)
Baker, Richard St. Barbe. *I Planted Trees.* London: Lutterworth, 1944.
Ball, Philip. *Life's Matrix: A Biography of Water.* Berkeley, Calif.: University of California Press, 2001.
Barry, R.G., and R. J. Chorley. *Atmosphere, Weather & Climate.* London: Methuen, 1976.
Bartholomew, Alick. *Hidden Nature: The Startling Insights of Viktor Schauberger.* Edinburgh: Floris Books, 2003; rev. ed. 2006.
———. *The Schauberger Keys.* Bath, UK: Schauberger Books, 2003. (Notes on Schauberger's worldview.)
———. "How Nature Works." *Living Lightly* 17 (2001).

———. "Nature is Sacred." *Resurgence* 225 (2004).

———. "Toward a Science of Nature." *The Network Review* 84.

———. "The Evolution of Earth and of Life," *The Network Review* 92.

———. "Viktor Schauberger," *Twentieth Century Visionaries.* Totnes, UK: Green Books, 2007.

———. "What is Living Water?" Micanopy, Fla.: *Caduceus,* 2007.

Bass, Karen, ed. BBC Natural History Unit, *Nature's Great Events: The Most Spectacular Natural Events on the Planet.* London: Beazley, 2009; Chicago: University of Chicago Press, 2009. (To accompany BBC six-part TV series, introduced by David Attenborough.)

Batmanghelidj, Fereydoon. *Your Body's Many Cries for Water.* Falls Church, Va.: Global Health Solutions, 1995. (Informative.)

———. *Water and Salt: Your Healer from Within.* Norwich, UK: Tagman, 2003.

Bennett, J. G. *Deeper Man.* Edited by A. G. E. Blake. London: Turnstone, 1978. (An exponent of the teachings of G .I. Gurdieff, for instance, the law of three.)

Bohm, David. *Wholeness and the Implicate Order,* rev. ed. London and New York: Routledge, 1995. (Originally published in 1980.)

Bortoft, Henri. *Goethe's Science of Nature.* Edinburgh: Floris Books, 2002. (Recommended.)

Boulter, Michael. *Extinction, Evolution and the End of Man.* London: Fourth Estate, 2002.

Brennan, Barbara Ann. *Hands of Light: A Guide to Healing Through the Human Energy Field.* London: Bantam, 1987.

Bruges, James. *The Big Earth Book: Ideas and Solutions for a Planet in Crisis.* Bristol, UK: Sawday, 2007.

Bunyard, Peter. *The Breakdown of Climate: Human Choices of Global Disaster?* Edinburgh: Floris Books, 1999.

———, ed. *Gaia in Action: Science of the Living Earth.* Edinburgh: Floris Books, 1996.

———. "The Real Importance of the Amazon Rain Forest." I-SiS, March 15, 2010.

Bushnell, D. "Seawater/Saline Agriculture for Energy, Warming, Water, Rainfall, Land, Food, and Minerals." http://web.mac.com/savegaia/flowerswar/Project/Entr percentC3 percentA9es/2008/12/5_mise_ percentC3percentA0_jour_en_cours_files/Dennis-Bushnell-saline-agriculture.pdf._(Accessed in 2008.)

Button, John, ed. *The Best of* Resurgence: *25 Years' Selection.* Bideford, UK: Resurgence, 1991.

Caldecott, Julian. *Water: Life in Every Drop*. London: Transworld, 2007. (Reprinted in 2010 as *Water: The Causes, Costs, and Future of a Global Crisis*. London: Virgin Books, 2010.)

Capra, Fritjof. *The Tao of Physics*. London: Wildwood, 1975.

———. "The Yin Yang Balance." *Resurgence* (May 1981).

Carson, Rachel. *Silent Spring*. Boston: Houghton Mifflin, 1963. (A classic.)

———. *The Sea Around Us*. New York: Harper, 1951. (Poetic.)

Chaplin, Martin. "The Importance of Cell Water." SiS 24 (2004): 42–45.

———. "Water: Its Importance to Life." Biochem. Mol. Biol. Educ. 29, no. 2 (2001): 54–59.

Clarke, Chris. "Entanglement: The Explanation for Everything?" *The Network Review* 86 (Winter 2004).

———. "The Implications of Modern Science for a New World View." *The Network Review*, 71 (1999).

Coats, Callum. *Living Energies: An Exposition of Concepts Related to the Theories of Viktor Schauberger*. Bath, UK: Gateway, 1996. (Most authoritative work on Schauberger's research.)

Cobbald, Jane. *Viktor Schauberger: A Life of Learning from Nature*. Edinburgh: Floris Books, 2005. (Recommended.)

Cloos, Walther. *The Living Earth: The Organic Origin of Rocks and Minerals*. East Grinstead, Sussex, UK: Lanthorn Press, 1977. (A Steiner earth science book.)

Consigli, Paolo. *Water, Pure and Simple*. London: Watkins, 2008. (Comprehensive and fascinating.)

Cook, David. *The Natural Step: Toward a Sustainable Society*, Schumacher Briefing, no. 11. Totnes, UK: Green Books, 2004.

Crawford, E. A. *The Lunar Garden: Planting by the Moon Phases*. London: Weidenfeld & Nicholson, 1989.

Darwin, Charles. *The Origin of Species*. In many editions, the first being *The Origin of Species by Means of Natural Selection, or the Preservation of Favored Races in the Struggle for Life*. London: Murray, 1859.

Darwin, F., ed. *Charles Darwin: Life and Letters*. London: John Murray, 1888.

Diamond, Jared. *Collapse: How Societies Choose to Fail or Succeed*. New York: Viking, 2005.

Diamond, John. *Your Body Doesn't Lie*. New York: Harper & Row, 1979.

Edwards, Lawrence. *The Vortex of Life: Nature's Patterns in Time and Space*. Edinburgh: Floris Books, 1993. (Important research on biological planetary influence.)

Emoto, Masaru. *The Hidden Messages in Water.* Hillsboro, Ore.: Beyond Words, 2001.

———. *The Secret Life of Water.* Hillsboro, Ore.: Beyond Words, 2006.

———. *The True Power of Water.* Hillsboro, Ore.: Beyond Words, 2005.

Endres, Klaus-Peter, and Wolfgang Schad. *Moon Rhythms in Nature.* Edinburgh: Floris Books, 2002.

Flannery, Tim. *The Weather Makers.* New York: Grove, 2005.

Forward, William, and Andrew Wolpert, eds. *Chaos, Rhythm, and Flow in Nature.* Edinburgh: Floris Books, 1993.

Fullerton, G. D., and M. R. Amurao. "Evidence that Collagen and Tendon Have Monolayer Water Coverage in the Native State." *International Journal of Cell Biology* 30 (2006): 56–65.

Glenn, E. P., J. J. Brown, and J. W. O'Leary. "Irrigating Crops with Seawater." *Scientific American* (August 1998): 76–81.

Goodwin, Brian. *Nature's Due: Healing our Fragmented Culture.* Edinburgh: Floris, 2007.

Gordon-Brown, Ian, with Barbara Somers. *The Raincloud of Knowable Things: A Practical Guide to Transpersonal Psychology: Workshops, History, Method.* Edited by Hazel Marshall. Dorset: Archive Publishing, 2008.

Graves, Tom. *Needles of Stone.* London: Turnstone, 1978 (A dowsing classic.)

Hageneder, Fred. *The Spirit of Trees: Science, Symbiosis, and Inspiration.* Edinburgh: Floris Books, 2005. (A lovely book.)

Hambling, Richard. The *Cloud Book: How to Understand the Skies.* Newton Abbott, Devon, UK: David & Charles, 2008.

Hamaker, John, and Donald Weaver. *The Survival of Civilization.* Burlingame, Calif.: Hamaker-Weaver Publishers, 1982.

Hanniford, Carla. *Smart Moves: Why Learning Is Not All in the Head.* Arlington, Va.: Great Ocean Publishers, 1995. (Detailed research into the educational benefits of Brain Gym exercises.)

Hall, Alan. *Water, Electricity, and Health: Protecting Yourself from Electrostress at Home and Work.* Stroud, Gloucestershire, UK: Hawthorn Press, 1997.

Harding, Stephan. *Animate Earth: Science, Intuition, and Gaia.* Totnes, UK: Green Books, 2006.

Henderson, Lawrence J. *The Fitness of the Environment: An Inquiry into the Biological Significance of the Properties of Matter.* New York: Macmillan, 1913. (Reprinted Cornell University Library, 2009).

Ho, Mae-Wan. *The Rainbow and the Worm: The Physics of Organisms*. Singapore: World Scientific, 1993. Rev. 3rd ed., 1998. (A seminal work.)

———. *Genetic Engineering: Dream or Nightmare?* Bath: Gateway, 1998; New York: Continuum, 2000.

———. "Quantum Coherence and Conscious Experience." *Kybernetes* 26, (1997): 263–76.

———. "Coherent Energy, Liquid Crystallinity, and Acupuncture." Lecture to British Acupuncture Society, October 2, 1999.

———. "Crystal Clear: Messages from Water." New Age of Water series. I-SiS, June 1, 2002.

———. "The Strangeness of Water and Homeopathic 'Memory.'" New Age of Water series, I-SiS, May 31, 2002.

———. "Water Forms Massive Exclusion Zones." New Age of Water series, I-SiS, 2004.

———. "Death of the Central Dogma." *SiS* 24 (September 3, 2004).

———. "Collagen Structure Revealed." New Age of Water series, I-SiS, October 23, 2006.

———. "Dream Farm." *SiS,* 38. Also "Dream Farm 2: The Story So Far." I-SiS, July 24, 2006.

———. "Two States Water Explains All." New Age of Water series, I-SiS, October 25, 2006.

———. "Quantum Jazz, the Tao of Biology." Keynote lecture presented in Global Philosophy Forum, Haverford College, Haverford, Pennsylvania, April 7, 2007. See full text of lecture at: www.i-sis.org.uk.

———. "Quantum Coherent Liquid Crystalline Organism." Energy Medicine Conference, Copenhagen, September 19, 2008.

———. "Science of the Organism & Sustainable Systems: Implications for Agricultural Policies." Briefing for "The Science of Sustainable Agriculture, An Innovative Paradigm" European Agricultural Policy Conference, European Parliament, Brussels, March 3, 2009. See full text of lecture at: www.i-sis.org.uk.

———. "Can Water Burn?" I-SiS, June 10, 2009.

———. "Medicine in a New Key," I-SiS, August 7, 2009.

———. "O_2 dropping faster than CO_2 rising." I-SiS, August 19, 2009.

———. "Epigenetic Inheritance: What Genes Remember." *SiS* 41 (December 1, 2009).

Ho, Mae-Wan, Sam Burcher, and L. C. Lim. *Food Futures Now: Organic, Sustainable, Fossil-Fuel Free*. London: ISiS/TWN, 2008. (Important.)

Hollick, Malcolm. *The Science of Oneness: A Worldview for the 21st Century.* Ropley, Hants, UK: O-Books, 2006.

Hood, K., C. Halpern, G. Greenberg, and R. Lerner, eds. *Handbook of Developmental Science, Behavior, & Genetics.* New York: Blackwell, 2009.

Hopkins, Rob. *The Transition Handbook: From Oil Dependence to Local Resilience.* Totnes, UK: Green Books, 2008. (Standard guide; important.)

Hosking, Rebecca. "A Farm for the Future." *Daily Mail,* 15 February 2009. (Also an impressive BBC2 film, February 19, 2009.)

Kilgour, William. *Twenty Years on Ben Nevis: Being a Brief Account of the Life, Work, and Experiences of the Observers at the Highest Meteorological Station in the British Isles.* Paisley, UK: Gardner, 1905. Reprinted 1985. (A record of the meteorological station from 1882–1904.)

Korten, David C. *When Corporations Rule the World.* London: Earthscan, 1996.

———. *The Great Turning: From Empire to Earth Community.* New York: Berrett-Koehler, 2006. (Inspiring and prophetic.)

———. *Agenda for a New Economy: From Phantom Wealth to Real Wealth.* New York: Berrett-Koehler, 2009. (Why Wall Street can't be fixed, and how to replace it.)

Kronberger, Hans, and Siegbert Lattacher. *On the Track of Water's Secret: From Viktor Schauberger to Johannes Grander.* Vienna: Uranus, 1995.

LaVilolette, Paul. *Genesis of the Cosmos: The Ancient Science of Continuous Creation.* Rochester, Vt.: Bear & Co., 1995.

Lipton, Bruce. *The Biology of Belief: Unleashing the Power of Consciousness, Matter & Miracles.* Carlsbad, Calif.: Hay House, 2008. (A seminal book.)

Lockley, Martin. "Intelligent Design Paradigm." *The Network Review* 87 (Spring 2005).

Lorimer, David, et al., eds. *Wider Horizons: Explorations in Science, and Human Experience.* Moreton-in-March, Gloucestershire, UK: Scientific Medical Network. 1999.

Lovelock, James. *The Revenge of Gaia: Earth's Climate Crisis and the Fate of Humanity.* London: Allen Lane, 2006.

———. *The Vanishing Face of Gaia: A Final Warning.* New York: Basic Books/Perseus, 2009.

Makarieva, A. M., and V. G. Gorshkov. "Condensation-induced Kinematics and Dynamics of Cyclones, Hurricanes and Tornadoes." Physics Letters A 373 (2009), 4201–4205.

Manning, Jeane. *The Coming Energy Revolution: The Search for Free Energy.* New York: Avery, 1996.

Marks, William E. *The Holy Order of Water: Healing Earth's Waters and Ourselves.* Great Barrington, Vt.: Bell Pond, 2001.

Marshall, Hazel, ed. *The Wisdom of the Transpersonal,* a trilogy uniting the work of Barbara Somers & Ian Gordon-Brown (q.v.).

McTaggart, Lynne. *The Field: The Quest for the Secret Force of the Universe.* London: Harper Collins, 2003.

Merrifield, Jeff. *Damanhur: The Real Dream.* London: Thorsons, 1998. (Account of an Italian artistic and spiritual community.)

Mistiaen, Veronique. "Guarding Russia's Sacred Sea." *Guardian Weekly,* 25 April 2008.

Moore, Alanna. *The Wisdom of Water.* Castlemaine, Victoria, Australia: Python Press, 2007. (Excellent, with unusual information; by an Australian dowser.)

———. *Stone Age Farming: Eco Agriculture for the 21st Century.* Castlemaine, Victoria, Australia: Python Press, 2001. (Permaculture, paramagnetism, dowsing, round towers, and ancient technology.)

Myneni, R. B., R. I. Negrón Juárez, M. L. Gouldon, R. F. S. Bernades, and H. Ga. "An Empirical Approach to Retrieving Monthly Evapotranspiration over Amazonia." *International Journal of Remote Sensing* 29 (2008): 7045–7063.

Narby, Jeremy. *Intelligence in Nature.* New York: Tarcher/Penguin, 2005.

National Geographic special issue on water. *Water: The Power, Promise, and Turmoil of North America's Fresh Water. National Geographic* 184, no. 5A (November 1993).

———. *Water: Our Thirsty World. National Geographic* (April 2010).

Okri, Ben. "The Moral Bankruptcy of our Civilization," *The Network Review* 98 (Winter 2008).

Ostrander, Sheila, and Lynn Schroeder. *Psychic Discoveries Behind the Iron Curtain.* Englewood Cliffs, N.J.: Prentice-Hall, 1970.

Ott, John. *Health and Light.* Greenwich Conn.: Devin-Adair, 1973.

Pembrey, Marcus. "Sins of the Fathers, and Their Fathers." *European Journal of Human Genetics* 14 (2006): 131–32.

Pogačnik, Marko. *Healing the Heart of the Earth: Restoring the Subtle Levels of Life.* Findhorn: Findhorn Press, 1998.

Pogačnik, Marko, and Karin Werner. *Nature Spirits & Elemental Beings: Working with the Intelligence in Nature.* Findhorn: Findhorn Press, 1997.

Prince of Wales, Charles. "Restoring Harmony and Connection: Inner and Outer." *The Network Review* 98 (Winter 2008).

Raethjen, Paul. "Dynamics of Cyclones." Presentation to ICHM Conference, Leipzig, Germany, 1953.

Ryrie, Charlie. *The Healing Energies of Water.* London: Gaia, 1998. (Well informed and beautifully illustrated.)

Safina, Carl. "For Evolution to Live, Darwin Must Die." *Observer,* 8 March 2009.

Sahtouris, Elizabet. *Earth Dance: Living Systems in Evolution.* iUniverse.com, 2000.

———. "Discovering Nature's Secrets of Success: A Potential Future for a Global Family." *The Network Review* 89 (Winter 2005).

Schauberger, Viktor. "The Dying Forest" [Der sterbende Wald], Part 1. *Tau* 51 (November 1936): 30.

———. "The Ox and the Chamois." *Tau* 146 (June 1939): 30.

———. *The Water Wizard (Eco-Technology,* vol. 1). Bath: Gateway, 1998.

———. *Nature as Teacher (Eco-Technology,* vol. 2). Bath: Gateway, 1998.

———. *Fertile Earth (Eco-Technology,* vol. 3). Bath: Gateway, 2000.

———. *Energy Evolution (Eco-Technology,* vol. 4). Bath: Gateway, 2000.

———. *Unsere Sinnlose Arbeit* [Our Senseless Toil], rev. ed. Edited by Schauberger-Archive and J. Schauberger. Bad Ischl, Austria: Verlag, 2003. (Originally published in 1933.)

Schiff, Michel. *The Memory of Water.* London: Thorsons, 1995. (Account of Jacques Benveniste's research.)

Schmauss, August. "Biologische Gedanken in der Meteorologie." *Forschungen und Fortschritte* 21 (1945).

Schulz, Andreas. *Water Crystals: Making the Quality of Water Visible.* Edinburgh: Floris Books, 2005.

Schwenk, Theodor. *Sensitive Chaos.* London: Steiner Books, 1965. (A classic on energy in water.)

Schwenk, Theodor, and Wolfram Schwenk. *Water: The Element of Life.* New York: Anthroposophic Press, 1989.

Schwenk, Wolfram, ed. *The Hidden Qualities of Water.* Edinburgh: Floris Books, 2007.

Seamon, David, and Arthur Zajonc, eds. *Goethe's Way of Science: A Phenomenology of Nature.* Albany, New York: SUNY Press, 1998.

Sheldrake, Rupert. *The Rebirth of Nature: The Greening of Science and God.* London: Rider, 1990.

Shiva, Vandana. "Climate Justice." *Resurgence* 257 (November/December 2009).

———. "Water Wisdom." *Resurgence* 259 (March/April 2010).

Somers, Barbara. *The Fires of Alchemy: A Transpersonal Viewpoint.* Edited by Hazel Marshall. Dorset, UK: Archive, 2004.

Somers, Barbara, with Ian Gordon-Brown. *Journey in Depth: A Transpersonal Perspective.* Edited by Hazel Marshall. Dorset, UK: Archive, 2002.

Spinrad, Paul. *The RE/Search Guide to Bodily Fluids.* New York: Juno Books, 1999.

Stevens, Peter. *Patterns in Nature.* London: Penguin, 1974.

Stewart, Iain, and John Lynch. *Earth: The Power of the Planet.* A six-part BBC documentary with accompanying book. London: BBC Books, 2007. (Background to the TV series, inspiring and informative; gripping photography.)

Stone, Robert. *The Secret Life of Your Cells.* Atglen, Pa.: Whitford Press, 1982.

Tame, David. *The Secret Power of Music: The Transformation of Self and Society Through Musical Energy.* Rochester, Vt.: Destiny Books, 1984.

Thomas, Lewis. *The Lives of a Cell: Notes of a Biology Watcher.* New York: Viking, 1974. (A classic.)

Thomas, Pat. "Behind the Label." *The Ecologist* (September 2007).

Thomson, C. Leslie. *Water and Nature Cure.* Edinburgh: Thomson-Kingston, 1955. Reprinted 1970.

Tompkins, Peter, and Christopher Bird. *The Secret Life of Plants.* New York: Harper & Row, 1973. (A classic.)

———. *Secrets of the Soil.* New York: Harper & Row, 1978.

Treven, Michael, and Peter Talkenberger. *Environmental Medicine.* (n.d.). (Quoting physicist Wolfgang Ludwig.)

Van der Kroon, Coen. *The Golden Fountain: The Complete Guide to Urine Therapy.* Bath, UK: Gateway, 1992.

Wilkens, Andreas, Michael Jacobi, and Wolfram Schwenk. *Understanding Water.* Edinburgh: Floris Books, 2005.

Wilkes, John. *Flowforms: The Rhythmic Power of Water.* Edinburgh: Floris Books, 2005.

Wilkinson, Richard, and Kate Pickett. *The Spirit Level: Why More Equal Societies Almost Always Do Better.* London: Penguin, 2009.

Wright, Machaelle. *Co-Creative Science: A Revolution in Science Providing Real Solutions for Today's Health and Environment.* Jeffersonton, Va.: Perelandra, 1997.

Zheng, J.-M., and G. H. Pollack. "Long-range forces extending from polymer-gel surfaces." *Physical Review E* 68 (2003): 1–7.

INDEX

Color illustration numbers appear in **bold**

BOOKS OF RELATED INTEREST

The Healing Power of Energized Water
The New Science of Potentizing the World's Most Vital Resource
by Ulrich Holst

The Water Prescription
For Health, Vitality, and Rejuvenation
by Christopher Vasey, N.D.

The Oxygen Prescription
The Miracle of Oxidative Therapies
by Nathaniel Altman

Science and the Akashic Field
An Integral Theory of Everything
by Ervin Laszlo

The Akashic Experience
Science and the Cosmic Memory Field
by Ervin Laszlo

Morphic Resonance
The Nature of Formative Causation
by Rupert Sheldrake

The Presence of the Past
Morphic Resonance and the Habits of Nature
by Rupert Sheldrake

The Basic Code of the Universe
The Science of the Invisible in Physics, Medicine, and Spirituality
by Massimo Citro, M.D.

INNER TRADITIONS • BEAR & COMPANY
P.O. Box 388
Rochester, VT 05767
1-800-246-8648
www.InnerTraditions.com

Or contact your local bookseller